EARL HAMNER

A BIOGRAPHY

EARL HAMNER

From
**WALTON'S
MOUNTAIN**
to Tomorrow

JAMES E. PERSON JR.

CUMBERLAND HOUSE
NASHVILLE, TENNESSEE

EARL HAMNER
PUBLISHED BY CUMBERLAND HOUSE PUBLISHING
431 Harding Industrial Drive
Nashville, Tennessee 37211

Cover photo of the Hamner house courtesy of Scott M. Hamner.

Cover design: Gore Studio, Inc.
Book design: Mary Sanford

Library of Congress Cataloging-in-Publication Data
Person, James E., 1955–
  Earl Hamner : from Walton's Mountain to tomorrow : a biography / James E. Person Jr.
     p. cm.
  Includes bibliographical references and index.
  ISBN 1-58182-455-6 (hardcover : alk. paper)
  1. Hamner, Earl. 2. Authors, American—20th century—Biography. 3. Television producers and directors—United States—Biography. 4. Blue Ridge Mountains Region—Social life and customs. 5. Rural families—Blue Ridge Mountains Region. 6. Virginia—Social life and customs. I. Title.
  PS3558.A456Z84 2005
  813'.54--dc22
                                                            2005012089

Printed in the United States of America
1 2 3 4 5 6 7—11 10 09 08 07 06 05

This book is dedicated to my wife,
Lista Joyce Haist Person

To our teens,
David and Rebekah

and to the memory of
our family storyteller,
Edna Hope Person Lowe

CONTENTS

FOREWORD

PHOTO BY TESS GAMBREL

Silas House.

When I was a boy growing up in the mountains of Eastern Kentucky during the 1970s, I idolized Earl Hamner. Sure, the other kids loved Evel Knievel and Clint Eastwood, but the two people who were most inspirational to me were Mr. Hamner and his creation, John-Boy Walton.

I grew up in a large extended family, in a house that was constantly being trekked through by various aunts, uncles, cousins, and/or friends we had known so long that they felt like family. All of these people came bearing stories. Not just stories, but great, breathless epics that everyone gathered around to hear. Sometimes my mother and her friends played the piano and guitars and sang. A whole gang of children was always present. There was little need to turn on a television when so many human voices were singing and telling stories and laughing. And also because of the busyness of our house, we rarely had the television on. What use was there settling into a show if someone was bound to show up and start one of their long, wonderful tales? However, there was one show that we never missed: *The Waltons*. If someone did wander in while the show was on—and it never failed that someone did—they'd simply settle down onto the couch and watch, too. It was a communal experience to witness the joys and trials of the Walton clan.

I watched John-Boy the closest, because seeing him was much like seeing myself on screen. I was a young boy growing up in a rural place who had always wanted to be a writer, and I didn't know anyone else like me except for John-Boy. I grew up in a town of about seven hundred people; there wasn't exactly a literary community. I read so much, wrote in my notebooks so much, that my family started referring to me as John-Boy. And because John-Boy eventually fulfilled his dreams and became a writer, I knew that I could too. My family had a strong work ethic that they had instilled deeply in me, but John-Boy drove home the notion that these same things applied to writing too. He was determined, he kept finding ways to expand his talent, and he was aggressive. Simply put, John-Boy Walton knew what he wanted, and he did everything in his power to fulfill his dream of becoming a writer. I would do the same, I told myself. Always inexplicably observant of such things, I also noticed the "Created by Earl Hamner, Jr." that appeared on the screen when each episode aired. I'm not sure how I knew—most likely through some of the reading I was always doing—but I knew that Mr. Hamner had been raised in a town much like mine and had found his way to fulfilling his goals in life. I realized that he was John-Boy to a great extent. I thought if he could do it, maybe I could, too.

Later on, in junior high, I was browsing the aisles of a used bookstore when I came upon a small, green paperback bearing Mr. Hamner's name. When I plucked it from the shelf, I was surprised to see that he had written a novel called *Spencer's Mountain*. Further research taught me that the novel was the basis for the television show. I could hardly believe how much I loved the book. These were my people. These were my uncles, my parents, my grandparents. Since then I have read that book dozens of times. I sought out his other books, such as *The Homecoming* (the first line still haunts me with its simple, firm beauty: "All day the cold Virginia sky had hung low over Spencer's Mountain."), *Fifty Roads to Town, You Can't Get There From Here,* and others. In all of these books I found something I could relate to and admire. No matter that they were set during a different time and under different circumstances than my own, I still found in all of them a resonance that has lasted in me to this day. At the heart of all of Mr. Hamner's work is hope. And that's something everyone can relate to, something we all clutch on to and desire the most. At a time when modern literature began to look toward the grotesque, the violent, and the cynical side of life, Mr. Hamner's work hung on to deceptively simple, well-told stories that actually made the reader feel good. Sure, there is pain and desperation in his work (at its core, *Spencer's Mountain* is a profoundly sad book in many ways), but in the end, there is always an essential good. Mr. Hamner didn't just write books or television shows—in all the mediums he tackled, he was a storyteller, first and foremost. Being told a story is the thing that all people crave, and in this time of national homogenization and family that is spread out across the world, it's the thing we need more than ever. Mr. Hamner knew that long before anyone else caught on.

As much as I love *The Waltons* (not to mention *Falcon Crest,* which everyone in my family was fairly obsessed with in the late 1980s), I have to say that Mr. Hamner's work in television has unfairly overshadowed his accomplishment as a writer of books. His novels are endearing, action-packed, and the kind of books that become beloved. Now that I am a teacher at a large university, I always assign *Spencer's Mountain* for my Appalachian Literature classes. It never fails to be the class favorite.

When I began my first novel, *Clay's Quilt,* while still in college, I had not forgotten the influence of Mr. Hamner's work. I named my main character, Clay, after Clay-Boy Spencer (who would become John-Boy Walton in the show). Everyone I grew up with looks back on *The Waltons* as a lasting memory of their childhood, mostly because it was a time that their whole families came together and agreed on something completely. But I am also reminded of those fine times I had alone while reading his books, times of stillness and silence that helped to fashion me into the writer I always wanted to be.

While on my first book tour for *Clay's Quilt,* I was at a book festival when I heard a strangely familiar voice behind me. I recognized the voice instantly as that of the man who had narrated *The Waltons.* One doesn't forget such a powerful baritone like that, especially one that was such a huge part of his or her childhood. I turned to find Mr. Hamner signing books right behind me and, after much hesitation, finally approached him in a daze of awe and stupidity. I had heard a rumor that Mr. Hamner was going to be present at the festival, but could not believe it. But just in case, I had brought along that battered, aging copy of the green 1962 paperback called *Spencer's Mountain.* When Mr. Hamner signed the book for me, he looked up with kind eyes and said, "And there you go, sir." And suddenly I felt compelled to tell him everything that I want you to know here: without his work, I would have never fulfilled my dream of being a writer. I have written three novels now, and everywhere I go, people ask me about my influences. I always list Earl Hamner at the top of my list.

That's why I'm so proud and delighted to be introducing this wonderful biography to you. James Person has crafted a book that lets us completely know Mr. Hamner and his work. This is a biography that speaks to many: fans of the television shows, readers of his novels, admirers of the fine man named Earl Hamner. Most of all, this well-written and thoroughly entertaining book will help to remind people of Mr. Hamner's work in all the fields he has trod, giving them each the equal coverage that they deserve. Mr. Hamner has forged a lasting legacy in the world of both television and literature, and this book gives careful insight into Mr. Hamner's craft, his life, and his special storytelling abilities. Perhaps being reminded of all these things will even inspire some other young writer looking for a hero like the one I found in Mr. Hamner.

SILAS HOUSE
25 JANUARY 2005

Silas House is the author of *Clay's Quilt* (2001), *A Parchment of Leaves* (2003), and *The Coal Tattoo* (2004). His work has received such prizes as the Award for Special Achievement from the Fellowship of Southern Writers, the National Society of Arts and Letters' Fiction Prize, and the Kentucky Novel of the Year, as well as two Pushcart nominations for his short fiction. He is a frequent commentator on NPR's *All Things Considered,* where he reads his fiction, and is a professor of creative writing at Spalding University's MFA Program and Eastern Kentucky University. He lives in Eastern Kentucky with his wife and two daughters.

The turnoff to Schuyler, Virginia, from the northbound lane of U.S. 29, the Seminole Highway.

PREFACE

*I have walked the land in the footsteps of all my fathers. I
saw yesterday and now look to tomorrow.*

EARL HAMNER, 1979

One day many years ago, at the publishing house where I work in
Michigan, a small group of us were discussing our favorite television
programs during a coffee break. One woman mentioned that she
strongly liked *The Waltons*—"because," she said, "the characters are
realistic and remind us all of what life can be like. And *should* be
like." The rest of us groaned, and someone piped, "Goodnight, John-
Boy!" *The Waltons*? Oh, come on! The young woman who had
declared her affection for *The Waltons* answered our jaded disbelief
with a smile and a simple question: "What's wrong with *The Waltons*?" There was a pause. Nobody among our little group of
thinkers could think of a good answer, so like all good sophisticates
who don't know what to say, we changed the subject.

As the conversation continued, I thought about a time several
years earlier, in late 1972. At that time, while visiting Southern California and walking down a sidewalk in Westwood Village one
evening, some friends and I passed *Waltons* star Richard Thomas on
the street as he stood in a queue outside a movie theatre, just off the
UCLA campus. (Wishing to respect his privacy, we passed by him

without saying a word.) Despite my silence on both occasions, I knew I owned an affection for that program and its creator, Earl Hamner. I had deeply enjoyed the adventures of the fictional Walton family as well as listening to Hamner's off-camera narration, which framed each episode. That voice—approachable, wise, and friendly, with the distinctive Scotch-Irish accent found in only one place on earth—reminded me of the land and the people I had known as a boy growing up in Virginia.

Over the years I learned that Hamner had written the novel *Spencer's Mountain,* upon which *The Waltons* was loosely based. And that he had written much else besides: including novels that owed much to Sherwood Anderson and his school; screenplays, such as the work he is perhaps most proud of, *Charlotte's Web,* and a now-famous adaptation of the novel *Heidi* which caused an uproar in 1968 when its airing pre-empted the decisive end of a professional football game (remembered today as "the Heidi Bowl"); and dramas, such as the moving *Appalachian Autumn.* He was one of the more prolific writers who contributed to the success of the classic television series *The Twilight Zone.* There were also the televised works for which he served as creator and executive producer for which he is most remembered: the warm, nostalgic *Waltons* and the tales of cold-blooded betrayal, hot-blooded lust, and boundless ambition depicted on *Falcon Crest.*

Many years passed, my career as an editor and writer progressed; and then, late in the summer of 2003, I was invited to an event sponsored by the Sherwood Anderson Literary Center at which Hamner would be present. Although I was unable to attend because of a death in my family back in Virginia, I did seek to read all the books Hamner has written, as well as any books about him, to learn more about his life. To my surprise, there was no full-length treatment of his life and works available. In the present volume, then, I seek to remedy this, and in so doing to bring recognition to this warm and good man who, over the course of a fifty-year career, has crafted a body of work that is memorable, life-affirming, and well worth revisiting.

Before the first line of this book was written, it never crossed the mind of Earl Hamner that his life and works might be worth serious consideration. He said as much to me in a letter, adding, "I am not being modest. I have always considered myself a storyteller and if my work has had any value beyond that then I would be delighted for you to explore the project. I will be happy to cooperate in any way I can." But to one of his friends he confided, "Who would want to write a book about this old fool?"

Well, as one old fool to another, I do. For I believe the reader will discover an interesting life spent pursuing the single goal of transferring the stories of his life into a form to be shared with readers and viewers, as well as the clearing-up of a source of mild puzzlement to anyone who has followed Hamner's career. On this point, perhaps a word of explanation will help.

Having written much and spoken often on the subject of my previous book, the American man of letters Russell Kirk, I have discovered that many good and well-meaning admirers of Kirk have seized upon one aspect or another of his multi-faceted career and elevated that particular portion of it into the whole of their understanding, the defining element, of the man. For example, some admirers see Kirk as a historian who merely dabbled in writing ghost stories, social criticism, novels, literary criticism, and other works. Others see him as a sympathizer with the Southern Agrarians above all. Still others see him primarily as an advocate of limited government. In each such case, these admirers have made the mistake of failing to see the integrated vision that informs all of Kirk's work, in every genre. And I have found that the same sorts of misperceptions are associated with Hamner. There are some who see him as "Mister Walton" and believe that everything else he has written outside that acclaimed television series is an odd foray into peculiar and somewhat embarrassing corners of interest. (Indeed, some have no idea that Hamner has done anything other than *The Waltons,* which has remained in syndication since the 1980s and the first two complete seasons of which have been released on DVD.) Others believe Hamner is a worldly wise individual who should be revered for the mature themes of *Falcon Crest* and *The Ponder Heart,* and see *The Waltons* as a mere finger-exercise that served as a distracting warm-up on the road to his attaining his true creative powers.

Readers of this book will discover the integrated nature of Hamner's career, finding that there is no real conflict between the warm folksiness of *The Waltons,* the offbeat fantasies of his *Twilight Zone* scripts, the unscrupulous ethic displayed in *Falcon Crest,* or the myriad other novels and scripts he has written and TV programs he has produced. Throughout these chapters, I will demonstrate that there are pervasive themes that run throughout Hamner's work, which shows a man forever taking a backward glance to his roots for direction in the way of what makes life worthwhile, who allows that vision to direct his steps forward, and whose depictions of life, in his books and televised works, reflect an assessment of how his characters and their choices conform to or drift from that guiding vision. In an eloquent and autobiographical narration Hamner contributed to "Founder's Day," an episode of *The Waltons* originally aired in 1979, he said, "I have walked the land in the footsteps of all my fathers. I saw yesterday and now look to tomorrow." Hamner has shrewdly intuited a truth, stated by William Faulkner, Aleksandr Solzhenitsyn, and many other wise writers, that a people who have forgotten their past, or who treat the past as a worthless succession of useless knowledge, have lost that which orients them and provides them direction in life.

At the conclusion of a letter to this writer, Hamner added modest words intended to reassure me as I set out to explore his life and work: "Let me assure you that if you find fool's gold instead of the fourteen-carat stuff you will not offend me if you abandon the idea." I have found that there is sufficient "fourteen-carat stuff" to make the writing of this slim volume worthwhile, as I hope the reader will agree.

Hamner's written works, especially his novels and certain of his teleplays, reveal a wide-ranging, lively imagination—as well as what he has called "the value of roots." In an interview, he once said, "I think [that] becomes more and more crucial when we become such a huge technology and so many of the so-called traditional values are being questioned and discarded. Even though families are said to be shattered these days, and God is said to be dead, if people can revisit the scenes and places where these values did exist, possibly they can come to believe in them again, or . . . to adapt some kind of belief in God, or faith in the family unit, or just *getting home again.*"[1] The enduring standards of conduct Hamner was taught as a boy, which were treated with lively imagination in *The Waltons,* have served as a sustaining influence in his own life, through times of lofty hope and immense disappointment. When he entered the world of writing for network television during the medium's infancy, he held to the hope that television would not only entertain but also elevate and instruct its viewers. This hope fluctuated mildly throughout much of his career and has plummeted during the era of "reality TV," with Hamner coming to a point at which he sees screenwriters who hold to his long-ago hope as waging a rear-guard campaign in a medium that has found appeals to humanity's lowest expectations profitable and desirable. And yet, amid the disappointments of recent years, Hamner works steadily away to write and produce intelligent, well-told programs for that considerable segment of the viewing public that longs for such. Amid banks of weeds and scrub, he plants an occasional rose.

A Journey to a Place Where the Road Just Stops

In his novel *You Can't Get There from Here,* Hamner has his young hero describe the route a person takes to get to a specific village in the foothills of Virginia's Blue Ridge Mountains. He describes it as a journey "to a place where the road just stops." That place is Schuyler, Virginia, where Earl Hamner himself, along with his seven brothers and sisters, was born and reared.

On a misty morning in mid-October of 2004, I found myself driving south into the heart of Virginia along the Seminole Highway, U.S. 29, south of Charlottesville. It is a divided highway, typical of so many of the better roads in the American South, lined with fields, forests aflame with autumn color, farms, and roadside shops. In the distance there lay the gentle but majestic Blue Ridge. Upon passing one small shop I recognized a family name from Hamner's book *The Homecoming*: Sprouse's Furniture. The thought flashed into my mind that I was entering Hamner Country.

Following the driving directions of young Wesley Scott from *You Can't Get There from Here,* I turned east off U.S. 29 at Highway 6, where a single, easily missed sign proclaimed *Schuyler.* Within moments I found myself traveling along a narrow country road amid a deep forest of second-growth timber, narrow creeks, and small farms. On the left, two horses cropped grass on a green hill-slope, as if posing for a painting. The road meandered on through the woods, over the Rockfish River, where deer and bears can sometimes be seen stooping to drink, and in the back of my mind I seemed to hear faintly Jerry Goldsmith's theme music to *The Waltons,* with its distinctive trumpet solo. Just about the time I began to believe I must have missed a turn, a sign loomed ahead indicating that a right turn would take me to Schuyler and the Walton's Mountain Museum. In a few minutes I passed the vast gray structures of the New Alberene Stone Company and arrived at the place where the road just stops (or, really, forks).

There on the left was Polly and Jim-Bob's Bed and Breakfast, a comfortable place to stay the night, and the Hamner house—a white, late-Victorian dwelling in which Earl Hamner's parents raised their eight children; recently purchased by a friend of the Hamner family, the house is now on the National Register of Historic Places. This is the building that the Walton house was modeled upon for television. (The exterior set used in the program, now painted a bright yellow, still stands on the back lot at Warner Brothers Studios in California.) It is empty now and in need of repair, and good-nights are no longer called out within its walls. Across the road from the Hamner house stands the former Schuyler Elementary School, now the home of the Walton's Mountain Museum, which displays many interesting artifacts related to the Hamner family, Schuyler, and *The Waltons.* A drive a little further along takes the interested visitor past the humble residential sections of Schuyler called Stump Town, Riverside Drive, and Gold Mine, and past a magnificent building that was at one time the small Daniel J. Carroll Memorial Hospital (where four of the Hamner children, including Earl, were born), now a private residence. This is the village where Earl Hamner lived as a boy and participated in the experiences and events that shaped his outlook on life and provided the raw material for his imagination.

Looking upon Schuyler, a person might wonder what it is about this secluded locale that could inspire a writer whose work would achieve world renown. It is a quiet place and humble, like the writer himself. Upon learning that this book was being written, Hamner told one of his friends, "I can't imagine anyone wanting to read a book about me, much less write one about me." But I believe that the reader who pushes on to read about the life and career of this fascinating man will find Hamner's doubts misplaced and will discover a delightful individual who has become one of America's favorite storytellers and a conservator of the truth that though the modern world disdains the past and elevates immediacy, wealth, and power, the true measure of life's meaning lies in love, grace, gentleness, and forgiveness. In Earl Hamner's world, as in the world of the central character in Mark Helprin's novel *Memoir from Antproof Case,* "You learn as well . . . that love can overcome death, and that what is required of you in this is memory and devotion."

NOTE

1. Quoted in Antoinette W. Roades, "Earl Hamner Jr.," *Commonwealth: The Magazine of Virginia,* April 1977, 29.

ACKNOWLEDGMENTS

In the writing of this book, I am grateful first and foremost to Earl Hamner himself, who graciously gave of his time in answering my questions and lending me valuable scripts, articles, books, videos, and photos that inform and compliment this short study. Along with Earl, Jane Hamner is much appreciated for her kindness and support. I also would like to thank the distinguished Appalachian novelist Silas House, a man whose career was greatly inspired by Hamner's own, for graciously agreeing to write the thoughtful foreword to this volume. In addition, I am grateful to Charles E. Modlin and Hilbert H. Campbell for granting permission to reprint a slightly revised version of my essay "All Their Roads Before Them: George Willard, Clay-Boy Spencer, and the 'Beckoning World,'" from *The Sherwood Anderson Review,* Winter 2003. Thanks are due also to Kirk Nuss and Pearl A. McHaney of Georgia State University for permission to use portions of "Interview with Earl Hamner, Jr.," which is reprinted from *The Eudora Welty Newsletter,* Summer 2001, copyright © 2001, by permission of *The Eudora Welty Newsletter* and Kirk Nuss. I am grateful to Scott M. Hamner for permission to use the photo he took of his father's boyhood home in Schuyler which appears on the front cover, to Glenn R. Hawkes for his kindness and help, and to Antoinette W. Roades for her insights and as the photographer who took several outstanding images of Earl Hamner reprinted in this book with her permission and that of the Virginia Chamber of Commerce. I wish to thank, as well, Rev. Tom Fowler of the Schuyler Baptist Church (Schuyler, Virginia) along with Caroline Hamner, Paul Hamner, Nancy Hamner Jamerson, John McGreevey, Don Sipes, Judy Norton, Stella Luchetta, David Harper, Isis Ringrose, Kami Cotler, Mary Beth McDonough, Eric Scott, Lynn Bayonas, Pauline Crum, Joe Conley, Michael Learned, Richard Thomas, Alex Paige, William P. Simmons, Lynn Hamilton, Harper Lee, Ellen Geer, William Schmidt, Patricia Neal, Harry Harris, Jeb Rosebrook, Manfred Wolfram, Hal Williams, Ronnie Claire Edwards, Paul Harvey, and the Hon. Gerald Baliles for sharing their insights on Hamner's significance; Ralph Giffin for his thoughts on Hamner and for permission to quote from the information provided on his fine Web site (www.the-waltons.com); Lisa Harrison and Kenneth Taber for each lending a hand at an important juncture; Carolyn Grinnell, for her remarks on Hamner, the loan of a key photograph, and her tireless work as president of the Waltons International Fan Club; Tony Albarella for sharing his thoughts on Hamner as well as his expertise on *The Twilight Zone;* Matt Adams and Claire Whitaker for their encouraging words and loan of great photographs; Elaine Klonicki for her infectiously enthusiastic support of this project and for providing me with a copy of an article she published on Hamner in the *Raleigh News and Observer;* the reference staff of the Novi Public Library, the Northville District Library, and the Harlan Hatcher Graduate Library at the University of Michigan for their assistance; Julie Heath and her associates at Warner Bros. for permission to reprint two photographs; Cindy Cline (Public and Technical Services Librarian) of the Margaret I. King Library at the University of Kentucky for locating and providing me with a photocopy of a rare and hard-to-obtain artifact; Carrie Throm, Director of Development and External Relations at the University of Cincinnati College-Conservatory of Music, for kindly providing photos of Earl Hamner; Deborah Rieselman, editor of *The University of Cincinnati Horizons,* for providing a copy of a key issue of the magazine, along with photos and her notes from Earl Hamner's lectures at the University during 2004; Laura Sharp at Warner Bros. for her valuable help; Thomas J. Pucher of the German *Falcon Crest* Fan Club for his support; Gleaves Whitney for his encouragement and for providing insights on Celtic-American culture; Audrey Hamner for her friendship and generosity, and for graciously providing me with photos, a personal tour of Schuyler, and her thoughts on her brother Earl's significance; and Woody Greenberg of Lynchburg College for supplying information about the Hamner papers and providing me with a videocassette and photos of an interview with Hamner and Michael Learned at the 2002 meeting of the Waltons International Fan Club. I wish to especially thank Will Schuck of the Sherwood Anderson Literary Center for acting as a valuable go-between at the beginning of my time of making initial contact with Hamner, when I was writing an essay on his work; and Ron Pitkin and editor Mary Sanford, along with their associates at Cumberland House, for their interest and support. I extend a huge thank-you to Duane Shell for sharing with me a selection from his trove of photographs of Hamner. I am grateful to a longtime friend of my family, Mrs. Annette Heindryckx, who first told me about Earl Hamner and *Spencer's Mountain* way back in 1971; it was in her home and in the company of her fine family that I first watched *The Homecoming* on television. I would like to thank also two dear cousins, Bettie Jane Leigh and Pam Hemmings; as well as my parents, James and Ellen Person, for their strong encouragement and support throughout the writing of this book. And finally, I am grateful to my wife, Lista, for her many hours of proofreading manuscript, offering advice, and in general making this work possible, and to our wonderful teens, David and Rebekah, for their patience with me—patience that was in large part rewarded when they met an enthusiastic and generous friend in Earl Hamner himself during a summer visit to California.

In the months during which this book was in preparation, two beloved members of the Hamner family passed away: Earl's eldest sister, Marion, and his youngest brother, Jim. Although I never had the pleasure of speaking with them, their words and presence live on in *Earl Hamner: From Walton's Mountain to Tomorrow* and in the hearts of those who knew and loved them.

JAMES E. PERSON JR.
NORTHVILLE, MICHIGAN
FEBRUARY 1, 2005

EARL HAMNER

Above, "Sparkplug" seated astride the family Model T, in a well-loved photo taken sometime in the late 1920s. *Right,* Earl Hamner Jr. as an infant, 1923.

1

AN INTRODUCTION TO THE LIFE
AND WORKS OF EARL HAMNER

*My people were drawn to mountains. They came when
the country was young and they settled in the upland
country of Virginia that is still misted with a haze of blue
which gives those mountains their name. They endured
and they prevailed; through flood and famine, diphtheria
and scarlet fever, through drought and forest fire, whooping cough and loneliness, through Indian wars, a
civil war, a world war, and through the Great
Depression they endured and they prevailed.
In my time, I have come to know them.*

EARL HAMNER, 1979

THE SCENE CALLED FOR SNOW, but there was none expected on that early-autumn day in 1971. Nevertheless the cast was assembled at the outdoor set in the Grand Tetons, the crew was in place, tape and sound were ready to roll, and the filming of Earl Hamner's Christmas novel, *The Homecoming,* was set to begin. The writer himself was on hand to observe. As Hamner looked on, director Fielder Cook called, "Action!" Cook then looked to the heavens and quietly said, "Now, Sir, if You please?"

And it began to snow.

And thus began one more improbable episode in a writer's career marked by unforeseen success and affection by readers, viewers, and critics alike. Writing during an era in which jadedness and cynicism were all the fashion among many prominent voices in American society—at the prospect of nuclear annihilation during the Cold War, the cultural shifts and excesses of the 1960s, the progress and outcome of the Vietnam Conflict, the loss of trust in public officials at all levels—Hamner tapped into a vein of longing for a return

One of Earl's favorite photographs of his boyhood home in Schuyler.

EARL HAMNER

to the mores and fondly remembered values of an unforgotten past, recounted in well-told stories. His novels *Spencer's Mountain* and *The Homecoming* have been translated into ten foreign languages and inspired the long-running television series *The Waltons,* which—though having finished its nine-year run over two decades ago—continues to attract viewers from around the world in syndication today.

In his role as a storyteller, Hamner has walked a careful line, sometimes navigating close to the overly sentimental—and some critics of his work have taken him to task for it. The expression "Goodnight, John-Boy!" and variations on it are used as a sing-songy taunt when sophisticates condescend to remember *The Waltons.* But for many who have appraised Hamner's overall body of work, there is a hard-to-define quality about it that has drawn them in and delighted them. In a review of Hamner's third novel, *You Can't Get There from Here,* Orville Prescott wrote what might be said of many of Hamner's works: "It is a little too sweet and its gossamer thread of story is too frail and artificially contrived. On the other hand, this is an appealing novel, one that makes one feel young and innocent and good just for the few hours it takes to read it." The renowned *New York Times* book critic went on to say, "It would be as difficult to dislike *You Can't Get There from Here* as to dislike a basket of spaniel puppies."[1] What is the quality that resonates with readers of Hamner's writings in an age in which "puppy-hating"—a fashionable stance of seeing-through-it-all and an emphasis upon debunking all instances of innocence and virtue—has long been in vogue? And what formed the mind, character, and skills of this remarkable writer, Earl Hamner?

"THE BEST OF ALL POSSIBLE TIMES"

"As far back as I can remember, I wanted to be a writer," claimed Hamner in 2002. Nothing is accomplished that ambition and decisive action don't bring into being—especially when the circumstances of one's early life indicate little promise. Born into a large, poor, Baptist family in Virginia's Blue Ridge on July 10, 1923, Earl

Earl Hamner Sr. Of this picture Audrey Hamner has said, "That's Daddy all over: full of the love of life."

Henry Hamner Jr. was the eldest of the eight red-haired children of Earl Henry and Doris Marion (Giannini) Hamner. His brothers and sisters, whose lives and personalities were to play such an important role in his career, were named Clifton (known to family and friends as Cliff), Marion, Audrey, Paul, Willard (Bill), James (Jim), and Nancy. During young Earl's formative years, the Hamner family lived in the mining-and-milling village of Schuyler (pronounced SKY-ler), in a house whose library consisted of two books: a copy of the Holy Bible and a how-to manual on bee-keeping. Those early years coincided with the period of widespread economic hardship known as the Great Depression. While his mother managed the family finances, kept house, and raised a growing family, Hamner's father worked in the local soapstone mill. Millwork and mining provided almost the only sources of livelihood to the citizens of Schuyler, which lies in rural Nelson County and was named for the village's first postmaster, Schuyler Walker. Founded in 1897, Schuyler lies in the heart of America's largest deposit of steatite, a substance used in the making of many household products, including certain paints, tailoring chalk, paper, kitchen counters, and the lining of laundry tubs and sinks.

Earl Sr. was by all accounts a fun-loving family man and an accomplished outdoorsman, respected in the community for his skills as a machinist and provider for his family. According to his children, he was like Huckleberry Finn in that "he could swear wonderfully"; a free-spirited man, he only infrequently joined his wife

EARL HAMNER

and children in attending services at the local Baptist church, preferring to attend when he thought it would do him some good. He enjoyed storytelling, hunting, fishing, and occasionally drinking a little too much—nipping in a bootlegged liquor known as "the recipe," which was distilled by a pair of elderly neighbors, a widow and her maiden daughter. Full of life, he would on occasion look lovingly at Doris and exclaim, "What a woman I married!" and then lift her in his arms and whirl her about. At other times he would gaze at his eight red-haired children seated around the kitchen table and declare, "All my babies are thoroughbreds." Doris Hamner, on the other hand, possessed what one neighbor, Isis Ringrose, described as a "righteous kindness": a devout woman, she was kind, quick-witted, and gracious, with a spine of steel. Earl and Doris bequeathed to their children many fond memories, none of them related to vast expenditures of wealth. Like many families that lived through those desperate times, the Hamners were poor, though they did not consider themselves as such; like others who lived through the Depression the Hamners reasoned that they, after all, were experiencing the

This is the building in which soapstone is milled at the New Alberene Stone Company in Schuyler. Hamner's father worked here until the company closed for a time in the early 1930s.

same circumstances as everyone else. This was the hand life had dealt them, they believed, and it fell to them simply to make the best of it. Unlike many townsmen and city-dwellers, the Hamners knew how to provide for their family needs, being rural people with handy skills at "making do" for clothing and shelter; attending to their own fruit trees, vegetable garden, and livestock; as well as fishing and hunting wild game for food. For entertainment, the family listened to the radio after supper each night, enjoying the music of the Grand Ole Opry as well as the comedy programs of Fred Allen, Jack Benny, and Edgar Bergen. By Hamner's own account, his family was close-knit in the midst of its poverty. "We were demonstrative in our love, kissing and hugging a lot, and often we would drink a bit of the recipe and end up around the piano with our arms around each other singing the old Baptist hymns," he wrote many years after the end of the Depression. The childhood he describes served as the model for scenes crafted into episodes of his novel *Spencer's Mountain* (1961) and the television series *The Waltons* (1972–81):

> All during the school year, my mother supervised all eight
> of us children as we gathered around the long wooden
> kitchen table to do our homework. Then one by one we
> drifted off to bed and there, sometimes with snow falling
> outside, we would call goodnight to each other, then sleep
> in the knowledge that we were secure. We thought we
> lived in the best of all possible times.[2]

Earl Jr. was an intelligent boy and a strong student. "My mother once told me that I was writing my numbers when I was two years old and reading by the time I was four. She was my first teacher, and when I started grade school I knew the first-grade primer by heart," he recalled many years later. At age six, Earl wrote a lively poem titled "My Dog," which was judged of such high quality as to be published on the children's page in the largest newspaper in the region, the *Richmond Times-Dispatch*. The poem puzzled Earl's father because his son wrote in a first-person voice of his new red wagon, his new blue sweater, and his six puppies—none of which the boy owned. The elder Hamner wondered aloud where young

Earl got such an imagination and where it would lead him. Writing was fine and all, he reasoned, but a man needed a practical trade of some sort. Many years later the son would write of his father's concern: "I think he worried about my having an ambition that seemed strange and unrealistic. He wanted a more sure way of my making a living for myself. . . . He worried about this over the years, and it wasn't until I invited him to the premiere of one of my movies at New York's Radio City Music Hall that I believe I set his mind at ease."[3]

Hamner's mother, Doris, signing an autograph for an admirer.

PHOTO BY ANTOINETTE W. ROADES

In the early 1930s, the soapstone operations in Schuyler closed, and Earl Sr. was forced to seek work elsewhere, eventually finding employment as a machinist at the DuPont chemical plant in the small city of Waynesboro, some thirty-three miles from home. Times being what they were, he accepted the job, though it necessitated his working and boarding all week in Waynesboro and then busing home on weekends, first making his way from Waynesboro over to nearby Charlottesville, then riding most of the way to Schuyler, and finally walking or hitchhiking the rest of the way. On the snowy Christmas Eve of 1933, while journeying home to Schuyler, Earl was forced to hitchhike the entire distance after he missed the last bus out of Charlottesville. Hours passed, and with no sign of her husband and no word of what had happened to his bus on the slick mountain roads, a worried Doris asked Earl Jr. to go look for his father. After a handful of false leads and minor adventures, the ten-year-old boy returned home, his mission unsuccessful. However, at about midnight the Hamner family heard a loud crash outside the house, the door burst open, and there stood a grinning Earl Sr. carrying a large sack filled with wonderful presents for his wife and each of his children—and a wild story about his having gotten that sack away from a rotund, white-bearded old fellow who had arrived at the house in a sleigh drawn by eight peculiar-looking deer. Many years later, this boyhood episode was retold with some variation and served as the basis for young Earl's novel (and television movie) *The Homecoming.*

Not until many years had passed and Hamner had moved away to New York did he learn that his family had been "economically deprived"—worse, that the Hamner family "lived in a 'depressed area' and that we suffered from a disease called 'familism.'" Hamner rejects this term, defined by sociologists as a type of social organization in which the family is considered more important than other social groups or the individual. "We didn't know we were afflicted with familism, we just thought we loved each other. Even today, with a highfaluting sociological name for it, I still prefer to call it love."[4] Hard times, he later said, seemed to bring together the inhabitants of Schuyler, with black people and white people enjoying friendships that reached across their respective communities and coming to each other's aid in times of need—this at a time when racial segregation was otherwise countenanced and even upheld by law. "The Depression was our common enemy," Hamner claimed.[5]

Earl Sr. had received little formal education, though Doris had graduated from high school, and it was the strong hope of them both that their children would complete high school and make their way in the world. Their eldest completed his high school studies and graduated at the top of his class of thirteen at Schuyler High School in 1940. He was now a tall, handsome young man at six feet, two inches in height, with a head of wavy red hair, and ready to leave home for an extended time for the first time in his life. With the encouragement of one of his teachers, he applied for and received a scholarship at the University of Richmond, a Baptist institution of learning that rose to prominence during the early twentieth century under the leadership of its longtime president,

Above, Hamner's paternal grandmother, Susan Henry (Spencer)
Hamner, with her pet parakeet,
Bird. *Right,* Hamner's paternal
grandfather, Walter Clifton
Hamner. *Below,* Hamner's maternal grandparents, Colonel
Anderson and Ora Lee (Mann)
Giannini. (Named after a Con-
federate army officer, *Colonel*
was his first name, not his rank.)

Frederic W. Boatwright. At Richmond, Hamner intended to pursue his dream of becoming a writer. But even with the scholarship, his expenses were only covered by great sacrifice on the part of the young man and his parents. Unable to fully afford a new, fashionable wardrobe for college, Earl borrowed a white dress shirt his father had set aside with his own (and only) suit, and Earl Sr. jokingly wondered aloud about how he could be properly "laid out" if he should die while his son was away at college. For his part, young Earl was eventually compelled to supplement his scholarship by working his way through college as a mail carrier, a census-taker, and a dispatcher for a trucking company. He also transcribed and typed a Civil War diary written by an ancestor of Dr. Garnett Ryland, the head of the University of Richmond's chemistry department, at a rate of fifty cents per hour's work, and spent his summers painting the university's dormitories as a way of returning some of the obligations of his scholarship.

As a student at Richmond, Hamner immersed himself in the traditional works of English and American literature required in his introductory courses, excelling in these but performing poorly in math classes. His studies were not helped by his need to work at the trucking company. "I worked from four in the afternoon until nine or ten at night," Hamner recalls. "Consequently my grades were not the greatest because I was fatigued most of the time. I remember that to go home I would catch a streetcar on a corner next to a bakery, and you cannot imagine the stunning experience of sitting on a streetcar-stop bench in the rain, hungry as hell, and waiting for the streetcar to arrive and breathing in the aroma of freshly baked bread."[6] He did find time to write what can be identified with little difficulty as an early draft of *Spencer's Mountain,* which his professor heavily marked up for its shortcomings and presumptions. (In his short life, the would-be author had kept a long-running journal of his observations of life in Schuyler but never spent significant time in any city larger or more cosmopolitan than Richmond, a fact painfully evident in this particular composition, which is set in the young protagonist's destination, New York City.)

Before Hamner could develop further as a student and writer,

America's entry into World War II interrupted his life as well as the lives of young men and women across the country. In 1943 he found himself in uniform in the U.S. Army, an institution in which he experienced a series of misadventures typical of many country-boy conscripts. After receiving basic training, he was assigned to a post in Fort Knox, Kentucky, where he was trained to drive the M4 "Sherman" tank—not an easy assignment for a tall man. After complaining that the top of his head was getting bloodied in the close confinement of the buttoned-up tank, he was sent to a specialized training program in engineering to learn calculus and geometry. Hamner, who by his own admission struggles with simple math, fared poorly in this assignment and was sent over to England to stand in reserve for the upcoming invasion of France. In England he underwent training in the important but immensely dangerous task of defusing land mines—"a job," Hamner later wrote, "where the life expectancy on the battlefront is about twenty minutes." Much to his relief, he was eventually assigned to the Quartermaster Corps and never had to test his skills at handling land mines. Like many soldiers, he began smoking heavily during this time, though he eventually quit this habit many years later, in the early 1980s.

Amid all the confusion and fear of wartime service, something favorable to Hamner's development as a writer occurred. While still Stateside, riding a troop train one day, he scraped acquaintance with a fellow soldier named Paul Nusnick. This friendly young man was from a cultivated Jewish family, and he was appalled to learn that Hamner had never read any work of modern literature and had never heard any piece of serious music performed. At the train's first stop, the troops disembarked and Nusnick steered Hamner into a nearby music store, where he played a recording of a movement from Tchaikovsky's *Third Symphony* in the store's listening room. Hamner was delighted by this first-time exposure to classical music. Sometime after this, when the two were assigned to a company and given a weekend leave, Nusnick took the young Virginian to a local public library, where he urged on his new protégé volumes of literature by F. Scott Fitzgerald, Thomas Wolfe, William Faulkner, Elizabeth Madox Roberts, and Sherwood Anderson. (Hamner remembers one novel in particular from this episode in his life: Anderson's *Winesburg, Ohio,* a series of tales of village life in turn-of-the-century Ohio. He later wrote of another of the modern writers he read during this period, "I remember Wolfe especially made me see that a kid from the backwoods in the Southern region could still become a writer.") At about this time, and in the months immediately afterward, Hamner began jotting notes for a novel that had already taken shape in his mind: a story of growing up in a small community in the mountains of Virginia during the Great Depression. In the years that followed, Hamner gave much credit to Nusnick for aiding his career by opening a door on the larger world. And throughout his years in the service, Hamner practiced his craft, writing sketches and stories whenever the chance arose.[7]

In August 1944, two months after the Allies' successful invasion of Fortress Europe, Private Earl Hamner came ashore at Omaha Beach. His unit, the Nineteenth Replacement Depot, was assigned to shadow the American fighting forces as the front moved inland during the Allied "breakout" from the hedgerows of the Normandy peninsula. Although Hamner never participated in the fighting, he was decorated on several occasions and, over time, was promoted to the rank of staff sergeant. He was prepared to be called upon to defuse land mines, later claiming that despite his having been assigned to a replacement depot behind the lines, "I knew I was going to die." Eventually, after his superiors learned he could type, he had the good fortune of being assigned to duty with the 542nd Quartermaster Corps as a clerk typist in liberated Paris, where he was stationed for the duration of the war. While in Paris, living and working at 105 rue Aubervillie, he continued taking notes for his novel, as well as writing short stories. These short pieces he mailed to various magazine editors in the United States, who promptly mailed them back. Hamner remembers, "They were printed rejection slips usually. 'This story does not suit our needs.' 'No manuscript accepted unless submitted through an agent.' 'Returned unread.' That is the rejection that hurt my feelings the most."

After returning to the United States after the war's end and being honorably discharged, Hamner found himself at loose ends.

Back in Virginia, he briefly considered an entry-level job writing for the *Richmond News Leader,* then worked for a short time at one of Richmond's radio stations, WMBG, which provided his first exposure to the behind-the-scenes work of radio. At WMBG, a country-music station, Hamner performed every task available except on-air announcing—learning along the way that working in radio might be an enjoyable and challenging venue for a would-be writer. Soon he took advantage of the G.I. Bill of Rights to apply for admission to Northwestern University, where he attended during the summer session of 1946, the only time he could be squeezed in as a student. Immediately after this he enrolled in the College of Music at the University of Cincinnati. There, Hamner entered a new program designed around writing for radio programs. At that time, radio was in its twilight years as a source of dramatic and comedic entertainment. Nevertheless, Hamner experienced two key events that proved crucial and beneficial to his longed-for career as a writer.

First, in 1949, a year after graduating from the University of Cincinnati, he enjoyed the first-time satisfaction of being paid for something he had written—a script crafted and submitted to a contest sponsored by the nationally syndicated radio drama called *Dr. Christian*—and hearing his own words coming over the airwaves for a national audience. Hamner's skill quickly caught the eye of the writing supervisor at Cincinnati's largest radio station, WLW, a 500,000-watt station that could be heard all over America and billed itself as "the Nation's Station." The young Virginian was offered a job on the station's writing staff; and for a year and a half he wrote for numerous radio programs aired by WLW, even serving as the narrator of a children's show called *The Days of the Giants.* Secondly, while in New York in 1949 to receive his award for winning the radio contest, Hamner met a fellow *Dr. Christian* honoree who later played a significant role in his entry into screenwriting: another ex-G.I. named Rod Serling, who would go on to create two legendary television series. At the time, Serling was also attending college in Ohio, at Antioch College in Yellow Springs.

Within a short time, Hamner followed the example of another Southern writer, Thomas Wolfe, by setting out to conquer New

York City, where artists and writers flocked for an environment conducive to working and getting their works known. He left Cincinnati, first turning over his responsibilities at WLW to Rod Serling. (Years later when Serling introduced Hamner to friends he would say, "I want you to meet the man who gave me my first job.") Arriving in New York, he was hired by a WLW alumnus, Van Woodward, a writer described by Hamner as "one of the finest men I have ever known." Woodward brought Hamner aboard at NBC, where he mentored the younger man and helped him refine his skills for a network radio audience. For his part, Hamner responded well to Woodward's tutelage and became known in a short time as a hardworking craftsman of well-made scripts for interviews with public figures on the program *Biographies in Sound,* of continuity material for *The Andy Williams Show,* and for on-air dramas. By the early 1950s, he had reached a plateau that served as a stepping-stone to new accomplishments: he began to be drawn to the exciting new medium of television, he began work in earnest on a novel, and he fell in love.

FAIRLY LAUNCHED AT LAST—IN LETTERS AND LOVE

As it came into being at NBC, television fascinated Hamner from the start. He perceived it as a medium that could educate, entertain, and elevate its viewing audience, and he wanted to be part of the rising tide of interest in TV. But he was told by his superiors at the network, "You're a radio writer. You write for the ear. Television requires writers who know how to write for the ear and the eye!" By politely badgering the right people at NBC, he got his chance and proved he was capable of writing for television. As his first assignment, he wrote a half-hour program on behalf of the Salvation Army, emphasizing the Army's role in helping "young women in trouble." The program featured singer Jane Pickens along with a largely unknown but rising young actress named Eva Marie Saint. Soon Hamner was writing occasional material for several NBC television programs, including *The Today Show* (during Dave Garroway's tenure as host), *The United States Steel Hour,* and *The Kate Smith*

Hour. But another major interest, something other than writing, entered Hamner's life during his years in New York.

In February 1954, a colleague at NBC, Susanne Salter, introduced Hamner to Caroline Jane Martin in a Manhattan restaurant, and he was smitten with her right from the start. For her part, Jane (as she is called) was strongly attracted to him; and in the weeks that followed their meeting, they went out on dinner-dates with other couples. Born in California and raised in the Midwest, she was an editor at *Harper's Bazaar* magazine and was a practical, quick-witted complement to the gregarious Hamner, with his down-home ways.

At the time, he was well along in the writing of one novel and had recently published another. This newly published work, set in the small-town South, was intended in part to be a counterblast to the then-current portrayal of Southern life as a fever-swamp of brutal imbecility as depicted by novelist Erskine Caldwell and his school. Ironically, upon the novel's publication in 1953, some reviewers described the work, titled *Fifty Roads to Town,* as a tale told *in the tradition of* Caldwell. "Mr. Hamner has a savage, *Tobacco Road* type of humor," wrote the reviewer for *Library Journal,* who added, "He does write better than Erskine Caldwell though."[8] *Fifty Roads to Town* was reviewed widely and favorably, and Hamner was thrilled that he had arrived as "a new novelist of unusual ability."[9]

Several months after his first novel appeared, he took Jane with him to Virginia to introduce her to his family. While on this visit to his home state, Hamner proposed to her in Roanoke. Jane accepted, and the two were married at St. Bartholomew's Cathedral in New York City on October 16, 1954. Within a few years the young couple welcomed two children into their lives, Scott and Caroline.

The young family lived in the midst of the literary and artistic capital of the United States, and periodically they brushed up against the major figures in New York's creative community. On one occasion Hamner fell into conversation with a man who lived next door to a summer place he and Jane had rented on Long Island. The man told Hamner that he worked at an advertising agency, but that he hoped to make his mark as a novelist and arose every morning at four o'clock to write for a while at his kitchen table before going to work in the city. Hamner asked what he was writing, to which the man replied, "I'm writing a funny little book." Hamner made a mental note to watch for his new friend to publish his novel—and in 1961 Joseph Heller finally published his "funny little book," *Catch-22.*

As the 1950s drew to a close, Hamner perceived that while television had supplanted radio as the electronic medium of the day, yet another change was afoot. In the early years of television's history in America, much of the programming was written and produced live in New York. However, this state of affairs was changing, with writing and production shifting to Southern California, where programs could be produced on tape more quickly and at less expense than live television. Hamner saw that the future of the medium lay in California. With his wife, two children, and their pet dogs, rabbits, guinea pigs, turtles, and a chipmunk, he left New York in 1961 and set out across the country. While his young family stopped in Davenport, Iowa, to stay with Jane's parents, Earl went on ahead to Los Angeles by airplane, taking along one of his children's pet turtles and hoping to get started as a writer of teleplays before bringing the rest of his family (and pets) to join him. He also brought a list of contacts supplied by his agent, Don Congdon. Among the names on this list was that of Ray Bradbury.

Hamner's earliest experiences in California have been described in detail in his wryly humorous memoir, *The Avocado Drive Zoo: At Home with My Family and the Creatures We've Loved.* First, he lived for a short time in a fleabag motel in Hollywood where, he soon learned, many rooms were rented by the hour to amorous couples. Ironically, the motel management indignantly asked *him* to leave because a maid discovered the turtle in his room, in clear violation of the establishment's "no pets" policy. Hamner next rented a small house in Studio City, just a few blocks from the major television studios and the Universal Studios lot. In this modest little house, Hamner, joined by his family, worked on his second novel and attempted to convince the staff at various television studios to give him an opportunity to prove himself as a writer. But in this endeavor he found himself in a distressingly familiar predicament, being told that he couldn't possibly write teleplays for film, having been a writer for live television.

Time passed with no success, and with his money running low, Hamner's situation became desperate. Then, during a get-together with one of the people on his contact list, Ray Bradbury suggested Hamner contact Rod Serling; and as a last resort he wrote and submitted two scripts to Buck Houghton, producer of Serling's successful new series, *The Twilight Zone.* Houghton and Serling liked Hamner's scripts and accepted them. They went on to put into production a total of eight scripts from the promising "new" writer, and from that time on, Hamner was never without work. Soon he and Jane began hunting for a house to buy in Studio City. In the meantime, to begin building his income, Hamner used the rented house's detached garage as his office, and he spent much of each day alternately typing and watching people on the street walk or ride past the open rollup door.

During the sixties, Hamner wrote material for several television dramas, notably *Wagon Train, The Invaders,* and the short-lived *It's a Man's World.* Of equal importance, he completed his second novel, a largely autobiographical work that had been percolating in his imagination and in draft form for almost two decades. As work progressed on this novel, Hamner decided to use a name from his family history as the name for the family in his book: the Spencers. As he sat typing this work in his open garage one day, a neighborhood eccentric happened by. This harmless man, known by the locals as Peter the Hermit, lived a few blocks away from the Hamners, in the guesthouse of a movie actor. On this particular day, Peter stopped to ask what Hamner was writing. Upon being told that a book was in process, Peter said, "Use the word *mountain* in the title and it will be a big success." As Hamner recalled many years later, "I had a different working title for the book, but my editor, Jim Silberman, came up with the title *Spencer's Mountain*! He was right, and so was Peter the Hermit! The book was most successful."[10] (So much so that Earl and Jane Hamner were able to use the advance on this novel to finally move out of the little rented house and purchase a larger house in Studio City, where they raised their children and where they still live today.) This work, concerning a teenage boy's coming of age in a mountain village in Virginia, was well received by critics and was adapted by *Reader's Digest* for its Condensed Books series. Further, *Spencer's Mountain* was selected by President John F. Kennedy for inclusion in a library of significant American books and sent to one hundred heads of state around the world. (While visiting London shortly after this development, an exuberant Hamner nodded toward Buckingham Palace and asked his wife, "I wonder if *she's* read it yet!")

Soon after the novel's publication, Warner Brothers bought the screen rights to it and began production on a film version of *Spencer's Mountain.* While Hamner was excited about this development—especially about the casting of Henry Fonda and Maureen O'Hara in leading roles—he was concerned about certain liberties the screenwriter made with his story, among them the shifting of the setting from Virginia's gently rolling Blue Ridge Mountains to the rugged Grand Tetons of Wyoming, where Hollywood production companies often traveled to film stories with mountain settings. In particular, Hamner was troubled by the screenwriter's leering treatment of sexual awakening (and sexuality in general), which departed markedly from the more innocent and wondering vision and tone of these elements in the novel. (The novelist, who had some degree of say in script development, succeeded in convincing the director to tone down the ribald dialogue written for the two characters modeled on Hamner's own parents—who were still living at the time and attended the film's opening at Radio City Music Hall.) In the end, Hamner had mixed feelings about the finished movie: a sense of accomplishment at having his novel adapted for a major motion picture in which there was much to admire, but mixed with a sense of faint disappointment at the way his plot was reshaped by the filmmaker.

Hamner later claimed that Jack Warner, president of Warner Brothers, felt that "he owed me one" for the studio's having bypassed him in the screenwriting chores for *Spencer's Mountain,* and that as a result Warner asked him to write the screenplay for a new film called *Palm Springs Weekend.* Hamner accepted this first screenwriting assignment and presented Warner Brothers with a completed script after checking himself into a hotel in the resort city of Palm Springs, California, and spending the Easter weekend of 1963 simply observing the antics of college students on spring break. The film, which starred Troy Donahue, Stefanie Powers, Andrew Duggan, Robert Conrad, Jerry Van Dyke, and Connie Stevens, among others, was a light romp in the tradition of the popular Frankie Avalon/Annette Funicello "teens-in-love" movies of the early sixties—though the City of Palm Springs was unhappy with Hamner's script. Upon reading it before filming began, the city attorney declared it "drivel," while a city councilman huffed that it made Palm Springs and its citizens look silly and called Hamner's script "the most terrible thing I ever read." The film itself became something of a cult classic, with Hamner claiming, "I still watch *Palm Springs Weekend* for laughs."

He published a third novel, *You Can't Get There from Here,* in 1965, and began work on a fourth, *Fenwick's Landing,* which was never completed. Like its predecessors, *You Can't Get There from Here* received favorable reviews and strong sales; but for the author, the best was yet to come. Five years after the appearance of *You Can't Get There from Here,* Hamner revisited the Spencer family in a short, largely autobiographical Christmas novel titled *The Homecoming.* At the urging of Malcolm Stuart, Hamner's agent at the time, a new company known as Lorimar Productions, headed by Lee Rich, expressed an interest in adapting the novel for a television movie, to be aired on CBS as a Christmas special during 1971. The special was filmed in Jackson Hole, Wyoming, and starred Patricia Neal, Andrew Duggan, Edgar Bergen, and Richard Thomas, along with a group of attractive child actors who later became regulars on *The Waltons:* Jon Walmsley, Judy Norton, Eric Scott, Mary Beth McDonough, David Harper, and Kami Cotler. *The Homecoming: A Christmas Story* was televised shortly before Christmas and drew a huge television audience who watched an imaginative retelling of Earl Hamner Jr.'s search for his father on a snowy Christmas Eve during the Depression. However, because Warner Brothers had purchased film rights to *Spencer's Mountain* a decade earlier, the screenwriter was forbidden to use many of the key place names and personal names from that novel. The screenwriter being Hamner himself, he changed the names of the story's central family from one name in his family history, the Spencers, to another name also in his ancestry, the Waltons.

"Mister Walton"

The success of *The Homecoming* spurred Lorimar and CBS to approach Hamner about developing a weekly television series based on the Walton family, set during the Depression years in fictional Jefferson County, Virginia. Hamner accepted, serving as co-executive producer, executive story consultant, writer, and narrator. Most of the original cast members from *The Homecoming* were retained, though there were a few key replacements. Patricia Neal (mother Olivia Walton) was replaced by Michael Learned because it was believed that Neal, having recently recovered from a stroke, would not sign on for a television series, with its rigors. (Ironically, Hamner later learned that she would have agreed had she been asked.) An actor somewhat younger than Andrew Duggan (father John Walton) was needed to play opposite Learned, and so Ralph Waite came to be selected for the role. And Will Geer took over from an ailing Edgar Bergen in the role of Zebulon Walton, the grandfather. Aired during the fall season of 1972, *The Waltons* was given little chance of survival against its rivals on the other two major networks: the highly rated *Flip Wilson Show* on NBC and *The Mod Squad* on ABC. The series indeed started slowly in gaining an audience base, but by Christmas of that year it had climbed to the upper tiers of the ratings. By season's end, it had knocked *The Mod Squad* off the air completely, taken market share from Flip Wilson's program, and garnered five Emmys. *The Waltons* became one of the most beloved television programs of the 1970s, enjoying a nine-season run on CBS and earning Hamner the nickname "Mister Walton." In addition to the series, he also found time to write the screenplay for the film *Where the Lilies Bloom* as well as the screenplay for an animated film he was especially proud of, *Charlotte's Web,* based on the novel by E. B. White.

At about the time *The Waltons* finished its run as a series in the early 1980s, Hamner read an interesting article in *Time* magazine concerning the wine industry in California's Napa Valley. He had long been intrigued by the culture of winemaking, as his mother was descended directly from Giovanni Antonio ("Anthony") and Maria Giannini. The Gianninis were one of two Italian families that came to Virginia at the behest of Thomas Jefferson in the hopes of establishing a successful winery at Monticello. This venture failed, and while one of the Italian vintners returned afterward to his native land, the Gianninis stayed and settled in Virginia. Hamner approached Lee Rich of Lorimar Productions with an idea about a series concerning a wealthy family of Napa Valley winegrowers, the Giobertis. Lorimar's representatives liked Hamner's concept and moved forward with the production of a new series, *Falcon Crest.* Starring Jane Wyman, David Selby, Robert Foxworth, Lorenzo Lamas, and Susan Sullivan, and with Hamner serving as executive producer, this series became a popular addition to the many night-time soap operas that dominated television during the 1980s, including *Dallas, Knots Landing,* and *Dynasty.* (Hamner had written radio soap operas earlier in his career and thought he would try his hand at this new development in nighttime television. To puzzled fans of the homespun Walton family and its values, Hamner explained his association with *Falcon Crest*—with its stories of love, lust, betrayal, and no-holds-barred struggles for power—by saying with a chuckle that stories of the Gioberti family represented his own "wicked side.")

Like *The Waltons, Falcon Crest* ran for nine seasons (and went into international syndication), but Hamner left the program after its fifth—for three reasons. First, he was exhausted and exasperated after spending two years defending himself in a lawsuit brought forward by an author who claimed Hamner had stolen the idea for *Falcon Crest* from one of her books. (When the case was eventually brought to trial, Hamner was completely vindicated, with the presiding judge announcing his verdict by stating, "I believe Mr. Hamner.")

This ordeal had preoccupied him and taken him away from his work for too long. Secondly, with increased involvement by the network in day-to-day operations, he had far less control over this series than he had enjoyed with *The Waltons,* and work on the set of *Falcon Crest* required that he work alongside not only his friends and allies from his *Waltons* days but also a small but influential circle of remarkably difficult people. Finally, he believed that the series had run its course and that he had nothing left to contribute to it. While he had greatly enjoyed working with the cast and crew of *Falcon Crest* during its first five seasons, he found the later incarnation of the series silly and not worth watching.

IN THE WAKE OF *FALCON CREST*

After his mixed experience with *Falcon Crest,* through the 1980s and on till the present time, Hamner has worked as the screenwriter or executive producer for numerous television specials and series, though none of the series enjoyed the long-lived success of the two for which he is best known. For the most part, these projects have about them the thoughtful, humanistic hallmark of "Mister Walton" (a name Hamner occasionally tires of, as it focuses upon only one aspect of his career), including even those programs that do not concern the Walton family. (There were six *Waltons* reunion specials aired during the 1980s and '90s.) During much of the time since the demise of *Falcon Crest,* he worked as co-executive producer of numerous projects with longtime business associate and noted Hollywood writer and television executive Don Sipes, one-half of the Hamner-Sipes Company, a company formed to produce independent film and television projects. Most notable among these are *Snowy River: The McGregor Saga* (1993–96), based on the poem "The Man from Snowy River" by Banjo Paterson, and *The Ponder Heart* (2001), based on the novel by a writer Hamner deeply admired, Eudora Welty. Showing their whimsical side, Hamner and Sipes also wrote an episode of *The Wild Thornberrys,* a cartoon for children broadcast on the Nickelodeon network.

Collaborating with Sipes, he also wrote a mystery novel, *Murder in Tinseltown* (2000), which spins a fast-moving, somewhat racy yarn while providing an insider's look at the cold-blooded alliances, deal-cuttings, back-stabbings, and goings-on in the making of a pilot for a television series. While the book draws upon Hamner's and Sipes's firsthand knowledge of such things, none of the characters is a portrait in full of either of the co-authors or of individuals they have known in Hollywood. However, one of the main characters, television screenwriter Justin Hargreaves, reflects at one point Hamner's own thoughts on the evolution of television and his place in it after forty years of working in that medium:

> I came into television writing with the greatest of hope and expectations. I thought it could change the world, and I wanted to dedicate my life to it. I felt proud to be part of it.
>
> Television could have been used to inform, to educate, and to humanize us all. Instead, it has become a cesspool.[11]

A Portrait of the Artist as a Virginian

Today, in his early eighties, Hamner has amicably ended his partnership with his friend Don Sipes (with whom he has lunch every few weeks). He delivers speeches across America about his experiences, records public service announcements for airing on radio, joins with former cast members of *The Waltons* to attend (when possible) reunions of the Waltons International Fan Club—held annually in Virginia and every few years in Los Angeles—and works "banker's hours" at his office in Studio City, California, where he crafts plays, answers correspondence, and explores new writing projects. He spends his evenings at home with Jane, his beloved wife of fifty years, and their pug dog, Charlie. (The couple's children have long ago grown up and embraced successful careers of their own, Scott as a writer and Caroline as a family counselor.) For recreation, Hamner goes fishing or tends his collection of some 50 bonsai trees. If he is no longer a familiar fixture on the studio lots of Southern California, he shows little discouragement about this turn of events. As he has

said on several occasions, "If I live to be four hundred years old and still have my faculties, I couldn't finish all the writing projects I have in mind."

As a man, Hamner is warm, friendly, garrulous, and generous, as well as an intriguing mixture of seeming contradictions. He is closely associated with that overworked term "family values," so beloved by rightward-leaning politicians today, yet his favorite comic strip is Garry Trudeau's "Doonesbury," with its twitting of all values and people who stand to the right of center on social issues, and one of his heroes is Eleanor Roosevelt, a public figure closely aligned with liberal causes. Hamner is identified with small-town values, yet the place he has lived for over forty years, Studio City, is hardly identified in the public mind with those values. He hymns the simple glories of rural Virginia, but he is a world traveler who has lived most of his life away from the Old Dominion by choice. He is the creator of both the folksy Waltons and the conniving Giobertis of *Falcon Crest*. How then to explain the mind of this man who enjoys the finer things in life, yet will fly off to lecture on the art of storytelling at the humble Elyria (Ohio) Public Library, primarily as a courtesy to a friend who had asked him? This Emmy Award-winning television figure who, at the height of his career, lent his renowned skills as a narrator to a thirteen-minute video presentation on the restoration of a historic Virginia iron foundry?

It would be easy to offer a reductionist explanation to the effect that there is within Hamner an ongoing psychic conflict between the influence of his freewheeling father and that of his more upright mother, or that the author is a cosmopolitan trapped inside the body of a rural Baptist. But no, in truth Hamner is a typical Virginian of his generation and ethnic stock—the Hamners are Welsh/Celtic in origin, hailing from the village of Hanmer in the uplands of Wales—which means a mixture of socially conservative outlook with a libertarian, let-sleeping-dogs-lie attitude toward that which "neither picks my pocket nor breaks my leg"; family-centered, fiercely so, rather than centered upon identity with a particular class or economic group, yet open to and curious about those outside the immediate clan; strongly drawn to setting down roots in hill-country, but fascinated by what might lie over the horizon in the lowlands and big cities; a rememberer of things past, but not one to let the worst of these memories blacken the present; and Christian (or at least theist) in belief and practice without being overly pious. Hamner is a lover of songs and of well-told stories, even off-color ones, regardless of "whose side wins" or which character gets thrown into the briar patch; a person who displays that generosity of spirit by which one is willing to admit that even one's opponents and enemies have their good points and are worth respecting for that; innately modest and self-deprecating, yet taking a perennially amazed, childlike pride when praised for his accomplishments; immensely patient and slow to anger, but ferocious when aroused; tending toward the sentimental in temperament but with a saving measure of level-headed common sense; and placing love of home, friends, family, dogs, and good conversation far above the value of money, though prudent in money matters. This "Virginian-ness" partly explains the apparent contradictoriness of Earl Hamner's life and work.

Of equal importance, Hamner is an inquisitive and observant student of human beings and how action springs from character. In conversations with him conducted during the writing of *The Twilight Zone Scripts of Earl Hamner,* Tony Albarella sought to explore the misperception of Hamner as a "soft writer," one who can write only about what novelist William Dean Howells long ago called "the more smiling aspects of life." "This 'soft writer' label," replied Hamner, "can negate the possibility that a writer can write anything other than that genre. For instance, when I wrote and produced *Falcon Crest* the question I was most frequently asked was: 'How can you do this kind of show after *The Waltons?* The answer, of course, is that the Giobertis of *Falcon Crest* were people, and any good writer can write with ease about people, whether they are rich vintners of the Napa Valley or modest hill folk of the Blue Ridge Mountains of Virginia."[12] In *The Waltons* Hamner wrote of essentially moral, decent, faith-filled people who faced life's problems according to that element of their character. In his scripts for *The Twilight Zone,* he presented people from varied backgrounds coping as best they can amid bizarre circumstances, and his depiction of them is as true to their essence as his depiction of the Walton family. Given their background and position, it is entirely unsurprising that the Giobertis of *Falcon Crest* behave as they do. As a student of human character, Hamner succeeded in portraying people from a variety of backgrounds and belief systems in a true-to-life manner. Offering further insight, he claims, *"Falcon Crest* may seem a startling change of pace from *The Waltons,* but in many ways the Gioberti family of *Falcon Crest* were the Waltons of today. The matriarch of the family, played by Jane Wyman, was proud of her family, and while she often was underhanded in doing so she did everything she could to nurture the rituals, history, and customs of her family. She was proud of her land, she valued the continuity of it, and I suspect she would have gone to any lengths to protect it. Come to think of it, that would make a good episode!"[13]

A COMMUNITY OF SOULS

What is it about Hamner's works that holds such positive fascination with the reading and viewing public? In an address delivered at an event at the Walton's Mountain Museum in Schuyler in 1997, Hamner declined to take credit for the values exemplified by the local people in years past, values now viewed as the lifeblood of *The Waltons.* He said of those values:

> They came from our parents, the people who nurtured us and who passed on to us the notions that there was dignity in work, satisfaction in having a job and doing it well, that we can and must be self-reliant and resourceful, that our country's laws are to be obeyed, that we have a right to practice the religion of our choice, the belief that our parents and grandparents not only deserve respect, but are to be treasured for the rituals and stories and rules of conduct that we all need to know and to pass on to our children if we are to call ourselves civilized.
>
> We didn't corner the market on these values, and I think they are more prevalent throughout our country than books and television and the movies would have us believe. We would be foolish to deny that drugs and crime

and scandal have taken their toll on us. But I believe that there is still more Judeo-Christianity than crime in this country, that there is more hope than heroin, more virtue than violence, and more good than evil.

If those values have been weakened today, they sustained our parents and their generation through some often mean and troublesome times.[14]

As noted earlier, Hamner sometimes wearies of being thought of in the public mind as solely "Mister Walton," though he is recurrently refreshed and made proud by the high esteem in which his famous series is held even today, and he is bound to the traditionalist values it affirmed. In the above quote, he describes a view of life that is not denial of life's harsh realities, but rather an acknowledgment of them and a need to face them with courage, dignity, and hope for a better tomorrow. This worldview is articulated in words close to Hamner's heart, expressed by one of his favorite writers, William Faulkner, in his Nobel Prize acceptance speech in 1950: Faulkner said in part that man "alone among creatures . . . has a soul, a spirit capable of compassion and sacrifice and endurance," and that it is the writer's privilege "to help man endure by lifting his heart, by reminding him of the courage and honour and hope and pride and compassion and pity and sacrifice which have been the glory of his past. The poet's voice need not merely be the record of man, it can be one of the props, the pillars to help him endure and prevail." (Hamner keeps a copy of Faulkner's acceptance speech tacked to a bulletin board beside his writing desk.) This vision affirms what has been called "the dignity of man."

It is a vision of life in which the lives of men and women are accounted as more than the flies of summer, but instead are seen as beings made for eternity, with each generation linking with its ancestors and future generations in a community of souls, living close to the soil—like Hamner's fictional Spencers, Waltons, Giobertis, and McGregors (from *Snowy River*). It is a vision that recognizes that although life is fraught with difficulties and "the sun goes down too soon for a poor man" (as Hamner's hard-working father lamented

Earl Hamner Jr. at about age six, in a photo taken in Schuyler.

time and again), human beings, after all, are created in the image of God. Commenting upon this view of life, this "moral imagination," in another context, the American man of letters Russell Kirk once wrote, "It is the strange faculty—inexplicable if men are assumed to have an animal nature only—of discerning greatness, justice, and order, beyond the bars of appetite and self-interest."[15] Each generation draws upon inherited customs, conventions, and ways of continuity to pass along to the rising generation, sensing rather than knowing that men are foolish to trade upon their own knowledge and the perceptions of a single lifetime in order to learn anew the norms of life. That way lies folly, rootlessness, and disorder. Opposed to this are the folkways, old stories, traditions, and manners of the family, united in community with its members and the larger community without and living on family land, or on long-familiar ground. On this point, Tony Albarella has commented on "the degree to which Earl and Virginia are intertwined. While a love of the people is evident in his work, it goes far deeper: Earl's very soul springs from the earth where he was born and raised." This lends to the sense of well-rounded genuineness about Hamner's work, with Albarella writing, "From the feistiness of *Falcon Crest* to the imagination of *Twilight Zone* to the warmth and tenderness of *The Waltons,* Earl's fiction is an extension of himself. His work is alive because he lives within it."[16]

It is all this that resonates with readers of Hamner's written works and viewers of his teleplays: for all the follies to which human flesh is heir, amid all the travails of economic hardship, here are well-told tales that affirm normative truths in a latent, non-didactic sense. During the course of over forty years, many people have contacted Hamner to say that the lives exemplified by the Spencers and Waltons either reminded them of their own upbringing during the 1930s, the way they wished life had been, or the way they wish life could be. It is no wonder *Spencer's Mountain* and *The Homecoming* and *The Waltons* series continue to hold such wide appeal—not only in the United States but around the world. In the subtitle of his book *Goodnight John-Boy,* Hamner described these works as reflecting "the values that have sustained us through good times and bad," and it is not surprising that these *values* (really *norms:* enduring standards, laws of nature that we ignore at our peril) have resonated not only among American readers and viewers but with an international audience as well. These norms were not conceived yesterday, but originate in the cultural history of a people and are given fresh life and fresh expression with each new generation. "The past is never dead," wrote Faulkner. "It's not even past."

The norms to which any healthy culture adheres are an element manifestly present in the work that first brought Hamner wide acclaim, the story of an Appalachian family named the Spencers.

NOTES

1. Prescott, "Wistful, Whimsical and Pure in Heart," *New York Times,* June 11, 1965, 29.

2. Hamner and Giffin, *Goodnight John-Boy,* 9. Many details of Hamner's early life can be found in the opening chapters of this book.

3. Ibid., 21.

4. Ibid., 9.

5. Hamner, telephone conversation with author, September 22, 2003.

6. Hamner to Person, January 7, 2004.

7. Quoted in Kimberly Dunham, "A Mosaic of the John Boys," *From the Hills* (Charleston, WV) no. 38 (1974): 7; and Hamner to Person, September 19, 2003. Of this time in his life, Hamner has also said, in his interview with Kimberly Dunham, "Certain writers were very influential in my own writing. One was a Kentuckian named Elizabeth Madox Roberts. I think she is one of the finest novelists we've ever produced. I have also been influenced a great deal by William Faulkner. . . . I am also a great admirer of Jesse Stuart. I was never fond of writers like F. Scott Fitzgerald. I admire Fitzgerald's work, but it seemed cold and a surface sort of work." Quoted in Dunham, 6. Hamner has read Stuart's complete works.

8. W. K. Harrison III, in an untitled review of *Fifty Roads to Town, Library Journal* 78 (October 1, 1953): 1686.

9. Gene Baro, "Significant Revelation of the Human Spirit," *New York Herald Tribune Book Review,* October 4, 1956, 6.

10. Hamner and Giffin, *Goodnight John-Boy,* 34.

11. Hamner and Sipes, *Murder in Tinseltown,* 151–52.

12. Albarella and Hamner, *The Twilight Zone Scripts of Earl Hamner,* 202.

13. Ibid., 18.

14. Hamner and Giffin, *Goodnight John-Boy,* 197. Hamner attended this event, the unveiling of a plaque in honor of his family, in the company of several former *Waltons* cast members. He ended his involvement with the Walton's Mountain Museum in 2002.

15. Kirk, *Enemies of the Permanent Things,* second ed., 1984, 119.

16. Albarella, Letter to *Charlottesville (VA) Hook,* May 29, 2003, 5.

2

THE STORY OF AN APPALACHIAN FAMILY:

Spencer's Mountain

*There is some of the same fitness in a man's building his
own house that there is in a bird's building its own nest.*

FROM HENRY DAVID THOREAU'S
WALDEN; OR LIFE IN THE WOODS, 1854

SPENCER'S MOUNTAIN HAD ITS ORIGINS in a dream of hope Hamner's father entertained during the darkest days of the Great Depression. It was a dream proffered to his family to give them hope for better days ahead, at a time when jobs at the soapstone quarry and mill in Schuyler, Virginia, had vanished.

Hamner recalls his father's hope: "'One of these days,' he would say, 'I'm going to have enough money to buy us a mountain and I'm going to build a house on it. It's going to have ten rooms and a fireplace and a front porch where we can all sit and rest of an evening. I'll put up what they call a "picture window" so we can see everything from a rainbow to a red bird flying over the Blue Ridge.'"

Earl Hamner Sr. never achieved his dream of accumulating enough money to buy a mountain or to build a new house, though he worked hard all his life. And yet, his eldest son later claimed, "he did achieve his dream in another way. He instilled enough confidence and security in me for me to become a writer and through my writing he built *Spencer's Mountain*. . . . The plot is simple and tells of how a father sacrifices his dream to give his son a college education."[1]

It is that and more. It is also the story of the writer as a young man, of his coming of age, and of his departure from home to make his way in the world. It is the story of a character similar in many respects to Earl Hamner Jr. as he grows up during the years of the Great Depression, experiencing the everyday joys and trials of life, the death of a beloved family member, the deathless love of his family, and most notably his father's self-sacrificing love. It is thus a story of endings and beginnings, awakenings and leave-takings.

In broad strokes, *Spencer's Mountain* tells of one year in the life of fifteen-year-old Clay-Boy Spencer, a boy in his final year of formal schooling in the village of New Dominion, Virginia, a close approximation of Hamner's native Schuyler. Clay-Boy is the oldest of the eleven children of Clay and Olivia Spencer—he a laborer in the local soapstone mill, she a full-time mother and homemaker, together the owners of undeveloped ancestral land on nearby Spencer's Mountain. Unlike his more refined, gracious, and church-going wife, Clay Sr. is something of a hard-drinking rascal and fun-loving scamp, a

Grade-school portraits of the Hamner children, ordered according to age. *Top row from left,* Nancy, Jim, Bill, Paul; *bottom row from left,* Audrey, Marion, Cliff, Earl.

man forever rejoicing at the simple pleasures of life or swearing a blue streak at life's injustices. He is immensely proud of his children, his "babies" as he calls them all: Clay-Boy, Matt, Becky, Shirley, Luke, Mark, John, Pattie-Cake, Donnie, Franklin Delano, and Eleanor. Clay's eldest son is a contemplative young man who helps raise the other children, excels in school, loves his large family and their neighbors, occasionally tires of being responsible (as the oldest) for raising the other children, and yearns for something that lies somewhere over the horizon of Spencer's Mountain.

Perhaps a word is in order at this point about the peculiar name Clay-Boy (and for that matter, John-Boy from *The Waltons*). At least until recent years, relations between Southern fathers and sons have been unique within American society for their closeness. For example, it is often the case that the father—rather than a brother or a best friend—is invited to assume the role of best man at his son's wedding. In years past it was common for the oldest son of a family to be named after his father—there are many Southern "Juniors"—and to be nicknamed in some manner to indicate this relationship. In some cases, the eldest boy is known throughout his life as "Son" or "Junior," even by his siblings. "Boy" is sometimes appended to a son's first name, at least until he reaches adulthood. (However, contrary to the speculations of at least one admirer, Earl Hamner Jr. was never called "Earl-Boy" by his family. His boyhood nickname, mercifully short-lived according to Hamner, was "Sparkplug.")

The episodic novel *Spencer's Mountain* opens on Thanksgiving Eve, with Clay-Boy standing in his yard at home and anxiously awaiting the arrival of his father's eight brothers and their families. After all the relatives have arrived, his bachelor Uncle Virgil gives Clay-Boy a gift, a new hunting knife. This is an important gift, because the young man is hoping to participate in the Spencer menfolks' annual Thanksgiving deer hunt for the first time in his life. This tradition puts meat on the table for the Thanksgiving meal. But the hunt offers a further attraction for the Spencer men. It is believed that somewhere on Spencer's Mountain there roams a mysterious white deer, and it is said that whoever should kill that deer will be "marked to follow a path unknown, a man marked for glory!"[2]

Clay-Boy joins the men early the next morning for the hunt, and within a few hours he encounters and shoots the white buck, giving the animal a death-thrust with his new knife. The boy is deeply shaken by this taking of an innocent life, but when he is joined by his father and uncles, he takes comfort in the words of assurance from his Uncle Virgil to his father: "It wasn't no boy killed that deer, Clay," he said. "It took a man to do it."[3] Clay-Boy has stood up to a test of courage and endured a rite of passage, however distasteful. With the Spencers living a simple, straightforward rural life, the taking of the deer is not mere sport for bored city-dwellers; the creature's flesh will provide venison for the Thanksgiving dinner (and beyond) as well as a handsome rack of antlers as a trophy. And the deer's death will "mark" Clay-Boy in some fashion, which will be revealed as the novel unfolds. Clay Sr. braces his son by saying, "Whatever you're marked for, boy, you'll stand up to it."[4]

Several reviewers have noted that it is unclear how successfully this first episode in *Spencer's Mountain* is understood and handled by the author himself.[5] In truth, the slaying of the virginally white deer by the phallic knife wielded by Clay-Boy, as well as his contemplations upon that act, form a thematic touchstone for all that follows in the book. In one sense it speaks of the young man's pending loss of virginity—in his understanding of sexuality (when he accompanies his father to have the family cow mated with a neighbor's bull) and in his sexual initiation with the mill-manager's flirtatious daughter. It also speaks to the boy's growing understanding of the meanness and glory that is human nature (as when his father goes to plead unsuccessfully with the richest man in the community for a loan to send Clay-Boy to college, then performs a signal act of sacrifice on behalf of his family's future), to his understanding of death, through the passing of his wise grandfather, Zebulon, and to his outlook on life: a continuum of change rooted in permanence. Human development, after all, does not pass through phases as a train passes through stations, as the Anglo-Irish writer C. S. Lewis once put it. Being alive, humanity, "has the privilege of always moving yet never leaving anything behind."

"Change is the means of our preservation," wrote the statesman Edmund Burke, and this truth is borne out vividly in the story of Clay-Boy Spencer's final year at home with his family. To attempt to keep children small and unchallenged by the world forever, as mother Olivia wishes for all her "babies," is to encourage a state of prolonged helplessness, dependency, and frustration, needlessly so. To avoid this state, Clay-Boy must mature, choose his path out of New Dominion, and prepare to leave the comfortable home in which his parents and grandparents have nurtured him. This comes about by decisive acts of the will, not by contemplation alone or by simply attaining a certain age. At the end of the novel's first episode, the carcass of the white deer is affixed to a carrying-pole by Clay-Boy's uncles and father, hunters all, and then the violent bear it away. This is to use the language of the Bible, one of the two books owned by the Hamner family during the author's upbringing, to describe a life of wise discernment and needful action. To achieve this marriage of wisdom and right action is maturity.

In a letter written to the Dial Press shortly before that publisher released *Spencer's Mountain,* Harper Lee (famed author of *To Kill a Mockingbird*) commended Hamner's skill as a portraitist, noting, "It is so easy to create a villain or an eccentric. It is so hard to create good people and make them unforgettable. Each character in *Spencer's Mountain* is memorable, because life itself flows in abundance from each. One finds pure joy in reading, for a change, a positive statement on the potentialities of man."[6] Aside from his remarkably lifelike portrayal of Clay-Boy—gawky, impatient, yearning to grow up and leave home but wanting to stay—Hamner crafts an especially powerful portrait of the young man's father. To some extent Clay Spencer resembles the stonecutter W. O. Gant from Thomas Wolfe's *Look Homeward, Angel.* Like Old Gant, Clay Spencer is a man who practically inhales all of life, though he is in love with life and his family, but Gant is an insensitive man who essentially embraces his own appetites. Each is a man of never-achieved ambition: Gant never carves his perfect stone angel, and Clay never builds his house on the mountain. Each is at once larger than life and immediately recognizable.

There is a Sisyphean aspect to Clay's efforts to be rid of the company-owned house in which he lives and to move into a house built by his own hands. In the same way Sisyphus, according to Greek mythology, was condemned by the gods to forever push a boulder up to the top of a mountain in the afterlife, only to have it roll back down at the moment of near-success, Clay is compelled each year to begin work on a task he will never complete. He earnestly wants to build his dream house and makes an honest effort to begin laying its foundation each spring; but he can never complete the job because of the demands upon his time by work, a growing family, or (more often than not) the siren-call of fishing. Each year time slips away from him, and soon it is winter when no work can be done. Every spring, Clay returns to his property on Spencer's Mountain only to discover that the cellar he dug last spring has largely vanished, with the rain and snow of winter having washed most of the fill-dirt back into it. Yet, for the sake of Olivia and the children, he clings stubbornly to his dream, believing like Thoreau that "there is some of the same fitness in a man's building his own house that there is in a bird's building its own nest." Ironically, it is during the year in which Clay has made the most progress on the foundation—actually progressing to the point of framing the house—that he decides to sell the property to pay for Clay-Boy's college education. The decision to sell the land is not made lightly, but only after considerable thought and a weighing of options. The decision is, in fact, painful. A few hours before he sells the property, Clay walks in agony of spirit to the site of his never-to-be-built house and destroys all he has accomplished to date:

> The horrible guttural cries of a man unaccustomed to
> tears forced their way through his throat, and tears and
> sweat rolled down his face together as he seized a sledge
> hammer and splintered each hand-hewn stud of the
> framework. Each blow he dealt the house fell as if on
> some living part of himself and Clay cried aloud with
> pain.[7]

After this decisive act and before he leaves the site, Clay grabs up a handful of dirt from Spencer's Mountain. He makes his way to the family burying-ground and sits contemplatively at the gravesite of his own father. There, alone, he speaks aloud of the world he faces and the decision he has made, hoping that in the world beyond this world his father can hear him and understand:

> "Times is changen on this old earth, Papa, and it looks like
> we're goen to have to change right along with 'em. I don't
> mean me and Livy and Mama, but there's some kind of
> world out there waiten for my babies and I aim to see 'em
> get whatever they can out of it.
>
> "I recken you know what's on my mind before I say it,
> Papa." Clay reached out the handful of earth and slowly
> let it fall through his fingers over his father's grave. "This
> is the last of the land. I'm sellen what's left of the moun-

tain. I know what that land meant to you and only Old Master Jesus knows what it means to me. I tried hard to build that house on it for Livy and the babies, but I just never could get around to it. . . .

"The sun goes down too soon for a poor man, Papa, and you know it yourself. There just ain't hours in a day to do all a poor man's got to do."[8]

Clay proceeds from the cemetery to the residence of Colonel Coleman, the general manager of the mill, and sells the property. After this he walks home, where a worried Olivia confronts him. He explains to her what he has done and why. Olivia understands Clay's decision but protests that it is not fair to their other children to sacrifice the property for Clay-Boy's benefit alone. Clay replies:

"I've put heart and mind to that already, honey," said Clay. "And I've decided we've still got to do it. The way I look at it, there's fine stuff in my babies. But it's like a river that's dammed up. All we'll ever get to see is what little bit pours over the top of the dam unless somethen comes along that breaks the walls down and lets the river flow. Well, somethen has come along. Clay-Boy is goen to college. If he goes down there and makes good then he's goen to help Matt get a start in life, and Matt will help Becky and right on down the line. All they need is a little start and God knows they might turn out to be doctors and nurses and lawyers and salesmen or even presidents. I used to vision the most we could for all of 'em was to get 'em through high school. I can see more than that now."[9]

Within a few pages, Clay Spencer has weighed present concerns against the needs of the future and the legacy of generations past. In his mind, each generation is linked intimately with the one that preceded it and the one that will follow, and he has taken steps to maintain that community of souls. This simple man intuits that the living would be foolish to depend upon the small fund of knowledge acquired in a single lifetime, as we are part of an unsung strand of individuals whose lineage disappears into the distant past, men and women whose choices for good or ill have brought us to this present day. From the standpoint of the present, he can see faintly into a future to which he owes a patrimony to those who will follow when he and Olivia are dust. As noted earlier, William Faulkner wrote, in *Requiem for a Nun,* "The past is never dead. It's not even past." In Clay's contemplations over the selling of his property, there is much more at stake than the mere happiness or spur-of-the-moment preferences of one man: there is also the future of the Spencer family and devotion to the traditions to which the family is heir. Our lives are not our own.

To craft a novel in which these truths are presented in a manner imaginative and heartwarming, yet realistic and (at times) uncomfortably earthy, requires a sure hand by the author. Hamner succeeds because the story of Clay-Boy and his family arises directly from his own experience, and because some fifteen years of apprenticeship in writing believable material for radio and television served him well as he prepared to write *Spencer's Mountain.* Describing it as "a splendid novel," Harper Lee wrote that it is Hamner's "perspective that I think I most admire. His subject matter was so fraught with temptations that sometimes I held my breath lest he go overboard, but I shouldn't have worried. Where a less gifted artist would have pitied, he showed compassion; where someone on the make for money would have inundated the reader with rural crudities, Mr. Hamner's good taste prevailed. His humor is true humor; it grows from his characters."

Clay-Boy's eight (by novel's end, ten) young brothers and sisters display all the characteristics of real children, with their tattling, their fears, their unerring choosing of the most inopportune times imaginable to begin misbehaving or to announce loudly that they have to use the toilet—preferably when visitors are in the house. The humor spoken of by Harper Lee lies in such natural situations. As she wrote, "I'd like to congratulate Mr. Hamner on his admirable control of his young people. Nothing in the world is drearier to me than ego-ridden fictional teenagers. They're all alike. Not so Mr. Hamner's youngsters. They reflect Mr. Hamner's faultless observation plus his truly innate sense of perspective."

Likewise Hamner avoids the temptation to sentimentalize the death scene of the grandfather, Zebulon Spencer, who was critically injured by the fall of a tree cut down by Clay during construction of the new house. Where other writers might say that the old man "died with a smile on his face, secure in the knowledge that his children and grandchildren faced a bright future" or words to similar effect, Hamner describes Zebulon's final struggle differently. As the children's grandmother holds the hand of her dying husband, the reader is told simply:

> When life ebbed away, when the blood no longer made its spasmodic voyage through the hand she held, she looked at his face. The fierce old beautiful visage relaxed, and something not quite a smile, but akin to it, took its place, a waxed artificial slack expression that was neither pain nor joy but was simply death.[10]

And yet the author will not leave the reader with a stark, almost naturalistic description. The humanistic aspect must be included, too, and so for honesty's sake, Hamner describes a scene with which any reader can identify who has ever been present at the death of a parent or spouse:

> Something she could not name rose from forgotten wells and the old woman remembered her husband in the vigor of his youth. He had been a man to be proud of and the tears that fell from her old eyes were the tears of a young girl. Her grief spent itself when at last she took her warm hand from the cold dead one and prepared herself to tell those who waited beyond the door.
> She opened the door and they knew.
> "The old man's gone," she said with dignity, and suddenly the arms of her sons were around her and they clung to one another and wept.[11]

Contrary to what some critics have said, all is not sweetness and optimism on Spencer's Mountain. It is a mixture of all the trials and joys faced by real people, told in language that is simple, in a style that is spare, and which owes much to a writer whose work Hamner encountered in the formative years of his career.

SHERWOOD ANDERSON AND *SPENCER'S MOUNTAIN*

Readers of *Spencer's Mountain* cannot but be struck by its many resonances with Sherwood Anderson's *Winesburg, Ohio* (1919). Like Anderson's masterpiece, Hamner's novel is a bildungsroman—a coming-of-age novel—which centers upon a teenage boy growing to manhood in an American village whose inhabitants have seldom seen life outside the world of work and putting food on the table. Like George Willard, the central character in *Winesburg*, Clay-Boy is given to introspection, has aspirations that extend far beyond the boundaries of his village, and has a strong-willed female teacher who sees education as the key to his launching forth into the larger world. Both young men have little knowledge of the ways of the world, want earnestly to enter the world of adulthood, and experience an awkward sexual initiation. Both suffer the loss of a beloved family member on the eve of their departure from the villages of their upbringing. Both novels end with the protagonists leaving town on their way to the big city, but with the sense that the place they have left has formed the canvas upon which they will paint the stories of their lives.

There are differences between the two novels, as well, based in large part upon the differing temperaments and artistic emphases of Anderson and Hamner, and it is insightful to examine the parallels and differences between them.

As noted in the previous chapter, Hamner has acknowledged that in 1943, while serving in the U.S. Army and traveling on a troop train, he met a fellow soldier, Paul Nusnick, who introduced him to the world of the arts, classical music, and literature—including the literature of Thomas Wolfe, F. Scott Fitzgerald, William Faulkner, and Anderson. As Hamner has written, "I read *Winesburg* while I was still in the army and I also started taking notes for *Spencer's Mountain* then. So I certainly must have been under Mr. Anderson's spell. Even if it were such a thin thread as my reverence

The Hamner family cemetery, near Wales Mountain in Schuyler.

for Faulkner who was so encouraged by S. A., it could be argued that he affected my work."[12] Anderson thus served as at least an indirect influence, through what the English divine and essayist John Henry Newman termed the *illative sense:* a method of reasoning and theory of knowledge beyond strict logic. It consists of knowledge that is borne in upon the mind from a source deeper than one's conscious and formal reason, combining intuition, imagination, experience, and much meditation upon one's reading and life experiences: a "supra-logical judgment," as Newman called it in his *Essay in Aid of a Grammar.* Hamner's friend Ray Bradbury, author of *The Martian Chronicles* and *Fahrenheit 451,* among many other novels and short stories, once described Anderson's influence upon his own imagination by saying that *Winesburg* dissolved into his ganglion in a manner that cannot be clearly discerned or adequately described;

Hamner used to listen to the sound of trains passing over this trestle across the Rockfish River late at night during his boyhood.

EARL HAMNER

one might as well attempt to detect the individual ingredients of a cake by tasting the finished product. "You might see a few apparitions of *Winesburg, Ohio* in my . . . book of-stories-pretending-to-be-a-novel, *Dandelion Wine*. But there are no mirror images."[13] As with Bradbury, the works of Anderson and the other writers Hamner discovered during his army years likewise *illated* into his mind and imagination. What resulted was a novel that blends an Anderson-esque style and wistfulness with a sense of hopefulness derived from Hamner's own inherited belief system.

"There Is a Time in the Life of Every Boy. . . ."

At a point early on in Hamner's novel, the reader is given a snapshot of Clay-Boy in a very George Willard–esque moment, sitting alone in a crab apple orchard. Significantly, he is in the midst of thoughts he cannot articulate, related to his prospects of achieving what is to him an impossible dream, attending college. He, after all—by killing the white deer—has been marked for something special in life:

> The air was cool but, sitting at the base of one of the old trees, Clay-Boy Spencer felt the warmth of excitement and expectation. He felt more than saw the change as the sun slipped away beyond the horizon and left the orchard in the cool blue light of fading day.
>
> Clay-Boy had come to the orchard to think. Something had happened during the day so unbelievable and so nearly impossible that he needed to be alone somewhere to let his mind absorb the thing gradually.[14]

But for the differences in the boys' respective names, those last two sentences could have been written by Anderson in *Winesburg*. Like Clay-Boy, George Willard is a young man given to long silences and the thinking through of what he observes in the lives of his family and his village's inhabitants. Both boys are a typical, uneasy blend of teenage awkwardness and blooming sophistication. In the chapter "Sophistication," Anderson muses upon George in the midst of one of the boy's reveries, in a simple yet eloquent passage:

There is a time in the life of every boy when he for the first time takes the backward view of life. Perhaps that is the moment when he crosses the line into manhood. He is thinking of the future and of the figure he will cut in the world. Suddenly something happens; he stops under a tree and waits as for a voice calling his name. Ghosts of old things creep into his consciousness; the voices outside of himself whisper a message concerning the limitations of life. From being quite sure of himself and his future he becomes not at all sure. If he be an imaginative boy a door is torn open and for the first time he looks out upon the world, seeing, as though they marched in procession before him, the countless figures of men who before his time have come out of nothingness into the world, lived their lives and again disappeared into nothingness. The sadness of sophistication has come to the boy.[15]

Where George sees life as sweet but meaningless, an endless procession of men and women passing out of nowhere into nothing, Clay-Boy sees it as containing a comforting secret: while desolation and death will in time call for him and for his family, life is informed and invigorated by family, tradition, continuity, and the promises of faith, hope, and love. There is the consolation of his mother's Christian faith and the memories of his family's plain, homely house at night, when his parents and the other children say their goodnights to each other. As Clay-Boy gazes in solitude at the plain-looking village, he dreams of going away to college and into the world beyond New Dominion and realizes his departure will be as much loss as gain. "'I'm going away from here,' he said aloud, and his voice to him seemed as filled with sadness as with victory." Clay-Boy "felt as if a curtain were being drawn across the scene, cutting him away from his family and separating them from him."[16]

"You Will Have to Know Life"
Clay-Boy is at the top of his class at the local high school: bookish and inclined toward a career as a writer. He is strongly encouraged

to pursue higher education not only by his parents but by one of his teachers, Laura Parker, who describes herself with a certain prideful defiance as "an old-maid schoolteacher who touches up her hair and adores Shakespeare" and as "the object of considerable ridicule already. Being laughed at is nothing new to me." It is she who politics among all the right people, attempting to arrange for a scholarship to the University of Richmond for Clay-Boy; and it is she who arranges with the general manager of the soapstone mill, Colonel Coleman, for a small lending library to be opened in New Dominion, with Clay-Boy on salary as the librarian, at the mill's expense. She does not take no for an answer from Coleman in regard to the library, or even from Clay-Boy when he balks at going to college. As she explains to Clay Sr., "Once in a while a child comes along with a hungry look in his eye. He's not content just to memorize facts. He wants to know, he has an inquiring mind, and everything he learns only whets his appetite to learn more. Your son is such a boy, Mr. Spencer. I've taught him everything I know and he's still hungry. If the day comes that I go past the mill and see him stooped over a polishing machine, I think I will give up the teaching profession."[17]

Laura serves much the same role in attending to Clay-Boy's fortunes as Kate Swift does in the life of George Willard. In Anderson's chapter "The Teacher," Kate—who is "not known in Winesburg as a pretty woman" but who possesses "the features of a tiny goddess on a pedestal in a garden in the dim light of a summer evening"—practically commands George to develop his talents as a writer in the world outside Winesburg, but first to learn about life and "to know what people are thinking about, not what they say." In George "she thought she had recognized the spark of genius and wanted to blow on that spark."[18] Thus, behind each of these young men is a strong-willed female teacher who wants the best for the boy she has known and taught and will not allow him to drift into aimlessness or become less than he ought to be. This fervent interest by an older female in her younger male charge has the potential for a more-than-Platonic relationship; and in the case of *Winesburg,* there is definitely sexual tension between George and Kate which Anderson makes explicit. At one point George takes Kate in his arms and attempts to kiss her, only to have his teacher remember her position, rouse herself from her momentary surrender to her student, and begin beating George's face with her fists. In *Spencer's Mountain,* there is no such suggestion of attraction between Clay-Boy and Laura.

"What He Wanted She Wanted"

During the early years of his writing career, Anderson was criticized by some genteel critics for an alleged obsession with sex. *Winesburg* itself gave these critics plenty of fuel for their attacks, with the author describing not only George Willard's musings about sexual relations, but also providing the exceptional story titled "The Untold Lie." Here Anderson relates a remarkable vignette containing complex truths expressed in simple terms. It concerns two farmhands, Ray Pearson and Hal Winters, who work land outside the village. Hal, a sturdy workman but a young hell-raiser by all accounts, has got a local schoolteacher, Nell Gunther, pregnant. His partner is Ray, an older, married man who has been worked to a frazzle by the responsibilities of life and supporting a family. He determines to warn Hal not to fall into the same trap of marriage that had ensnared him years before. As evening falls, Ray runs across a field to stop Hal, who is swanking down the road into Winesburg for a night out on the town, and he shouts out arguments to himself, almost (in effect) practicing what he intends to say to Hal while justifying his own bitterness about life and his thwarted dreams:

> "There was no promise made," he cried into the empty spaces that lay about him. "I didn't promise my Minnie anything and Hal hasn't made any promise to Nell. I know he hasn't. She went into the woods with him because she wanted to go. What he wanted she wanted. Why should I pay? Why should Hal pay? Why should anyone pay? I don't want Hal to become old and worn out. I'll tell him. I won't let it go on. I'll catch Hal before he gets to town and I'll tell him."[19]

As readers of this story know, Ray eventually catches up with Hal but doesn't have a chance to warn him about marriage. Hal does all the talking, informing Ray that on his own he has decided to marry Nell, settle down with her, and have children. The story ends as Hal strides away into the gathering twilight toward a new chapter in his life while Ray shuffles homeward, back across the field. He now remembers the simple pleasures of home-life with his wife and children. Weighing that memory with the knowledge he failed to impart to Hal, he muses aloud: "'It's just as well. Whatever I told him would have been a lie,' he said softly, and then his form also disappeared into the darkness of the fields."[20] In the end, Ray stumbles upon the unforeseen truth of his earlier words, learning that, in truth, what she wanted he wanted, too.

The most serious crisis of Clay-Boy's teenage life arrives when he finds himself alone in the woods during a stroll with Claris Coleman, the well-off and sexually precocious daughter of the general manager of the company that employs many of the men living in the village, including Clay-Boy's father. From the remarks she makes to Clay-Boy during their every private conversation, it is plain that sexual intercourse is never far from her mind; she is forever steering the conversation in order to tell the puzzled young man, in a recurrent display of psychological projection, that sex is the only thing on his mind. For his part, Clay-Boy exhibits all the fumbling wonder of a sexually awakening male as he contemplates a girl he has known all his life. "Last summer they had been buddies, as close as companionable brothers and sisters. Perhaps it had to do with the fact that Claris had spent a year in college. Clay-Boy had matured too, and whatever it was that was new between them neither of them was able to speak about to the other."[21]

When Clay-Boy and Claris eventually find themselves alone in a secluded clearing on Spencer's Mountain one hot day, the young man discovers that what she wanted he wanted. Claris takes up her usual flirtatious taunt about sexual adventure:

> "You're always thinking about it. I can tell. I can read
> minds and I've known all along you brought me up here
> just to try something."
> Clay-Boy was wordless. Suddenly he realized that it

could very well happen. He had dreamed of it, imagined it, anticipated it, yearned for it, and now it seemed that the mysterious and impossible thing could actually happen.[22]

As indeed it does—with the twosome chasing each other like little animals, much like the lovely Helen White and George Willard do in wild innocence at the deserted Winesburg fairground, in the story "Sophistication." Earlier in *Winesburg*, George had experienced sexual initiation with Louise Trunnion. But where George's sexual adventure is accompanied by a certain bravado and the prideful self-assurances that Louise "hasn't got anything on me" and that "nobody knows," Clay-Boy's Baptist conscience is troubled after his sexual initiation. Although he initially feels tenderness toward Claris immediately after the act, within a short time he is worried that Claris might be pregnant and that his own life might take an unforeseen turn, with no college and no prospects other than to do whatever is necessary to "do right" by Claris. For her part, Claris, knowing that she has worried Clay-Boy with hints that she may be pregnant, playfully torments him in the days and weeks immediately following their tryst by hinting that she has a big announcement she needs to confide to him. As it turns out, her untold lie—finally revealed—is that she is not pregnant; she has merely transferred to the women's college at the University of Richmond to be near Clay-Boy, news that he greets with relief and joy.

Departure

In the life of each of these fictional young men, there comes a time of departure from the familiar surroundings of home and family. In the weeks immediately preceding their leave-taking, each has lost an important family member to death: George, his mother; Clay-Boy, his beloved paternal grandfather. In *Winesburg*, George comes to the train station alone to leave Winesburg and travel to the big city, where he will pursue his dreams. He boards his train, barely missing a chance to say goodbye to Helen White—just the sort of anticlimactic moment reflecting an opportunity missed or denied that Anderson specializes in throughout the novel. (For example, one thinks of the failure of George's mother, Elizabeth, to ensure that her carefully hoarded money—which might have served to deliver her from the dullness of her existence as Tom Willard's drudging wife—comes into George's hands, in the story "Death." Where Elizabeth's sacrifice is for naught, Clay Spencer's sacrifice of his own dreams, by selling his property on Spencer's Mountain—along with his dream of building a new house on that land—is fruitful, as the money he gains by the sale pays for Clay-Boy to attend college.) As he sits waiting for the train to depart, George counts his money and thinks back on his father's parting words: "'Be a sharp one,' Tom Willard had said. 'Keep your eyes on your money. Be awake. That's the ticket. Don't let anyone think you're a greenhorn.'" As he gazes out the window, George thinks not of the drama of the moment at which he has arrived, but of homely scenes from everyday life in Winesburg which have nevertheless taken on an aspect of timeless, twilit beauty, with their memory creating what the poet T. S. Eliot termed "a lifetime burning in every moment." In one of the many passages of quiet beauty crafted by Anderson in *Winesburg, Ohio,* George

> thought of little things—Turk Smollet wheeling boards
> through the main street of his town in the morning, a tall
> woman, beautifully gowned, who had once stayed
> overnight at his father's hotel, Butch Wheeler the lamp
> lighter of Winesburg hurrying through the streets on a
> summer evening and holding a torch in his hand, Helen
> White standing by a window in the Winesburg post office
> and putting a stamp on an envelope.[23]

It is interesting that George's last thought before dozing off in the train-car is of Helen; it is at once true to life in terms of human behavior in the typical coltish male of George's age in life and a testimony to Anderson's knowledge of human psychology. Anderson closes his novel and the story of George's life in the village of Winesburg by stating simply that when the young man awakened and again looked out the window of the train, "the town of Winesburg had disappeared and his life there had become but a background on which to paint the dreams of his manhood."

Unlike George and his thoughts of Helen, Clay-Boy's last thoughts before leaving to begin his college education are not of his girl, but of his family. He too has been instructed by his father not to be betrayed by his own inexperience while in the big city. On the morning of his son's departure, Clay advises the young man, "Don't get mixed up with bad women if you can help it, boy. They'll ruin you." A little later he says, "Don't borrow money, play square with everybody and look 'em straight in the eye." The novel closes with Clay's final words of advice and his son's departure:

> "Give 'em hell, Son," said Clay.
> "Goodbye, Daddy," he said, and held his father's
> strong rough hand in a quick handshake, and then the bus
> was there and he was on it.

During their childhood years, the Hamner children went fishing near this hydroelectric dam across the Rockfish River.

Schuyler Baptist Church, where the family attended Sunday-morning and Wednesday-evening services.

For a few minutes after he reached his seat his eyes were clouded with tears, but when they were clear again he saw that the bus was nearing the top of a steep mountain road.

"Goen far, son?" asked an old farmer sitting next to him.

"Right far," the boy said, and watched as the bus arrived at the top of the mountain and went on into the beckoning world.[24]

That is the last prospect the reader is given of Clay-Boy Spencer and George Willard. Their creators crafted no novelistic sequels—though *The Waltons* does provide an imaginative sequel of sorts to *Spencer's Mountain*—and we do not learn what became of them from the time they ventured into the wide world until the day they too disappeared into the darkness of the fields; but both Anderson and Hamner have skillfully drawn the reader along to the point where it is understood that these young men, shaped and strengthened by both the love and the hard knocks they have experienced during their youth in small villages, nevertheless have a better chance than many to realize the dreams of their manhood, wherever those dreams might lead them. In bringing Clay-Boy and George to this point, Hamner and Anderson have walked a path marked by many of the same landmarks but with differing overlooks. And in the case of each writer, words used by novelist Henry Miller to describe Anderson's work apply: "The style was as free and natural . . . as the glass of ice water which stands on every table in every home and restaurant"—though in truth this style had been acquired through long apprenticeship.[25] In a blurb written for the first edition of Hamner's novel, the prolific Appalachian novelist and short-story writer Jesse Stuart said, "The sheer beauty of simple writing in *Spencer's Mountain* is powerful. It's the way the English language should be written. It's the kind of prose that flows like a young wind in spring . . . or with the smoothness of the blue Ohio River in summer."

A little more than ten years after the publication of *Spencer's Mountain,* the novel was adapted to form the framework, characterization, and series of story lines for the long-running television program *The Waltons*. However, it would be a mistake for readers familiar with only the onscreen saga to assume a straight one-for-one correspondence between *Spencer's Mountain* and *The Waltons*. The similarities and differences between these works will be explored in the following chapter.

NOTES

1. Hamner, "A Wonderful Journey—The Books of Earl Hamner," http://www.the-waltons.com/booksbyearl.html.

2. Hamner, *Spencer's Mountain*, Dial Press, 1961, 12. All allusions to *Spencer's Mountain* refer to this edition.

3. *Spencer's Mountain*, 19.

4. *Spencer's Mountain*, 19.

5. See especially John Cook Wyllie, "A Boy Grows Up in Nelson County, Virginia," *The New York Times Book Review*, January 14, 1962, 40. The critic emphasizes the novel's importance as a work that stresses "breaking free of rural chains," for "the past is suddenly dead, even if it is still lovely." This is to overstate Hamner's intent, as he believes that in an increasingly complex, rootless, and technological world, it becomes increasingly crucial that the traditional values learned among small communities and wise, virtuous families and mentors be revisited, as well as the communities and people themselves, to conserve and restore in one's own life the outlooks and beliefs that make life worthwhile.

6. Lee to the Dial Press, 1961. This otherwise undated letter was printed in full on the back cover of the first edition. All further references to Lee's remarks are from this prepublication letter.

7. *Spencer's Mountain*, 231.

8. Ibid., 233.

9. Ibid., 236.

10. Ibid., 199.

11. Ibid., 199.

12. Hamner to Person, September 19, 2003.

13. Bradbury, "Green Town, Somewhere in Mars; Mars, Somewhere in Egypt," in *The Martian Chronicles*, Avon Books, 1997, x.

14. *Spencer's Mountain*, 65.

15. Anderson, *Winesburg, Ohio*, Penguin Books, 1976, 234. All allusions to *Winesburg, Ohio* refer to this edition.

16. *Spencer's Mountain*, 67–68.

17. Ibid., 86.

18. *Winesburg, Ohio*, 162–63.

19. Ibid., 207.

20. Ibid., 209.

21. *Spencer's Mountain*, 104.

22. Ibid., 208.

23. *Winesburg, Ohio*, 247.

24. *Spencer's Mountain*, 247.

25. Miller, "The Storyteller," in *Homage to Sherwood Anderson: 1876–1941*, Paul Appel, Publisher, 1970, 118. This essay was originally published in a special issue of *Story* magazine in 1941, shortly after Anderson's death. One other note might be added about an aspect of Hamner's writing style: his spelling of such words as *havin'* and *goin'* as *haven* and *goen,* a convention he borrowed from the fiction of Elizabeth Madox Roberts. He believes this phonetic spelling better serves the way a word sounds when spoken.

Hamner relaxes on the front porch of the Walton house on the Warner Brothers lot.

On the twenty-fifth anniversary of the debut of *The Waltons,* Carolyn Grinnell, president of the Waltons International Fan Club, presents Hamner with a handmade cross-stitched star, which she modeled upon the stars on the Hollywood Walk of Fame.

3

TO ENDURE AND PREVAIL:

The Homecoming and *The Waltons*

*My grandfather used to say that nobody owns a moun-
tain; but getting born, and living, and dying in its shadow,
we loved Walton's Mountain and felt it was ours.*

FROM EARL HAMNER'S SPOKEN PROLOGUE
TO *THE HOMECOMING*, 1971

*"There ought to be a view around the world
From such a mountain—if it isn't wooded
Clear to the top."*

FROM "THE MOUNTAIN," BY ROBERT FROST

"IT'LL NEVER WORK."

The key decision-makers in the world of network television believed from the beginning that the American viewing public would not likely embrace a series about a rural family living in the shadow of a mountain in Virginia's Blue Ridge. Did they not have it on the authority of Erskine Caldwell and of James Dickey's novel *Deliverance* that Southern hill folks are by and large an appalling collection of inbred, banjo-picking hillbillies beneath the dignity of the jaded modern? Indeed, so. The executives suspected *The Waltons* would never last through its first season. They were wrong.

Instead, that series, *The Waltons,* became one of the best-loved and most-watched programs in television history. Over the course of nine seasons, from 1972 to 1981, many Americans tuned in to CBS every Thursday night to watch an imaginative recreation of life in a close-knit family reminiscent of Hamner's own as they endured and prevailed amid the Depression and the early years of World War II. To its admirers, especially those who had lived during those long-ago years, *The Waltons* represented a fond backward glance to a time when love, hard work, virtuous conduct, and a sense of pulling together for the common good not only helped American families survive but made life worth living. To the program's detractors, however, *The Waltons* was merely an exercise in saccharine nostalgia.

To give the hostile critics their due, the series did tap into a vein of nostalgia. In the twilight years of the American youth movement of the mid to late 1960s, with its emphasis upon sexual adventuring, protesting American involvement in the Vietnam conflict (and the American military in general), throwing down the established order, and sneering at all things beloved by earlier generations, a wave of nostalgia came to the fore in American culture. This was manifested during the early seventies by a fashion for collecting and displaying memorabilia of days past: old photos, movie posters from Hollywood's golden era, soft-drink signs from store displays, penny-banks, and dozens of other artifacts from the 1930s and earlier. Amid a faltering economy, strong evidence of political corruption, and immense social upheaval, many younger people wondered if things had always been as unsettled and unsettling as they were in the present era, and if there was any truth to the old stories told by their parents and grandparents of quiet joy amid struggle and hardship during the Great Depression. Hamner's short novel *The Homecoming,* the television special it inspired, and *The Waltons* arrived on America's cultural landscape at precisely this time of widespread reassessment and yearning for a simpler life.

Hamner himself acknowledged this aspect of the program in the "Guidelines" he wrote about the series during its planning phases. In this unpublished document, he wrote to his associates at Lorimar Productions, "As in *The Homecoming* we will be telling warm stories about the Walton Family who live in the Blue Ridge Mountains during the mid-thirties. We never mention a specific year and the time is roughly: The Depression. . . . In each show we wish to capture as much color of the times as possible: Radio broadcasts, songs of the thirties, Burma Shave signs, NRA posters, etc. We feel that this is important not only for authenticity but for the nostalgia today's audiences feel for the recent past."[1]

If nostalgia is indeed "a device that removes the ruts and potholes from memory lane," as in humorist Doug Larson's quip, it is also true that there is much to be learned from stories relayed orally across generations as to truth, and living in a fulfilling manner, and triumphing over circumstances. There are indeed ruts and potholes in memory lane, but there is also history. In *The Homecoming* and *The Waltons,* Hamner spoke to America's historical consciousness, which had been numbed by the rapid and jarring events of the post–World War II era. Writing of the importance of a people's collective memories, historian Wilfred M. McClay has claimed, "In the end, communities and nation-states are constituted and sustained by such shared memories—by stories of foundation, conflict, and perseverance. The leap of imagination and faith, from the thinness and unreliability of our individual memory to the richness of collective memory, that is the leap of civilized life; and the discipline of collective memory is the task not only of the historian, but of every one of us. Historical consciousness draws us out of a narrow preoccupation with the present and with our 'selves,' and ushers us into another larger world—a public world that 'cultures' us, in all the sense of that word."[2] This is important because, as the eighteenth-century English statesman Edmund Burke has noted, "People will not look forward to posterity, who never look backward to their ancestors." During the 1970s—a decade riven by the worst economy since the Depression, political corruption in the highest office in the land, the collapse of American resolve in Southeast Asia, and widespread cynicism—*The Waltons* gave many Americans a weekly glimpse of a time when hope was the nation's lifeblood, during an almost-forgotten era in their history as a people.

THE HOMECOMING

The Waltons had its origin in *Spencer's Mountain,* and in Hamner's prequel to the Spencer saga published in 1970, *The Homecoming.* This short novel recounts a single day in the life of the Spencer family, Christmas Eve of 1933, and it closely parallels events from Hamner's own early life. As the novel's author wrote in a summary description contributed to Ralph Giffin's fine *Waltons* Web site:

> In 1933 we were in the grip of the Great Depression. The soapstone mill and quarry upon which our village depended had closed and with it went payrolls, the company operated commissary, the cheerful sounds of a busy industry and a pleasant sense of security. People struggled to keep their families fed. In my family we relied on our family vegetable garden, my father's hunting and fishing, fruit and berries that were free for the picking. For some modest monetary income, my father took a job forty miles away in Waynesboro. He worked there five days a week and returned home on Friday evening. To get home he had to take a bus to Hickory Creek where Route 6 meets Route 29. From there he would either hitchhike or walk the six miles [to Schuyler].
>
> On Christmas Eve of that year my father was late arriving home. A heavy snow had fallen and there were reports of accidents on Route 29. My mother was worried

and, in the age-old practice, the mother sent the oldest son to look for his father. That is what happened to me that night, and the events of that night became the inspiration for this book.[3]

Earl Hamner Sr. had died less than a year before his eldest son wrote and published *The Homecoming*. Earl Jr. acknowledges that the significance of his father's life was very much on his mind as he wrote this short work. As the novel opens it is Christmas Eve day, and the Spencer family of rural New Dominion, Virginia, awaits the arrival of Clay Senior, who is due home after a week's work at his job in Waynesboro. On this snowy day, everything seems to be going wrong for the rest of the family, with the children housebound, irritable, scrapping with each other, and getting on their mother's nerves as well. After a heated debate over the existence of Santa Claus, accompanied by some name-calling and tattling, the children are brought into line by their mother, Olivia, who sends fifteen-year-old Clay-Boy out to the forest on Spencer's Mountain to cut the family Christmas tree. The boy is glad to get away for a while, and he spends his first minutes in the woods engaging in a newly acquired habit he has come to enjoy and keeps secret from his parents, smoking a cigarette. As Clay-Boy finishes his smoke and is about to begin the important task of felling the chosen tree, he is drawn to the sight of a deer struggling in a tangle of brush and snow. He begins gingerly removing fallen branches to free the floundering doe, but in the midst of this deed he is confronted by a white buck, offspring of a mysterious white deer that has roamed the mountain since time out of mind. Enraged because Clay-Boy is apparently threatening its mate, the albino deer charges at the boy, who escapes serious injury on the creature's antlers and hooves by diving under the lowest boughs of the tree he had been cutting and then cowering away from the beast each time it charges at him. With each assault, the deer drives its rack into the tree's foliage, tearing it furiously as it tries to impale the boy. Finally, startled by a torch Clay-Boy has hurriedly crafted and set ablaze, the white deer backs away, enabling the boy to free the still-struggling doe. Both deer then disappear into the for-

Hamner prepares to read his narration to an episode of *The Waltons.*

est. Shaken, Clay-Boy cuts another tree to replace the damaged one and drags it back to the house. In this early chapter, he has had to fend for his life and has experienced a lesson learned by many teens regardless of their background, a theme recurrent in the rest of the novel, that there are times in life when it seems that no good deed goes unpunished.

Back at the house, Clay-Boy learns that his father is long overdue getting home and that his mother's parents, Homer and Ida Italiano, have arrived at the house for supper while he was away. The reason for Clay's delay is unclear, though Ida—a wispy, disapproving woman of narrow views modeled fairly closely upon Hamner's own maternal grandmother—has an opinion; she announces in front of the family that her son-in-law is probably off drinking in the company of the local bootleggers, a pair of elderly sisters who are known for distilling and giving freely of a concoction they primly call "the Recipe." There follows a tense supper, and then a visitor arrives: a local boy called Birdshot Sprouse, who is mentally challenged and recognizes the Spencer children as friends. He brings news that a kindly missionary is over at the village store, ready to hand out wrapped second-hand gifts to the children of New Dominion. Birdshot and Clay-Boy take the other Spencer children to the store to watch—and to watch only, as Olivia has warned them that her family accepts charity from nobody. Despite her mother's warning, the youngest child in the family, Pattie-Cake, impetuously accepts a charity gift, which turns out to be a doll with a broken face that frightens the little girl to tears. The Spencer children trudge back home, having learned a bitter lesson their father had spoken to them many times in the past: "Nobody ever gave away anything worth keepen!"

A blizzard is now blowing outside, and Olivia suspects that there may be traffic accidents on the area roads and fears the worst. She sends Clay-Boy out into the wild night to look for his father, urging her son to seek out a truck-driving neighbor, Charlie Sneed, who can drive him as far as the Hickory Creek turnoff in his search. Over the course of the next few hours, Clay-Boy faces a number of unexpected obstacles and never finds his father. First he finds Charlie's truck parked at the local pool-hall, but he discovers that Charlie himself is under arrest for poaching and cannot help him. Sheriff Ep Bridges, who has taken Charlie in hand, sarcastically ventures a guess that Clay might be holed up with a handful of other poker-playing men in the local "colored" church, where New Dominion's black people worship on Sundays, and where the village's white men play poker at other times. Depicted as something of a bully, puffed

Hamner relaxes on the front porch of the Walton house, sometime during the 1970s.

up with the authority granted him, the sheriff condescends to give Clay-Boy a ride to the First Abyssinian Church while driving Charlie to jail, but not before questioning the boy's motives for wanting a ride. Let off at the church, Clay-Boy discovers a Christmas Eve service in progress, and he inadvertently stirs anger and suspicion in the congregation by walking uninvited into a church regularly desecrated by poker-playing white men. But Rev. Hawthorne Dooley, shepherd of the church, proves to be a friend indeed, welcoming the boy to the service as a guest and thus dispersing the hostility of his flock. At the service's conclusion he takes Clay-Boy on horseback to the ancestral home of the not-quite-respectable Staples sisters (distillers of the Recipe), where Ida Italiano believed Clay might be in the first place. But he is not there either.

At the Staples house, Clay-Boy is fussed over and admired by the elderly sisters, Miss Etta and Miss Emma, elegant and genteel ladies who display a long-established, humorous affability with each other, their thoughts almost completely in thrall to memories of long ago. For the boy's benefit, Miss Etta recounts the story of a day when she was visited by her only suitor, a handsome man with a name straight out of a sentimental, post–Civil War Southern novel, Ashley Longworth. This young man, she says, showed up for a visit one autumn day in 1902, and before parting he kissed Miss Etta as "a shower of leaves fell around us"—before being run off the place by her father, never to return. As is made plain in this novel—and in several episodes of *The Waltons*—she treasures this memory and has rehearsed it and retold it until everyone who knows her can practically recite it themselves, especially the sentimental line about the shower of leaves, often burnished in retellings to "a shower of golden leaves." Finishing her reverie, Miss Etta joins her sister in trying to help Clay-Boy get home in the snow-blanketed Virginia countryside. Fortunately, they own a sleigh and a mare for pulling it—perfect for transportation on snowy country roads. Hitching the mare to the sleigh, the sisters drive Clay-Boy back to his house, leaving him at the front gate.

At the end of his odyssey into the night, Clay-Boy returns to the house without his father, having been thwarted at every turn by nature, circumstances, and the idiosyncrasies of human nature. And for all his trouble, he brings to his mother only a container of the Recipe given to him by the Staples sisters—which Olivia gratefully (and a bit surprisingly) accepts, explaining that it will serve as a needed ingredient in the frosting for her holiday applesauce cakes. (Earlier in the novel, tee-totaling Olivia had fantasized idly about blowing up the Staples house and its distillery with dynamite.)

Hope is running low for the family at this point. A few minutes before midnight, Olivia and the children tramp out to the barn to see if it is true that at midnight on Christmas Eve, away from human view, animals drop to their knees in reverence to the newborn Christ-child and speak in human voices. Hidden in the barn, the family witnesses an unconvincing "half-miracle": Chance, the cow, does drop to her knees, but she does not speak—for which the children blame young Pattie-Cake for making too much noise. As the family files back to the house in disappointment, Olivia sadly reflects that there are no such things as miracles. She has also silently taken stock of her children and seen them as creatures in need of care beyond her ability to give:

> Children are such fragile things, she thought. Arrows shot from her body, gone now beyond any calling back. She catalogued them in her mind. Clay-Boy, so smart and ambitious. Becky, so independent, so capable and vulnerable. Shirley, so beautiful and so maternal. Matt, so self-reliant and full of love and promise. John, with the talent born in his hands to play music on a piano. Mark, all business one minute and wanting a hug in the next. Luke, the handsome wild one with his eye already on some far horizon, and Pattie-Cake, too spoiled to turn her hand for herself, too pretty and sweet to spank. What will become of them all, God only knows. Life be good to them. God, help us all.[4]

Hope is nearly gone. But at about one o'clock in the morning, there is a loud crash outside the house, the front door opens, and a beaming Clay Spencer walks in, to the delight of Olivia and the children. He explains that he had missed the last bus out of Charlottesville, hitchhiked almost the entire distance, and then walked the six-mile stretch from the Hickory Creek turnoff. Exultantly, he greets his children and grabs Olivia, whirling her around the floor in a half-hug, half-dance. Clay comes bearing presents for the entire family, having spent almost his entire paycheck on Christmas gifts—though he claims in the children's presence that he had taken these treasures away from a mysterious portly stranger he had caught prowling about the house near a sleigh drawn by eight odd-looking deer. Among the presents are a number of writing tablets for Clay-Boy, proof of Clay's support of his eldest son's desire to become a writer. Across a gulf of nearly forty years, Earl Hamner Jr. takes this opportunity to express his love to his father:

> "I wonder how news got all the way to the North Pole that you wanted to be a writer," said Clay with a grin.
> "I guess he's a right smart man," said Clay-Boy, his throat almost too full to speak.[5]

Clay has provided a gift for everyone but himself, and he explains that he experiences Christmas every day in the love of his family. In giving to his wife and children, he has spent down his paycheck to almost nothing, for which Olivia takes him gently to task:

> "You must have spent every cent of the paycheck," she said. She tried to sound cross but somehow she didn't succeed.
> "Just about," he admitted cheerfully.
> "What are we goen to live on this comen week?" she asked.
> "Love, woman," he said, and this time he did not seize her in his arms and waltz madly about the room, but kissed her gently and took her hand in his.[6]

Although based in fact, this simple story bears a mythic element, faint but definitely present, in Hamner's retelling. On an evening of great expectation, Christmas Eve, the gift-giver arrives at midnight dispensing love for his bride and his children, freely and in overflowing abundance. He is the exception to the claim that "Nobody ever gave away anything worth keepen," as he empties himself of his wealth; and when his bride asks how the family can abide without money, the gift-giver tells her to give no thought to the morrow—what they will eat, what they will wear—for love will be their security. Did Hamner intend Clay Spencer to serve as a Christ figure? Probably not, but the hints and whispers of a much older story pervade *The Homecoming,* which expresses perhaps above all a son's great love for his father, and a father's great love for his family. As the novel closes, everyone retires to bed, goodnights are called, and all is well at the house in the shadow of Spencer's Mountain. "Around the house the world lay bright as day. The moon blazed down its cold light on the earth that was touched with magic. An ancient wind sighed along the ridges of crusted snow. Angels sang, and the stars danced in the sky."[7]

In terms of style, *The Homecoming* is similar to *Spencer's Mountain,* meaning that Hamner makes use of simple, spare, declarative sentences, reminiscent of Sherwood Anderson's style in their lack of ornamentation. At some points in the narrative, it is plain that it was written by someone with screenwriting skills, with Hamner writing

Hamner and Fielder Cook, director of *The Homecoming,* at a dinner party

brief character summaries of the Spencer children such as would appear in a script. At various points early in the novel, he swiftly sketches in such descriptions as that of Becky, "who was thirteen and had a mind of her own," and "Pattie-Cake was eight and took everybody literally," and "Alone with his wife, Homer was tender and dependent, an indulged child as much as a husband, but when they were in the presence of others he found it necessary to deride Ida's talents and personality." In works by many other novelists, these characteristics would be demonstrated in conversation and incident over the course of the novel, so that the reader makes these inferences; in Hamner's novel, no inferences are needed, as the author states these descriptions from the outset, early in the novel, so that he can proceed swiftly with the plot. As for the plot itself, Hamner was able to take a slight but memorable episode from his early life and invest it with a sense of myth and realism, a compelling story conveying greater truths than its simple form might suggest. And like *Spencer's Mountain, The Homecoming* was rendered into a Readers' Digest Condensed Book.

FROM PAGE TO SCREEN

As noted in an earlier chapter, when *The Homecoming* was adapted to the small screen in 1971, the names of many characters were changed in the teleplay to satisfy legal concerns with Warner Brothers, who had purchased the screen rights to *Spencer's Mountain* in 1962. The Spencers thus became the Walton family. (The decision-makers who planned the program searched for a "solid-sounding, typically American" name, Hamner recalls, and at his suggestion settled upon the name "Walton," which is a name from his own ancestry as well as the name of a signer of the Declaration of Independence, George Walton of Georgia.) Clay-Boy became John-Boy; Becky Spencer became Mary Ellen Walton; the Spencers' middle daughter, Shirley, became Erin Walton; musically talented John became Jason, Mark became Jim-Bob, and Pattie-Cake became Elizabeth. As originally conceived by Hamner, the two "middle sons" of the Spencer family, Matt and Luke, were to correspond to two Walton boys, Ben and Stuart; but for cost-saving purposes these characters were combined into one Walton son, Ben, at the insistence of Lorimar Productions. Miss Emma and Miss Etta Staples became Miss Mamie and Miss Emily Baldwin. But the names of the paternal grandparents, Zebulon and Esther, along with the storekeeper, Ike Godsey, and the children's mother, Olivia, remained the same. Not surprisingly, given that Hamner was the screenwriter, much of the program's dialogue was lifted directly from the book; and thus this episode—above all episodes of the series it inspired—captures the real-life language of the Hamner family during the 1930s. "What a woman I married!" exults John Walton, as he lifts Olivia and whirls her about. "All my babies are thoroughbreds," he boasts of his red-haired children at another point. For the most part, the language and actions of John are the language and actions of the elder Earl Hamner.

Translated to television, the simple story was told compellingly, and the casting was superb, especially that of the children. As an ensemble, the entire cast worked effectively under the guidance of director Fielder Cook; they looked and acted like a real family, rather than a collection of actors thrown together and merely *called* one. Given its nostalgic theme and the presence of veteran actors Patricia Neal, Andrew Duggan, and Edgar Bergen in the cast, it is little wonder that the program was watched by a huge television audience upon its debut on December 19, 1971. Here were sympathetic characters, immediately recognizable, likeable, and realistic. When Mary Ellen, played by Judy Norton, strikes a boxer's pose and commands John-Boy to stand up and fight like a man, when she laments that her thirteen-year-old figure is undeveloped, and when she heatedly calls her siblings "a bunch of piss-ants" after they jeer at the bird's nest she wants to hang on the family Christmas tree, there is much in her portrayal that is remarkably true to life. For his part, actor Richard Thomas defined the character of John-Boy, bringing to his interpretation a coltish earnestness in depicting a fairly gawky, sensitive boy who is on the verge of manhood, who yearns to express his thoughts and stories in writing, and who is tiring of serving the role of "some old mother duck": watching over the other children, keeping them together as a group when they go anywhere outdoors, breaking up arguments, wiping away tears, and in general keeping the Walton brood in line. Hamner had seen Thomas portray a somewhat similar character in the film *Red Sky at Morning* (1971) and determined that this was the actor he wanted to hire to portray John-Boy Walton.

Patricia Neal brought an astonishingly accurate command of the peculiar accent of Scotch-Irish Virginians, an accent that is sometimes mistaken for an English accent by people unaware of the state's unique heritage. Her Olivia is a compelling presence, superbly acted, though somewhat different than the Olivia of the novel; having something of the gracious, well-mannered martinet about her from the start, she becomes progressively more short-tempered as Christmas Eve wears on with no sign of her husband. She demands to know why John-Boy has gotten into the habit of locking himself in his bedroom, implying that she suspects him of doing something unspoken and shameful behind the closed door. (It turns out John-Boy is spending those stolen minutes writing in his journal of his thoughts on growing up in a large family and life in the Blue Ridge.) She also scolds her oldest son for "joy-riding with a pair of old-lady bootleggers" when he returns home without his father, and then loudly orders him to step outside the house and pour the contents of the Baldwin sisters' gift into the snow. Here, in another change from the novel, John-Boy explains quietly that the flask sent by the sisters contains only eggnog. Deflated, Olivia seems to shrink into herself, spiritually worn out by worry over her husband's fate. Her embrace of humility and declaration that the only miracle she is seeking is the return of John Walton makes the sudden, almost unforeseen reunion with her husband that follows particularly effective.

Hamner himself was enlisted to narrate the framing narration, to which he brought a sense of affecting authenticity; he sounded like a man who had actually lived through the grim Depression but had come through in hope. As the writer of the teleplay, he altered several scenes in tone and substance in the translation from the printed page to television. The early scene involving the eldest boy's encounter with the white deer was cut entirely; and several characters in the book were deleted, notably Birdshot Sprouse and Olivia's parents, Ida and Homer Italiano. In the television version, this set of grandparents was replaced by the father's parents, Zebulon and Esther, who live with the family. In the adaptation, the gift-giving missionary was changed from a well-meaning, compassionate individual into a long-winded, sanctimonious woman given to florid flights of speech. Purists might note that the accomplished character actor Woodrow Parfrey's portrayal of storekeeper Ike Godsey has about it more the sense of a brisk clerk in a New England mercantile store than a Southern country storekeeper. To viewers and critics these changes mattered not at all, as they had had no effect upon the simple and irresistible power of the story. *The Homecoming* was a hugely successful addition to the small clutch of perennial holiday specials aired on the three major networks in the years before cable television, and it was rerun for many years, becoming a minor classic of the genre.

"*The Homecoming* could have been a disaster," Hamner wrote less than a year after the program's airing. He added words of remarkable modesty: "The writing leaned toward the sentimental and the situation lent itself to mawkishness." However,

> Thanks to the direction of Fielder Cook, the actors played against the sentiment, and we walked that fine line between honest sentiment and sickening sentimentality. If you saw *The Homecoming* you may recall a scene in which Mary Ellen asks her mother if she thinks she is pretty. Olivia replies, without missing a beat of the work she is doing, "No, I think you're beautiful." No tear in the eye, no touching, just a matter of fact statement. In the series we want to be guided by the direction of *The Homecoming,* to always walk that fine line between excessive sentimentality and believable human warmth.[8]

THE WALTONS

If the 1950s were the golden age of television in general, the early 1970s were a golden age in the history of CBS alone. At that time the "Tiffany Network" boasted such immensely popular series as the groundbreaking *All in the Family, M*A*S*H, The Mary Tyler Moore Show, The Bob Newhart Show,* and *The Carol Burnett Show.* Amid all this richness, network CEO William Paley strongly urged that the success of *The Homecoming* be parlayed into a series, to debut in the fall of 1972. The new series would differ from the above-named programs, being a family drama depicting the day-to-day challenges of growing up in an American village in the South during the Depression.

As CBS and Lorimar Productions began preparations for the new program, Hamner wrote down his vision of how the characters and "feel" of the series ought to be, saying:

> There is one quality which each of these characters share and that is a kind of innocence. This comes from their being a single family unit, isolated to a large degree from the larger world, and it produces a kind of sweetness, a sense of wonder about the world, a kind of naiveté. For instance, when they speak of "the depression" they only know its effects. They have no idea of the complicated economic forces that brought it about. Remember too that the time is 1933 and we were all a more innocent and trusting people then than we are today.
>
> This "sweetness" and innocence should not be confused with a lack of strength. As the scripts will indicate from time to time, the Waltons are descended from pioneer stock and in settling the country, the weak in body and spirit did not survive. Only the strong survived, and this should be reflected in the kind of people we cast and in the interpretation of their roles.
>
> That the Waltons are poor should be obvious, but there should be no hint of squalor or debased living conditions usually associated with poverty. The house should reflect the fact that Olivia is a good housekeeper, and even though clothing has been handed down from older to younger children, it is in good repair. Physically the house

should reflect that John is a "fixer of things." A sagging door, a broken window, a leaky faucet, would be repaired immediately.[9]

In the development of *The Waltons,* much of the original cast of *The Homecoming*—including all the "Walton" children—was retained, as was Hamner as the narrator. But some key substitutions were made. Patricia Neal was replaced by a younger actress, Michael Learned, as Olivia Walton. This change necessitated the search for an actor a few years younger than the talented but fiftyish Andrew Duggan to portray John Walton. Ralph Waite auditioned and got the part. Edgar Bergen was in declining health and thus unable to act in a series. He was replaced by Will Geer in the role of Zeb Walton, the

Hamner (in foreground) poses with the central cast of *The Waltons.* With Richard Thomas in the center, the cast consisted of (clockwise from left): Eric Scott, Will Geer, Mary Beth McDonough, Jon Walmsley, Judy Norton, David Harper, Ralph Waite, Michael Learned, Kami Cotler, and Ellen Corby.

grandfather. Joe Conley replaced Woodrow Parfrey as Ike Godsey. In *The Homecoming,* two New York actresses, Dorothy Stickney and Josephine Hutchinson, had delivered delightfully quirky and memorable portrayals of the "old-lady bootleggers," but for a weekly series a pair of California-based actresses were needed. Into the breech stepped Helen Kleeb and Mary Jackson, who portrayed the Baldwin sisters for the entire run of the series.

Each of the children in the Walton family was based upon one—or, in the case of Ben Walton, two—of Hamner's siblings. John-Boy, the eldest and a would-be writer, was based upon Earl himself. Judy Norton portrayed Mary Ellen, a feisty girl of independent spirit, a problem-solving go-getter, anxious to get on with life, whose character is based upon Earl's oldest sister, Marion. Jason Walton (portrayed by Jon Walmsley), the brother with musical talent, was based upon Cliff Hamner, Earl's oldest brother. (Interestingly, Cliff Hamner did not possess the talents of a musician; his sister Marion and his brother Jim were the musically talented members of the family.) Shy, pretty Erin (Mary Beth McDonough) was a portrayal of the "middle daughter" in the Hamner family, Audrey. Practical, headstrong, and occasionally hot-tempered Ben Walton (Eric Scott) was a blending of two Hamner boys, Earl's brothers Paul and Bill. The quiet but ambitious youngest Walton boy, Jim-Bob (David Harper), was based upon Earl's youngest brother, James. And the youngest Hamner, Nancy, inspired the character of lovable Elizabeth, played by Kami Cotler.

In his unpublished "Guidelines" to the new series, Hamner had encouraged his colleagues at Lorimar Productions that in producing *The Waltons* a key direction would be "to always walk that fine line between excessive sentimentality and believable human warmth." Speaking of himself in the third person, he added:

> *Believable human warmth* is a good phrase to remember
> when dealing with the Walton family. In the first place
> they are actual human beings, based on author Earl
> Hamner, Jr.'s own family and many of the events we are
> dramatizing took place in Earl's growing up in the Blue

Ridge during the depression. Let us keep in mind that these people, now grown men and women, will be watching themselves portrayed, and portrayed tastefully.

Because few actors, writers, directors or producers really know mountain people, there is sometimes a tendency to portray them as either *Beverly Hillbilly* types or as comic-strip characters out of *Barney Google.* These characters should never be played for "cuteness" or for reached-for humor.

There is humor here, but it comes out of character. When Grandpa, for instance, claims that his son is handsome because he "got his looks from his Daddy," he halfway means it because the old man is a little vain. When Elizabeth states that she intends to have puppies rather than babies when she grows up, the statement comes from her innocence, not an attempt to be funny.[10]

The cast was set, the first stories were written, production began, and the result was one of the proudest achievements in television history. Ironically, at the beginning CBS executives had small hope that this down-home family drama would succeed in its Thursday evening timeslot, positioned directly opposite *The Mod Squad* on ABC and *The Flip Wilson Show* on NBC. But both these competitors were several years along as established series, and *The Waltons,* despite its setting and themes, was fresh and appealed to the nation's sense of nostalgia and soul-searching during the twilight years of the Vietnam-War era. Fans of the show were enthusiastic about it from the beginning, when the first episode—titled "The Foundling"— aired on September 14, 1972.

Even with its fervent fans, from the start the series fared badly in the ratings against the well-established shows on NBC and ABC, just as the executives had feared. Upon learning that the series was struggling for its life in the early weeks, admirers mounted a letter-writing campaign to CBS urging that it be retained. *Detroit News* television critic Frank Judge encouraged his readers to write directly to CBS President Robert D. Wood and to tell him that despite the

At the 1975
Emmy Awards
ceremony,
Hamner stands
with Jon Walm-
sley and Ellen
Corby.

Hamner stands with
(then-CBS president)
Robert D. Wood, Richard
Thomas, and Bob ("Cap-
tain Kangaroo") Keeshan
to receive a George Fos-
ter Peabody Award in
1972, for exhibiting
"excellence, distinguished
achievement, and merito-
rious service" in the field
of broadcasting.

COURTESY OF EARL HAMNER

Hamner and his Emmy,
awarded in 1973 by the Academy of Television Arts and Sciences for his role in creating
The Waltons. (The Academy
awards the Emmy to individuals and programs for achieving excellence in the television
industry.)

new program's stiff competition, "Television needs *The Waltons* far more than CBS needs to win every rating race it enters."[11] Across the country, similar efforts were mounted. These widespread pleas for patience on the part of CBS were honored, and within a few weeks *The Waltons* flourished in popularity. By December of that year, it was an established hit, at the very top of the ratings. Near the end of its first season, *The Waltons* scored impressively at the Emmy Awards, with honors going to Richard Thomas for Outstanding Continued Performance by an Actor in a Leading Role in a Drama, Michael Learned for Outstanding Continued Performance by an Actress in a Leading Role in a Drama, Ellen Corby for Outstanding Performance by an Actress in a Supporting Role in Drama; John McGreevey for Outstanding Writing Achievement in Drama (Single Program of a Series—"The Scholar"), and the program itself for Outstanding Drama Series, Continuing, for which Hamner, executive producer Lee Rich, and producer Robert L. Jacks received the award.

Acerbic TV critic John Leonard, writing under his pseudonym "Cyclops" for *Life* magazine, was moved to write of the show, "Confronted with wholesomeness, a critic wants to stab it to death with his 19-cent Bic ballpoint pen." Yet, "I liked *The Waltons*. Only a churl would not."[12] Leonard was not alone in this belief. During the nine seasons of its run, *The Waltons* attracted a large, faithful audience, especially among viewers in rural areas, small towns, small cities, and particularly in the South and Midwest. It was somewhat less popular in large cities. On some Thursday evenings, as many as 50 million viewers tuned in. Looking back, admirers are hard pressed to name their one favorite episode, though there are a small number of episodes that are widely recognized as exceptional. These include:

- "The Foundling," written by John McGreevey and beloved as the first episode in the series. A deaf six-year-old girl named Holly is abandoned at the Waltons' door. The family takes her in and cares for her, even learning sign language and teaching it to the little girl to better communicate with her. Elizabeth gets jealous because of all the attention lavished upon Holly. In the end, with Holly's assistance, Elizabeth is rescued after being trapped in a locked trunk. And Holly's parents reclaim their daughter after gaining a new respect for a daughter whose physical challenges they had once found overwhelming. In a letter to the author, McGreevey recalled, "I had the great pleasure of working with Earl and writing more than twenty subsequent episodes, for which I garnered two Emmy nominations and one Emmy. *The Waltons* experience was a turning point in my career and I will be forever grateful to Earl for the opportunity which he gave me."

- "The Scholar," which earned John McGreevey an Emmy for best writing in a dramatic series. A neighbor of the Waltons, Verdie Grant, faces her daughter's college graduation with the embarrassing knowledge that she herself cannot read or write. Afraid that she might embarrass her daughter, she asks John-Boy to teach her these skills—but to tell her secret to nobody. One day Elizabeth observes John-Boy tutoring Verdie and tells the local teacher, Miss Hunter. Upon learning that her secret is out, Verdie angrily accuses John-Boy of betraying her trust; but in the end she learns the truth, forgives her mentor, and learns to read. This episode introduced Lynn Hamilton in the role of Verdie Grant, whose character appeared recurrently during the series' run.

- "An Easter Story," which was conceived by Hamner and written by John McGreevey for a two-hour episode. Olivia is unexpectedly stricken with polio and becomes bedridden. The family agonizes as she does not respond to traditional treatment. Spiritually tormented by seeing this tragedy strike his good and gentle mother, John-Boy researches a new treatment practiced with some success in Australia by Sister Kenny, who pioneered the successful treatment of polio with physical therapy. With the family's assistance, Olivia tries the revolutionary treatment, though the local doctor holds out little hope for recovery. But shortly before sunrise on Easter, Olivia wakens and walks, taking her first steps toward full recovery. In a subplot to this episode, Jason enters a music contest and wins first prize for a song he writes and performs in honor of Grandma Walton (portrayed by the delightfully vinegary Ellen Corby) titled "The Ironing Board Blues." (The late Miss Corby is a favorite of *Waltons* fans. As she developed the character of Esther Walton, she told Hamner, "Young man, you have so many sweet characters in this show that the viewers are going to die of sugar diabetes. I'm going to put some *vinegar* into this role!" Miss Corby's longtime friend and caregiver, Stella Luchetta, told the author in a telephone interview, "Ellen liked Earl a lot and enjoyed working with him. And she loved being on *The Waltons*.")

- "The Gift," written by Carol Evan McKeand, explores the reality of death and dying among young people and their parents. One of Jason's and John-Boy's closest friends, Seth Turner, is diagnosed by Dr. McIvers as suffering from leukemia and having only a year to live. Seth, his mother, and the Walton family are stunned by this news. Jason copes with Seth's diagnosis by angrily shutting himself off from everyone. But Seth, after initially running to the forest to "rage against the dying of the light," accepts the fact of his coming death. The son of a musician, he realizes that the "music" he has known and loved all his life—the call of the whippoorwill in the evening, the rumble of a train crossing the Rockfish River trestle, and other sounds of country life—must be savored and their simple goodness shared with beloved friends. Seth insists upon crafting a recorder from the limb of an apple tree as a gift to Jason, so that the music of life will not die. With the help of Seth, John-Boy, and Grandpa, Jason accepts the gift of the recorder and takes his first steps toward learning to play the instrument, though he is overcome with emotion to see that Seth has carved the name "Jason Walton" on it. Ron Howard guest-starred as Seth, and his father, Rance Howard, played the role of Dr. McIvers. In an anecdote included in *Goodnight John-Boy*, Jon Walmsley reminisced about the episode: "Ron Howard played my best friend, Seth Turner, who was dying of leukemia. I had always been a fan of Ron's from *The Andy Griffith Show* and had grown up with people telling me I looked like him. When I first met Ron on the set, his first words were, 'You're the guy everybody says I look like!' Ron later told me that 'The Gift' was his favorite episodic performance, and that he had landed a starring role in *The Shootist,* John Wayne's last film, as a result of the producers' watching 'The Gift.'"

- "The Conflict," written by Jeb Rosebrook, is another two-hour episode that is considered a fan favorite. As the Blue Ridge Parkway is constructed, elderly Aunt Martha Corinne Walton's cabin is scheduled for destruction by the highway contractor because the cabin lies in the new road's right-of-way. Aunt Martha Corinne (Grandpa Walton's sister-in-law) refuses to move, and there is a tense confrontation between the Walton family and the road builders—culminating in John-Boy's being wounded by a gunshot. In the end, Aunt Martha Corinne acquiesces to the inevitable; and as the program ends, she sweeps out her cabin one last time, explaining that she intends to leave her home in the same spotless condition she found it on her wedding day many years earlier.

A portrait of the *Waltons* cast in about 1979—with a few extra "characters." *Back row:* writer Rod Peterson, Hamner, writer Claire Whitaker, writer/producer Claylene Jones, and director Harry Harris. *Middle row:* Jon Walmsley, Michael Learned, Ralph Waite, Leslie Winston, Eric Scott, Mary Beth McDonough. *Bottom row:* David Harper, "Reckless," Kami Cotler, Judy Norton, Marshall or Michael Reed.

COURTESY OF CLAIRE WHITAKER

EARL HAMNER

Portrayed by Beulah Bondi, Aunt Martha Corinne reminds many of this episode's admirers of a kindly grandmother or aunt they remember from long ago.

- "The Quilting," which tells of a mountain custom whereby the women in small communities gather to sew a quilt for a young woman once she reaches a marriageable age. In this case, the young woman is Mary Ellen, who resents the idea that she must conform to this custom, resents the expectation that she must marry someday, and defies Grandma, who has organized the quilting. Grandma and Olivia exchange sharp words about Mary Ellen (who is determined to boycott the quilting), and a rift between the Walton women is opened. On the day of the quilting, John-Boy gives his oldest sister a heated but reasoned talking-to and convinces her that if she should attend the quilting she would not be constrained to marry anyone, and that her presence would heal the strained relations between their mother and Grandma. In the end Mary Ellen attends the quilting after all. The rift is closed peaceably and to everyone's satisfaction. This fine episode was written by Rod Peterson and Claire Whitaker.
- "The Firestorm," which tells of how John-Boy, as founding editor of *The Blue Ridge Chronicle,* attempts to keep his readers apprised of the political situation in Europe by printing excerpts from *Mein Kampf,* the bible of the Nazis. His act is misunderstood by the community as an act of advocacy, and Rev. Fordwick (portrayed by John Ritter) denounces John-Boy's actions and holds a public burning of German books. John-Boy intervenes at this ugly event by pulling an unburned book from the blaze and asking German-speaking Mrs. Brimmer to read the first page aloud to the assembled crowd. She does so, and then translates the sentence she has read: "In the beginning God created the heaven and the earth, and the earth was without form and void. And darkness was upon the face of the deep. And the spririt of God moved upon the face of the waters. And God said, 'Let there be light.'" Shamed by this, the crowd disperses—concluding another strong story written by Rod Peterson and Claire Whitaker.

- "The Pony Cart" concerns a visit to the Walton home by Aunt Martha Corinne, a role reprised by Beulah Bondi. She helps Ben renovate an old-fashioned pony cart; but otherwise she is an unsettling influence in the Walton household, disrupting the lives of each family member. Eventually she is asked to leave, but en route to her home she reveals to John-Boy that she is dying. He returns to his parents' home with Aunt Martha Corinne, who spends her final days with the only family she has. She dies and is interred in the family cemetery next to her husband's grave. Writer Jack Miller produced a poignant teleplay for this episode, and Beulah Bondi received an Emmy for her performance.
- "The Achievement," which records a time of heartbreaking transition in the Walton household. John-Boy travels to New York and, through persistence, convinces a publisher to accept his first book. He returns to his home in Virginia to share this glad news with his family but also to announce that he is leaving home to live in New York. On the evening of this announcement, John-Boy stands outside the house and listens to his family members calling goodnight to each other, a family ritual. Recognizing that this is a moment of both exciting opportunity and wistful sadness, he softly says, "Goodnight, everybody. I love you." This episode marked Richard Thomas's final regular appearance as John-Boy in the series. This powerful episode, which could have been ruined by overwriting or excessive sentimentality, was instead kept within the bounds of honest experience and sentiment by writers Dale Eunson, Andy White, and Earl Hamner himself. It was directed by Harry Harris, who directed most of the episodes of *The Waltons* during its run.
- "The Children's Carol," a two-hour episode, written by John McGreevey and set during the early years of World War II. As Mary Ellen and her soldier-husband, Curt, seek to resolve tensions in their marriage, the Baldwin sisters take in two English children, a girl and a boy, whose parents were killed by a German aerial bomb during the London Blitz. The boy, Pip, has been rendered mute by the horror he has witnessed. Unable to

handle the traumatized children, the Baldwins ask the Waltons to care for them for a time, and the family agrees. Little by little, Pip and his sister, Emma, warm to the Waltons—especially Grandpa. But after overhearing and misunderstanding a private conversation in the household, the English children run away, believing that the Waltons are preparing to send them away anyway. John, Olivia, and Erin track them down and rescue them from certain injury at an army airfield. Pip is so frightened and relieved by this close call that he speaks for the first time since his parents' death. Returning to the Walton home, Emma and Pip are confronted with undreamed-of good news when Jim-Bob, communicating with London via short-wave radio, allows the English children to speak with their mother, who is alive after all and wants them to come home. Pip was portrayed by Kami Cotler's brother, Jeff.

- "The Anniversary," written by Rod Peterson and Claire Whitaker, focuses upon events directly from Hamner's life. As John and Olivia's twenty-fifth wedding anniversary approaches, Olivia decides to surprise her husband by having a telephone installed in the house. Now they will no longer need to use the telephone at Ike Godsey's store to place calls. For his part, having long promised Olivia that he would build a new house for her on Walton's Mountain, John realizes that after many years of marriage, this promise cannot be kept. Instead, he builds Olivia a gazebo atop the mountain and takes her there on the day of their anniversary so that they may dance together to music from an old phonograph and toast their marriage with champagne. Soon they are joined by their children and by Grandpa and Grandma; and together the Walton family joins in celebrating John and Olivia's long, happy marriage. Admirers of this episode have commented upon the natural chemistry that exists between Ralph Waite and Michael Learned as a husband and wife very much devoted to and at ease with each other.

- "The Empty Nest" was the first episode of the seventh season, as well as the first episode filmed after the death of Will Geer, one of the most beloved members of the cast. Grandpa Walton's death is acknowledged from the outset in this two-hour program, which deals with the family's coming to terms with this loss. This episode—still another written by Rod Peterson and Claire Whitaker—concludes with the family gathering at Zeb's grave and then, one at a time, speaking aloud their love for him, each bidding him an affectionate goodbye.

- "Founder's Day," which was written by Kathleen Hite. It concerns a college assignment given to Jason, the musically talented member of the family, to write a serious musical composition capturing the essence of life as experienced by the composer. Contrary to his professor's wishes for a formal work along classical lines, Jason writes and performs a piece grounded in the folk music of the Blue Ridge, titled "Appalachian Portrait." The professor is won over by Jason's accomplishment, which is highlighted for the benefit of the television audience by Hamner's voice-over narration: a stirring and heartfelt tribute to the heritage of his family and the land they have lived on, which has given them sustenance and a sense of rootedness, orientation, and community over several generations.

- "The Waiting," also written by Kathleen Hite, concerns the anguish of John and Olivia as they sit at the hospital bed where John-Boy lies in a coma. (A reporter for *Stars and Stripes*, he had been traveling in a plane in wartime Belgium when the craft was shot down by German fire.) As the story ends, John and Olivia, still maintaining their vigil, join hands to pray before an evening meal at their son's bedside. As the prayer is spoken, John-Boy moves his arm and blindly joins his hand to his parents'. This was the first episode featuring Robert Wightman in the role of John-Boy.

- "The Revel," which Hamner named as his own favorite on one occasion. This was the series' final episode and was written by his son, Scott, and directed by Harry Harris. It concerns a party planned by the Baldwin sisters to honor their girlhood friends and classmates. But the invitations they send are returned as undeliverable, and the sisters lament that they have outlived everyone they knew in their youth. It seems that their party, their "revel," will be a very lonely affair, but the Walton family and their friends, learning of the predicament, come to the party and surprise the Baldwins. The revel is a success, and at its height John-Boy shows up, just in from New York, to make the revel complete. In a short tribute included in *Goodnight John-Boy,* Scott Hamner wrote of his sense of honor at having written this final episode and, in so doing, contributing to the storytelling tradition exemplified by his father: "The Revel," he wrote, "exemplified core values espoused in the show: the celebration of family and the rising above individual differences for the greater good."[13]

Admirers of the show have their own favorites, in addition to these—perhaps the foremost of these being a powerfully moving tale of young love titled "The Love Story," written by Hamner himself. As executive producer of the program, and executive story consultant, Hamner worked with a trusted core group of writers and directors to ensure that the series hewed fairly close to the spirit if not the letter of his life's formative experiences. Contrary to what some critics have said, *The Waltons* was never intended to suggest that this was the way *everyone* behaved during the Depression; rather, the program showed how a small community of people, living in a particular place and time, coped with daily life during a most difficult era. Each episode presented some element borrowed from an actual event in the lives of Hamner and his family, such as the community's coping with a bear that has wandered into its midst, meeting a Jewish person for the first time and wondering how (if at all) this "exotic" person is different from everyone else, Earl's borrowing of a typewriter, his father being puzzled by his son's inclinations toward writing, and his departing from home in Virginia to live in New York, to name a few.

How to describe the series? In an article published in the *Raleigh News & Observer* in 2001, writer Elaine Klonicki summarized the series succinctly, writing:

> In *The Waltons,* the character of writer Earl Hamner Jr.
> was called John-Boy, and he was the oldest son. No matter

what John-Boy experienced in a particular story, each episode was wrapped up nicely in Hamner's own voice, expressing gratitude for his family and the values he was taught growing up in the Blue Ridge Mountains of Virginia during the Depression.

Those tributes were often the most touching parts of the show. Critics called *The Waltons* saccharine and unrealistic, but the family members weren't portrayed as perfect, and they faced many challenges. They often stumbled along the way, even the adults, but each family member struggled hard to live life under the framework of the family's principles and values. Honesty, hard work, respect, responsibility, self-sacrifice, compassion, and kindness— today they package it and call it "character education."[14]

When John-Boy's character was written out of the series for a time, the other family members, along with other members of the Walton's Mountain community, were placed in more prominent roles in each episode. In this capacity, they stepped forward to maintain the warm, down-to-earth character that was the hallmark of the program throughout its run. The Baldwin sisters showed forth the quality of aging with dignity and humor amidst broken dreams—for the legendary Ashley Longworth would never return to Walton's Mountain, despite Miss Emily's fondest hopes. The Godseys, Ike and Corabeth, sought to build a successful marriage despite remarkable differences in temperament. Ike, portrayed by Joe Conley, was content to be a simple country storekeeper all his life, while Corabeth, brought marvelously to life by Ronnie Claire Edwards, was a complex character—a warm-hearted and generous woman underneath several layers of insufferable snootiness, a thwarted aristocrat who was constantly trying to bring a sense of elevated culture to rustic Walton's Mountain. "*The Waltons* was the best-written and best-produced show I was ever associated with," Edwards recently said. "I feel very fortunate to have been a part of it. And one of the most satisfying things about it to me was not only the role I was given, but the fact that Earl allowed my character to be redeemable from time to time."[15]

EARL HAMNER

Over time a number of actors joined the cast of *The Waltons* in recurring roles, and they share with Edwards a sense of gratitude at having been part of the program. This supporting cast included Tony Becker as Drew Cutler, Lynn Hamilton as Verdie Foster, Hal Williams as Harley Foster, Lisa Harrison as Toni Hazelton Walton, Leslie Winston as Cindy Brunson Walton, Morgan Woodward as Boone Walton, John Crawford as Sheriff Ep Bridges, John Ritter as Rev. Matthew Fordwick, Robert Donner as Yancy Tucker, Peggy Rea as Rose Burton, Martha Nix as Serena Burton, and Lewis Arquette as J. D. Pickett, among many other talented actors. In addition, a great number of actors who are well known today made guest appearances on *The Waltons.* A partial list of these guests includes Sissy Spacek, Ron Howard, Rance Howard, Sian Barbara Allen, Merle Haggard, Ellen Geer, Dean Jagger, Ned Beatty, Paul Michael Glaser, Kathleen Quinlan, Linda Purl, Gerald McRaney, Cleavon Little, Wilford Brimley, Abby Dalton, and Lloyd Nolan.

By Hamner's own admission, family life in the Walton household is a bit idealized: it is truthful in essence, though some aspects of fact are veiled to protect his family's privacy. As he once explained, "I would not put in[to the series], for instance, that my father used to curse a great deal. I wouldn't want to put that on television and I haven't stressed it in the books. He also drank, not really a heavy drinker, but when he did drink he would not come home because my mother disapproved of it. So I don't think those are compromises, but they are simply selections that I have made in order to present a larger facet of the family."[16] In an interview with Hamner, Margaret Fife Tanguay wrote, "Since *The Waltons* is autobiographical, I was interested to know how his real family felt about seeing their lives unfold on television. Of course they had already experienced this 'exposure' to a limited degree in the publication of *Spencer's Mountain.* 'Not shock, but delight at reliving those times,' Hamner told me. 'You know, Thomas Wolfe "couldn't go home again" because of the things he'd written, but I can go home, and do, because I've written with affection about our life together.'"[17]

Beyond that, on any given week, the Walton family faithfully reflected life as experienced by the Hamner family during the 1930s as Earl, his parents, his siblings, and the inhabitants of their village contended with such "saccharine and unrealistic" themes as theft, displacement from one's home, death in wartime, life-endangering injuries, kidnapping at gunpoint, vandalism, arson, miscarriage, and despair; though episodes also dealt with lighter issues such as handling loneliness; caring for injured animals; and coping with the honest mistakes, misunderstandings, and hardships common to everyday life. Further, in a 1995 interview, Richard Thomas said, "People used to attack the show for being too sweet, too idealistic. But it honored the lives of ordinary people, and the simple passages of their lives have as much significance on Walton's Mountain as they do in Buckingham Palace. Growing up is growing up. Getting old is getting old. Coming to terms with your children is coming to terms with your children."[18] Kami Cotler attributes this to the fact that Hamner, drawing upon the things he learned during his formative years, "was able to look at all the different characters and personalities he grew up with and find a way to prize them *with their flaws*. People sometimes accused the show of being saccharine, and sometimes it probably is saccharine. But there are also moments of human frailty or friction that he also captured, that I think really did resonate with people. And I think that if it was completely saccharine, and we weren't dirty and grubby and barefoot and bickering and noisy and doing all the things real groups of children do, it wouldn't have been as meaningful for people."[19]

Asked how the program's writers kept the series sensitive without becoming overly sentimental, Hamner replied:

> What we attempted to do was to create full-blooded, full-bodied people. None of them is a perfect character. Olivia was extreme in her views of the Baptist Church. Grandma is almost a bigot. John, as opposed to the father in *Father Knows Best,* never really knows best. He feels his way along and he does what he thinks is best. Sometimes it isn't the right thing. The problem for the writer who doesn't know the show that well is that these people are already so good that if you write them nice, then they

come off boring and saccharine. The secret then is to toughen them up, to go away from what is expected.

As an example, we once did a show where a book salesman came to town, and instead of sending the money he got back to the book company he was putting it in his pocket. The reason he was doing it was to buy a Christmas present, which was a doll, like one that Elizabeth had. There was a scene at the end of the show where Elizabeth stands holding the doll and the man departs without the money for the Christmas present for his daughter. Someone who didn't know the show might say, "Oh, that sweet little girl—she's going to give him the doll for his own child," but she didn't do it. That was an example of pulling away from the expected to keep the characters tough.[20]

The program did not depict the bizarre world of novelist Harry Crews's South, nor the grasping world of William Faulkner's scavenger-like Snopes family, but it did portray on a weekly basis a Faulknerian theme articulated in Faulkner's Nobel Prize address and closely echoed in Hamner's narration to "Founder's Day": the Walton family, like the Hamner family, like many families who lived through the Depression, "endured and prevailed." As envisioned by Hamner, the Waltons bear witness to the truth pronounced by Faulkner, that man "alone among creatures . . . has a soul, a spirit capable of compassion and sacrifice and endurance"; and with each episode Hamner and his fellow writers sought "to help man endure by lifting his heart, by reminding him of the courage and honour and hope and pride and compassion and pity and sacrifice which have been the glory of his past." In the epilogue to "Founder's Day" Hamner says, in part:

There is something within us that tells us all we will ever know about ourselves. There is a destiny that tells us where we will be born, where we will live, and where we will die.

Some men are drawn to oceans; they cannot breathe unless the air is scented with a salty mist. Others are drawn to land that is flat, and the air is sullen and is leaden as August. My people were drawn to mountains.

They came when the country was young and they settled
in the upland country of Virginia that is still misted with a
haze of blue which gives those mountains their name.
They endured and they prevailed; through flood and
famine, diphtheria and scarlet fever, through drought and
forest fire, whooping cough and loneliness, through
Indian wars, a civil war, a world war, and through the
Great Depression they endured and they prevailed. In my
time, I have come to know them. . . .
I have walked the land in the footsteps of all my
fathers. I saw yesterday and now look to tomorrow.

With richness in the casting, writing, production, and popularity, what brought about *The Waltons'* demise as a series? First, as a strong ensemble series, it was strongly dependent upon a sense of continuity in the cast. Over time, several key cast members departed—due to professional-development concerns, health concerns, and in the case of Will Geer, death—and the show lost its central energy as a result. As each of the "originals" departed, the cohesiveness of the show declined, though the writing and production remained consistently strong.

Hamner himself has suggested that the show remained strong as long as it was concerned with common, day-to-day events during the Depression. After the fifth season ended, and with Richard Thomas's departure, a decision was made to jump forward several years in time—and suddenly all the children were practically grown up and getting married (while continuing to linger at the Walton house), with new names to keep track of, the 1940s underway, and World War II looming. Evidence suggests that viewers disliked this shift in time, which became more pronounced with the periodic *Waltons* specials that were aired during the 1980s and '90s—when the passing of several decades was conveyed, though the family members hardly seemed to age. When the series went beyond its original premise, it began to sag. As Horace Newcomb and Robert S. Alley explained in their important study, *The Producer's Medium*, in the "post-Depression" seasons of *The Waltons*:

EARL HAMNER

This new world looked much like our own, and, at the same time, our memories of the war and its immediate aftermath have little of the power of the Depression. The people and their problems were remote, shadowy. The series took on a thinness in the final years, and when early episodes of *The Waltons* now reappear as the show is syndicated through the country, these reruns are reminders of a different time and place, reminders almost as powerful as our own family memories. We have known these people, visited with them before, and now they are gone. Watching the show in rerun is much like looking into a family photograph album.[21]

Finally, and this too is Hamner's opinion, the show had reached the end of its natural life cycle. Every television program, he has explained, no matter how popular and well done, has a natural ebb and flow of rising and falling appeal. Freshness fades. Over time, a point is reached where it is best to stop. *The Waltons* reached that point in 1981 and ended production with a strong episode. (Even the program's most fervent fans concede that the final two seasons lacked much of the vigor and appeal of the earlier seasons.) Even then, such was the closeness of the cast, which had grown to see itself as almost a real family, that Michael Learned and Ralph Waite made a point of reassuring their "children" that although the series was ending, they would always love and remember each other fondly. The "family" had much to be proud of, if only because their series ran to over two hundred episodes over the course of nine full seasons on the same night and at the same time every week—the much-coveted timeslot of Thursday night at eight o'clock—a feat extremely rare in network television.

THE WALTON LEGACY

There is a view around the world from Walton's Mountain. Watching the program in syndication, some German viewers have declared that they believe the series is set in the Vienna Woods. The series is beloved in India, with Hamner occasionally receiving fan letters from the subcontinent. Families who view the program in Sweden and in Greece identify with it, as do the Irish and Australians. In England, *The Waltons* continues to be especially popular with television audiences. In the United States (and today, from around the world), fans of the series have written often to Hamner to say that *The Waltons* reminds them of the way they remember their childhood during the Depression, or the way they wish their childhood had been.

In an essay published in *The Horn Book Magazine* in 1943, contributor Irene Smith saluted Laura Ingalls Wilder, writing that the *Little House* books "speak so eloquently of the courage that made our country big and free, of the family solidarity that is its cornerstone, and the decency that flames in its ideals." Smith added that the series "reminds a needy world today of the canniness of the pioneer, the strength and joy of the builder, and the dreams of free individuals working toward a better future. Young present-day readers

In *The Waltons,* Hamner based his fictional railroad town of Rockfish on the small city of Scottsville, which is roughly thirteen miles from Schuyler. The Dew Drop Inn, where Jason Walton and his band performed, is a real restaurant where musicians still appear.

can learn from Mrs. Wilder that vicissitudes must be faced, and that real happiness is not measured by material possessions."[22] Wilder's *Little House* books, published during the Great Depression, lifted the spirits of her readers, encouraging them to believe that perseverance is worth the effort. One may argue that, with *The Waltons*, Hamner performed a similar feat during the 1970s, another period of economic hardship and national uncertainty. With very little editorial adjustment, Smith's words could apply to Hamner's accomplishment, too.

To the program's admirers, the central characters on the program resonate as real people, with viewers describing the Waltons as the sort of people who lived their lives in a way that made it possible for all that is good, homely, lovable, and worthwhile in life to survive to the present day. In his short, concluding narration to several episodes, Hamner speaks of how the pull of tradition and the call of modern ways were blended harmoniously through love, patience, and charitable compromise during his formative years. Elaine Klonicki summarized what many have expressed to Hamner about *The Waltons*: "Like John-Boy, I'm finding myself increasingly grateful for my upbringing, and for many other things in my life, and increasingly respectful of the natural beauty of this Earth, which is highlighted on the show."[23] To the program's detractors, the *Waltons* characters are idealized types created to appeal to its viewers' insecurities and sense of wishful thinking. But this is simplistic. In an article published in *The New York Times Magazine* in 1973, novelist Anne Roïphe puzzled over the question of how *The Waltons,* a show she considered maudlin and sentimental, managed to draw her in every week to watch, sometimes reducing her to "ridiculous tears." She offered the following explanation, which provides one of the more thoughtful insights of those viewers who have a love-hate relationship with the program:

> An age or so away, primitive man danced wild steps
> around night fires to scare away evil spirits and to comfort
> himself that he was not helpless against the demonic,
> destructive forces in the universe. Man has always

invented stories, gods and heroes to give him a sense of understanding and control of the lightning, the thunder, accident and death. I think we use our television set in many of the same ways. We huddle about its blue light looking for relief, control and understanding, magic to be worked on all those confusing forces that push us about. *The Waltons* may be romantic nonsense, may bear only superficial and misleading resemblance to real life, but it is very good magic. It is a good, workable dance to scare away the evil spirits of loneliness, isolation, divorce, alcoholism, troubled children, abandoned elders—the real companions of American family life, the real demons in the living room.

Roïphe goes on to speak of the "dichotomy in our society between what we believe—the image we would choose of ourselves—and the social realities," and notes that many modern people strive to fashion their lives along lines that seem to come so easily to the Waltons. Of their success in that quest, she writes, "Never mind that we all fail; it's a journey worth taking," for, living with a hopeful goal, "Who knows what the American family can become?"[24] John Leonard wrote, "More people than one would guess from reading contemporary novels grew up in such families [as the Waltons] and are stronger and happier for it; what John Cheever called the 'sense of sanctuary that is the essence of love' abounds. If we didn't have fathers like John Walton (Ralph Waite, who explains to his little girl that she was found 'hiding behind one of your mother's smiles'), at least we wished we did, and we knew that such fathers existed."[25] Actor Judy Norton has recently said, "Many families still aspire to be like *The Waltons*. The future of the culture is led by the arts and the dreams of the artists. People watch shows and wonder, "Is that possible?" and then they set out to find out. I suspect there are many families today that are closer because in some way, either subtle or not, they were inspired by *The Waltons* to work a little harder to create a better family."[26]

Hamner himself is pleased that viewers have found life-building qualities in *The Waltons,* but he professes that he never intended the series to provide lessons in living or for specific episodes to have a "message." While the teachable moments, family sing-alongs, and the saying of goodnight to family members at bedtime as depicted in *The Waltons* are outside the experience of many viewers—and provide fodder for the self-styled sophisticates who despise the program—they were common enough in the Hamner household during the 1930s. "I've always considered myself a storyteller above all," Hamner has said on numerous occasions. If

Kami Cotler with Earl's sister Marion during a break on the set of *The Waltons.*

there are messages in *The Waltons,* it should not be ascribed to a desire to preach on the part of Hamner, who merely recorded how a single family of fundamentally kind, mutually supportive people raised in a specific faith tradition respond to the events and circumstances of their lives together.

Through the stories of the Walton family of Jefferson County, Virginia, television viewers in America and throughout the world have touched a time and a way of life that are emblematic, however imperfectly, of life as they believe it is meant to be lived. In the words of Robert Butler, one of the series' directors, "There always seemed to me to be a kind of fresh-air, sun-washed clarity about the show. I felt that the writing staff's ideas, their notions on character and humanity and fair play, were lucid and light, familiar and comforting, and easily accessible to all of us. The simplicity of the Walton life, its dignity and stature, the affection and love in those people, was deep and honest and even-handed always. Simplicity and honesty and the warm sunshine born of decency—that's the way I always felt whenever I worked on this series."[27] Those very qualities in the successful *Wal-*

tons inspired a host of family-oriented programs during the seventies, such as *The Family Holvak, Eight Is Enough, The New Land, Little House on the Prairie, Family, The Fitzpatricks,* and another series conceived by Hamner himself, *Apple's Way.* (*Apple's Way* was rushed into production to capitalize upon the success of *The Waltons.* Unfortunately, being hurried into production hurt the show, as Hamner was unable to properly conceive of and develop the series, which suffered from overt moralizing that its target audience found unappealing.) Of the program that started this trend, Hamner said at the time, "I think people are hungry for a sense of security, and the Waltons represent that. They're hungry, too, for real family relationships—not just rounding up the family for a cookout, but real togetherness where people are relating honestly."[28]

On one occasion he was asked by writer Kimberly Dunham what advice he would offer to anyone who wanted to change his or her family life to reflect a more "Walton-like" aspect—aside from simply watching the program. Hamner replied by citing the need for people to lead "examined lives" and then act upon their beliefs: "I think in any case if you can achieve some kind of serenity within yourself, then you can impart it to other people; and I think it helps a great deal to come to terms with one's own self, if you can articulate to yourself who you are and what you are with honesty. And one of the best ways I've found—and I did it when I was growing up—is to keep a journal, as John-Boy does. It not only gives you a record of your own growth, but it provides you with a habit of writing."[29]

Where is Walton's Mountain? It is a country of the mind, based upon a real place and real people, set in a time that is slowly fading from America's collective memory. Where is Walton's Mountain? Hamner's sister Marion answered this question once, saying "It's a place where my brother was happy." Through *The Waltons,* many people in the United States and around the world have visited that place and touched that happiness for a short time. And the series has stirred in them a sense of longing for simplicity and honesty in a sunwashed land amid a supportive family of good people.[30]

NOTES

1. Hamner, *"The Waltons:* A Guideline." Unpublished MS, 1972. In all quotations from this piece I have retained Hamner's punctuation.

2. McClay, "The Mystic Chords of Memory: Reclaiming American History," *Heritage Lecture,* no. 550, 1995, n.p.

3. "The Homecoming," http://www.the-waltons.com/booksbyearl.html.

4. *The Homecoming,* 112.

5. Ibid., 120.

6. Ibid., 122.

7. Ibid., 123.

8. Hamner, *"The Waltons:* A Guideline." Unpublished MS, 1972.

9. Ibid.

10. Ibid.

11. Judge, "Let's Save a Show," *Detroit News,* September 15, 1972, 14C.

12. Cyclops [John Leonard], "Wholesome Sentiment in the Blue Ridge," *Life,* October 13, 1972, 20.

13. *Goodnight John-Boy,* 182.

14. Klonicki, "Reality in a Television Survivor," *Raleigh News & Observer,* January 30, 2001, 9A. Hamner so admired this essay that he quoted it in full under Klonicki's original title, "What's Your Reality?" in *Goodnight John-Boy.*

15. Edwards, in a telephone conversation with the author, October 12, 2004.

16. Quoted in Kimberly Dunham, "A Mosaic of the John Boys," *From the Hills* (Charleston, WV) no. 38 (1974): 9. This now-hard-to-obtain periodical was a publication of Morris Harvey College (now the University of Charleston). Dunham's article consists primarily of a remarkably insightful interview with Hamner.

17. Tanguay, "Earl Hamner, Jr.: The Man behind *The Waltons," Authors in the News,* Vol. 2, edited by Barbara Nykoruk, 135–36.

18. Quoted in Deborah Starr Seibel, "John-Boy Says 'I Do'," *TV Guide,* February 11, 1995, 25.

19. Cotler, interview with the author, October 16, 2004.

20. Quoted in Irv Broughton, ed., "Earl Hamner, Jr.," in *Producers on Producing: The Making of Film and Television,* 194. Here Hamner refers to the episode titled "The Five-Foot Shelf," which originally aired in March 1974. It was written by John Hawkins and directed by Ralph Waite.

21. Horace Newcomb and Robert S. Alley, *The Producer's Medium: Conversations with Creators of American TV,* 159.

22. Smith, "Laura Ingalls Wilder and the Little House Books," in *The Horn Book's Laura Ingalls Wilder: Articles About and by Laura Ingalls Wilder, Garth Williams and the Little House Books,* edited by William Anderson, 1987, 19.

Smith's essay was originally published in the September–October 1943 issue of *The Horn Book Magazine.*

23. Klonicki, "Reality in a Television Survivor," *Raleigh News & Observer,* January 30, 2001, 9A.

24. Roïphe, "*The Waltons:* Ma and Pa and John-Boy in Mythic America," *The New York Times Magazine,* November 13, 1973, 40, 146.

25. Cyclops [John Leonard], "Wholesome Sentiment in the Blue Ridge," *Life,* October 13, 1972, 20.

26. Norton, in a letter to the author, October 8, 2004.

27. *Goodnight John-Boy,* 93.

28. Quoted in Joseph N. Bell, "The Real Waltons," *Good Housekeeping,* November 1973, 82.

29. Quoted in Kimberly Dunham, "A Mosaic of the John Boys," *From the Hills* (Charleston, WV) no. 38 (1974): 10.

30. The virtues of *The Waltons* are celebrated by the activities of several organizations, including:

The Waltons International Fan Club, P.O. Box 1055, Kernersville, NC 27285
Carolyn Grinnell, President
e-mail: Olivia@viafamily.com
Publishes a newsletter titled *The Blue Ridge Chronicle*

Friends of The Waltons, The Walton's Mountain Museum
P.O. Box 124, Schuyler, VA 22969
e-mail: waltonmt@cstone.net
Publishes a newsletter titled *The Blue Ridge Chronicles*

The Waltons Friendship Society, Riding Gate House, Riding Gate
Wincanton, Somerset, BA9 8NG England
Contact: Irene Porter
e-mail : Ijohnrene@cs.com
Publishes a newsletter titled *MAILBOX*

4

THE INCONSOLABLE WOUND:

Fifty Roads to Town and Hamner's Other Novels

But to return to the aims of men: their minds seem to seek to regain the highest good, though their memories seem to dull their powers. It is as though a drunken man were seeking his home, but could not remember the way.

BOETHIUS, FROM *THE CONSOLATION OF PHILOSOPHY*

ON ONE OCCASION DURING HIS years with NBC Radio, Earl Hamner interviewed Katherine Anne Porter, a writer renowned for her slim but distinguished corpus of short fiction. He asked her how she came to write her stories, and about the nature of the creative process. Porter replied that an idea for a story would arise in her mind unexpectedly, and that over time details would suggest themselves and attach themselves to that story in much the same way iron filings are drawn to a magnet. Eventually, she said, the story practically begs to be written, and then she knows that it is time to commit it to paper.

Hamner identifies closely with Porter's assessment of how the initial stages of the writer's work progress. In his novels, he ruminated for years on the ideas that formed them—*Spencer's Mountain* being the prime example of this. At the same time the first draft of Hamner's initial account of the Spencer family was taking shape, the idea for still another novel began to suggest itself to the aspiring writer. This occurred during the late 1940s, while Hamner was still in Cincinnati and working at his first job as a writer for radio. This, the first novel Hamner was to publish during his career, explores various aspects of an element of life that had proven so vital to his early life and the theme of much of his work: love—but in this case love that has been twisted, thwarted, longed for, and found at last.

HAMNER'S FIRST VOYAGE OUT: *FIFTY ROADS TO TOWN*

For many years, since the days of his boyhood when he had observed traveling revival meetings in Schuyler, Hamner had been fascinated by aspects of Pentecostal Christianity—particularly the phenomenon of *glossolalia,* commonly known as "speaking in tongues." Seeing the phenomenon firsthand at these revival meetings prompted questions in the young man's mind. Are modern-day occurrences of this act truly an outpouring of the Holy Spirit, as described in the second chapter of The Acts of the Apostles, or the fruit of mass-hysteria and the power of suggestion, or possibly something else? Upon what sorts of people does the "spirit" fall? Whatever the source of this phenomenon, are there dangers associated with engaging in it?

With these questions in mind, Hamner took a month-long leave of absence from his job at radio station WLW in Cincinnati during the fall of 1948 and traveled to the Ouachita Mountains in Arkansas. He had a specific purpose in mind for this short sabbatical: he wanted to try his hand at writing a novel, one that explored the themes that were suggesting themselves to him in regard to his thoughts on "speaking in tongues." He rented a small stone cabin in the woods

The dashing young writer, early in his career.

near Mena, Arkansas, and with nobody around for many miles, he tapped out the early chapters of his first book, *Fifty Roads to Town,* keeping an eye out for snakes the entire time, as they seemed to be everywhere—even inside the cabin.[1] Several years later he finished this work—in which serpents play a key role—and carried the manuscript with him to the offices of Random House in an effort to convince editor Belle Becker to publish it. Becker told him she would look at it, but that the chances were slim that Random House would publish a first novel by an unknown author. Before leaving the editor's office, Hamner placed his manuscript in a pile of other manuscripts Becker was planning on taking home to read over the weekend. On the Monday after that momentous weekend, Hamner was contacted by Becker, who said that this was an excellent novel—too good for a new author, she said—and that she would personally recommend it to the renowned publisher Bennett Cerf, head of Random House. Within the year, 1953, the novel was published. At the time Hamner was twenty-eight years old, launched at last as a writer of fiction, and published by a major house.

The Inconsolable Wound

"This was my first book," Hamner later wrote. "I have always had a special place in my heart for it because it was a challenge. I had never written a book before, had taken no writing classes, and it was written at night after putting in a full day's work as a radio writer. In it I attempted to write about people of the backwoods and to endow them with dignity and depth. So often I had seen the people portrayed as simple-minded hillbillies in books by such writers as Erskine Caldwell and in plays like *Dark of the Moon*. I think I accomplished what I set out to do with these characters and there is even a certain amount of poetry in the writing that I am proud of."[2] Indeed, the book is written in a style markedly different from his others, possessing an eloquently literary style entirely unlike the spare style of *Spencer's Mountain* and his other works.

Hamner himself has summarized the book more succinctly than any of his critics, writing, "All my life I had been fascinated by something called 'the unknown tongue,' a kind of physical seizure experienced by some fundamental religions."

> I had seen people experience it and at times they seemed to go into a kind of ecstasy. The book is centered on a country girl, Althea, who yearns to speak "the unknown tongue." She believes it will bring an end to her loneliness, to enable her to communicate her secret and precious thoughts. What she learns in the course of the book is that love is the key to the language she is seeking. A less ethereal approach to communication is taken by an itinerant evangelist when he comes to town with his [dreams of] twelve female disciples. Preacher Otha throws the little town into turmoil with his fiery sermons. Under his spell the people in his congregation reveal secrets about themselves they had never known before.[3]

Fifty Roads to Town is set in the fictional Virginia mountain village of Edensville. In all of life here below, every Eden is visited by a serpent, and Edensville is no exception. The heat-baked village is stirred by the arrival one day of a tent evangelist, Rev. Otha, who claims to specialize in bringing "old-timey, fourteen-carat, one-hundred-per-cent, Christ-blessed, plain-spoken, straight-from-the-shoulder, fighting-mad, God-sent, sky-blue, man-craved, soul-saved, God-bathed, no-holds-barred revival" to a world in dire need of it. In truth, Otha—though earnest and at times sympathetic and well-meaning—is a mesmerizing deceiver, like a poisonous snake that charms its prey to the point of unmoving fascination before striking. At the outset of the novel, this minister of the Gospel is advancing through a state of messianic delusion, believing himself to be not a servant of God but the true risen Christ Himself. Directed into town by a local resident, Fate Bibbs, Otha drives into Edensville from Tennessee, after having only recently buried his teenage protégé and lover, Tessie, who was fatally bitten by a rattlesnake while attending a snake-handling service presided over by a rival evangelist. As Otha approaches Edensville, he muses upon Tessie's charms and envisions the day when he will be attended by his own twelve apostles, all of them women, all of them willing to minister to him in ways distinctly unspiritual. He sets up his large tent in the pasture of young Althea's mother, Ossie Peeler, a woman defeated by life in the dull village and married to a mentally impaired man, Hubey, who keeps his own homemade coffin propped on sawhorses in his backyard, urinates on the ground for his own fascinated amusement, and carries in his shirt pocket a live, injured goldfinch, its wings bound. Hubey's mind had not always been such. He had been a typical unimaginative married man until the day he scuffled with Ossie's illicit lover, who broke a liquor bottle over Hubey's head. From that moment until the end of his life, he possessed the mind of a child, with thoughts occasionally punctuated by the concerns of a leering, sexually active man. For the most part, though, Hubey is fascinated by dreaming of the life offered by the advertisements in the Sears and Roebuck catalogue, and of mounting up on the wings of a bird and flying away.

Hubey's aged mother, Sabbatha, is another "character," in every sense of the word. She lives under her son's roof, despises Ossie as a heartless, faithless tramp, and is given to walking out to the family burying ground periodically to talk with her dead husband. Sabbatha is certain that she and God are on intimate terms; in fact, she speaks with him regularly and is sure the Almighty agrees with her every opinion—including her spiteful, self-righteous views about nearly everyone in the village. And in a house on the edge of the Peeler property lives a lonely, sorrowing old widow called Miss Mattie, whose children have all died or moved away and forgotten her. Her mind no longer tethered to reality, Miss Mattie wanders about the inside of her trash-strewn house singing at all hours of the day and night.

Thus far in the narrative, during this laying of the novel's groundwork, Hamner has described a scenario from Southern country life that is strongly reminiscent of Flannery O'Connor's Southern Gothic fiction. What follows continues in a similar vein, venturing into realms of degradation of which O'Connor knew and wrote—and then ascending to the light of wisdom, mercy, and redemption. The stage is set for drama, for despite its name Edensville is no Eden: its residents live out their lives in dust-choked, decadent boredom, without purpose, their lives a mere running exercise in paying lip-service to a strict and narrow form of Christianity while engaging in gossip, slander, and the begetting of numerous inbred children, most of whom die in infancy. That and collecting a monthly relief check from the federal government, because nobody in the village works, thus ensuring a life of aimless boredom. Life in Edensville is in some ways a living death. At one point Hamner describes one character as she stands in her yard on a hot afternoon. At such a time, it seems to her,

The new recruit: Hamner in 1943, shortly after being inducted into the U.S. Army.

EARL HAMNER

that everyone but her had died and she was alone in a strange place and as far as she could see there was nothing but dust and drooping grass and desolation. The afternoon might never end.

"Oh, God!" she cried, and her voice fell out into the dead air where nothing heard her except the bumblebees buzzing in the honeysuckle vine.[4]

The only rose blooming in this desert of ashes is beautiful, nineteen-year-old Althea Peeler, who closely resembles her mother, Ossie, in physical appearance. Perhaps as Ossie once was, Althea is pure of heart but no naïve fool, an honest seeker after God without being insufferably pious. In a conversation with a girlfriend who has spoken in tongues, Moselle Winthrop, Althea seeks without success to learn how to acquire that spiritual gift. She senses that her fellow seekers who enter into frenzied worship under Otha's guidance "had known something which she had not known, had been some place that she would like to go, some place denied to her, some land of the unknown tongue. All things could be understood there. There was possible all communication between people and with God. She felt that once having been there she would have answers to the questions she had asked herself."[5] She longs to transcend her humble surroundings and be made complete in Christ or in love or in some other manner.

Although life in Edensville is dull, its story is far more than one of dullness alone, and the reader would be mistaken to see *Fifty Roads to Town* as simply another "revolt from the village" novel, similar to those works written early in the twentieth century by the likes of the American writers Edgar Lee Masters and Sinclair Lewis. As it was with *Spencer's Mountain,* Hamner once again owes a literary debt to Sherwood Anderson, whose *Winesburg, Ohio* depicted not only village dullness but also the complexity and lovable nature of its fictional Ohio town's inhabitants. Those obscure people, along with Althea Peeler, and to some extent the other inhabitants of Edensville, possess what literary scholar C. S. Lewis has termed *sehnsucht:* an intense longing for Joy and Love. In one of his own novels, Lewis describes this as "the inconsolable wound with which man is born." This "wound" is characterized by the unexpected, beautiful, yet sweetly painful epiphany such as a person experiences at the sound of the wind among sea-oats, the prospect of distant blue mountains at day's end, or the sound of a faraway train-whistle heard late at night. It is a longing for fulfillment, spurred by reveries of something only faintly remembered yet utterly real, with clues to the source of these reveries residing in the fondest memories of one's childhood. Althea clutches at what she believes will bring her to the fount of that vision, first by enjoying the company of her boyfriend, Eubank Ryan, whom she chastely loves and whose highest dream in life is to become a bus-driver for Greyhound, marry Althea, somehow purchase a truck, and leave Edensville to live with her in Richmond. Althea's affection for Eubank is recurrently mixed with puzzlement over his moodiness and fierce possessiveness. She also seeks fulfillment in the fiery sermons of Otha, whose honied words convince her that speaking the unknown tongue—not loving God, or obeying the commands of Christ, or loving her neighbor as herself—will fill her dull life with purpose, meaning, and the ability to communicate her most deeply held thoughts amid a fellowship of understanding people.

Before long Althea swims into Otha's predatory line of vision. Within a short time after his arrival, Rev. Otha has enjoyed sexual congress with Ossie, attempted to rape Althea (while whispering that he will "save" her), and spellbound the people of Edensville, leading them into temptation and delivering them to evil by way of acts of religion-driven sexual frenzy. His career as a spellbinder in Edensville reaches its crescendo in a service that ends with a number of believers confessing their most tantalizing sins in the presence of all, speaking in "the unknown tongue"—while Althea looks on in longing and frustration—and descending into a writhing orgy of sexual groping from which Althea flees hurriedly, followed by Eubank. When he catches up with her, at a pasture fence some distance from the evangelist's tent, the two tumble to the ground together, shrug out of their clothes, and spend a night of blissful lovemaking interspersed with earnest, articulate sharing of each other's dreams. She

EARL HAMNER

Right, Private Earl Hamner stands for a photograph while stateside. *Below,* The Hamner siblings in 1950. Earl, in a plaid shirt, stands with his hand upon the shoulder of his sister Nancy, who stands beside Marion, Jim, and Bill. Cliff and Paul kneel in front. (Not pictured is Audrey, who had recently married and was on her honeymoon.)

speaks to Eubank of her desire to marry him, leave the village, and spend her life making him happy. He speaks to Althea about his own desire to spend his life making *her* happy as a faithful husband and provider.

When Eubank awakens early the next morning, he discovers that Althea has arisen already and presumably gone home. But he is driven to a blind rage when he sees, from a distance, a woman who looks remarkably like Althea walk out of the preacher's tent and walk to the Peelers' house, followed a minute later by Otha himself. The woman is in fact Ossie, but the possessive Eubank is so driven by a desire for vengeance that he runs to the house, bursts in, and hurls himself upon Otha for committing acts to "ruin my girl." The two men engage in a fistfight that wrecks the inside of the Peeler house and results unexpectedly in the sudden, violent death of Hubey. Otha accidentally stabs Hubey to death with a butcher knife after the simple-minded man interferes during the fight with Eubank.

After Hubey's death, the novel moves swiftly toward its conclusion. Otha flees the scene of the crime, takes refuge in an abandoned mine in the wooded hills, and collapses into sleep. When he awakens, it becomes apparent to the reader that Otha's mind is completely overthrown; the preacher believes himself to be in Christ's tomb and that he is truly the resurrected Messiah. Hunted down and captured by a lynch mob, Otha is rescued from certain death by the now-rational and merciful Eubank, who takes him unresistingly into custody and drives the fallen and bound messiah to the insane asylum in Waynesboro, where he is institutionalized. "In the end," writes *New York Times Book Review* critic Charles Lee, "everybody has reason to remember Otha"—including the desperately frustrated Ossie, the silly Hubey, their beautiful daughter, Althea; and Ossie's long-grieving mother.[6] Fate (in the form of a man by that name) brought Otha to Edensville, but it is by the free will of men that the captured preacher, a ruined wreck of a man, is driven from the village.

Like every other character in the novel, Otha is a complex and rounded character, not a latter-day cardboard cutout of novelist Sinclair Lewis's false prophet, Elmer Gantry. With psychological complexes that originate in his vanished, deeply troubled boyhood, Otha honestly wants to serve God and believes—rightly—that he is unfit to serve as an evangelist. His sins of the flesh are not so much a hypocritical flouting of his responsibilities as a man of God as they are acts of protests of his unworthiness. Yet, in time, because of the power he wields by his commanding physical appearance, the handful of healing miracles he sees at each service (among other "healings" that fail), as well as his ability to sway large audiences, Otha falls for the oldest lie on record, that he will become as God.

With the fall of Otha, Christianity has not been discredited; instead, the truth of human fallenness has been affirmed, as well as the truth that Jesus' commands to love God and love one's neighbors as oneself are at the true heart of the faith. Faith, hope, and charity remain; and these virtues are displayed not in rigid self-justification—as exemplified by Otha and the townspeople of Edensville—but in the many acts of faith, hope, love, and mercy that are part of everyday life. At the burial of Hubey's body in his homemade coffin, the local Baptist minister affirms this in his closing oration. This truth is also borne out in the novel's opening epigraph, which gives Hamner's first work of fiction its title. The epigraph is from "The Chant of the Brazen Head," by the minor nineteenth-century English poet Winthrop Mackworth Praed, and it reads:

> I think while zealots fast and frown,
> And fight for two and seven,
> That there are fifty roads to town,
> And rather more to heaven.

After returning to Edensville from Waynesboro, Eubank realizes that the false "risen Christ" has bestowed a blessing upon him unaware, for he has been given custody of Otha's truck and now has a mode of transportation to take himself and Althea away from Edensville forever. The deceiver has been driven out of Edensville, but the memory of his influence remains, and Eubank and Althea—innocent despite their actions on the previous night—cannot remain in the village. They must leave, and they make plans to depart shortly after Hubey's funeral. Among the novel's closing passages, the description of Althea's departure from her home is particularly moving as it explores the mysteries of time and the timeless, of memory and the things that last:

> As Althea looked for the last time on the place she was leaving she realized that good-bye was just a word. No matter how many times she said good-bye to the people and the things she was leaving behind, they would still go with her as they were at that moment, and that she was not leaving them behind at all, but was only putting them out of her sight. Althea herself might change, but all that had happened, a wish she made, the feel of the quilted comforter, the face of Sabbatha, Miss Mattie's singing, the color of morning, all these would be forever with her. After she left, those who remained would go on into a life where they too would change so that if and when they came together again in the world there would be between them moments they had not shared together, events of great and small import which would make strangers of those who remained behind and those who went on to another part of the world.[7]

The novel concludes with the funeral of Hubey and with the betrothed young couple leaving the village for Richmond in Otha's truck. Assigning her will to Fate (Bibbs)—the man who had originally directed the false prophet into the village—Ossie decides to stay in Edensville to wait for the return of her lover from long ago. Sabbatha reflects upon her own life—a mixture of great joy and immense sorrow, all to which she is bitterly resigned—and trudges toward the family graveyard for what will be her final talk with her departed husband, believing her work on Earth to be complete.

In his assessment of the novel, Charles Lee of the *New York Times Book Review* describes *Fifty Roads to Town* as "picturesque in its psychological oddities and setting. But it does not so lose itself in hillbilly comedy and terror as to alienate the reader's sense of compassion. Indeed, it goes to the sorrowful core of the human condition." Likewise, reviewer H. J. Shinn of *Saturday Review* added, speaking of Hamner's characters, "You leave them, in short, with your sympathies, not just your curiosities, aroused."[8]

In contrast to these views, other readers have found *Fifty Roads to Town* a work with a markedly darker vision of the land and people it describes. Literary scholar John M. Bradbury found the novel a typical work of the "Southern Renaissance" in that it treats the country preacher as "a subject of ridicule, often for criticism on the grounds of his bigotry and intolerance." He added, "Earl Hamner, Jr., combines lust and a true Christ-complex in his itinerant Virginia preacher of *Fifty Roads to Town* (1953), and produces a curious mixture of low comedy and serious criticism."[9] Similarly, scholar Richard K. Meeker found the novel "rather hard to label," noting that in it Hamner "is obviously exploiting the eccentricities of Southern Virginia country people, but there is no perceptible theme. He begins in the Erskine Caldwell tradition by introducing Otha, a fanatical faith healer, to the town of Edensville. The novel could have been an exposé of religious fanaticism, but Hamner takes us off to several families in town to witness their degeneration. Our sympathies are meant to be with Otha, mad as he is, because his intentions are honest. At the end he is so confused that when he wakes up in a cave, he thinks he is the risen Christ and tells a local boy that, if anyone asks for him, he has gone to Galilee. The only normal people left by that time wisely plan to move to Richmond."[10] Writer Margaret Fife Tanguay offered a similarly dour view of Hamner's vision of Southern hill-life as presented in *Fifty Roads to Town*, saying, "These mountains are full of hillbillies, bootleggers, distorted love and lust. The mountains are a trap. They stifle all growth. The characters' only hope is to leave, to escape to city jobs and better pay."[11] Perhaps this is true, but Hamner's novel is written more in sorrow and sympathy than in anger. For despite their proclivity to sin, the characters in *Fifty Roads to Town* are all to some degree recognizable and able, to some degree or another, to gain the reader's sympathies. Thus this novel does not represent a backhanded slap at the hill people Hamner knew and loved; rather it is a portrait of those people in all their complexity. The novel is an accomplished warm-up exercise by a young writer who was to some extent struggling to organize and present his own vision of modern Appalachian life, finding his voice as an author, and laboring in a field already being worked by other hands.

The style of the novel is far more literary than Hamner's other novels, as when the author describes the diverse crowd at a rural Tennessee revival meeting with stark accuracy, writing, "Perhaps the one thing they all had in common was the frost-bitten look of poverty." Possibly the strongest example of Hamner's style of simple eloquence in *Fifty Roads to Town* comes at the beginning of Chapter Four, where he describes in poetic imagery night flowing into the Virginia countryside from the sea, like a specter.

> At night in Virginia, across the old fought-on earth, there comes a special kind of darkness. It seeps in from the sea and, carried on the wind of tall dead planets, it drifts across the tideland. It comes from the sea and it swallows little towns with the old names. Flowing westward, the night sifts along the rivers of old Virginia, along the James and the York and the Rappahannock. It hovers over the Dismal Swamp and then it goes inland.
>
> Crossing Smithfield the darkness falls on fields where peanuts grow, and even while the chickens cluck apprehensively in their huts at Waverly the night is on them and past them and all of Surry County sleeps. Now the damp smell of night is on Hopewell, reaching toward Richmond, and the sad city of Petersburg is sadder because night is on it and it is afraid, for night is when the sounds return of battles lost long ago, and the trenches are unquiet.
>
> Over Richmond, the night goes on, sweeping across its quiet lawns, touching the heads of its dead heroes with damp hands, and goes on to the country beyond. Up in old Amelia County they light the kerosene lamps and the Negroes sit in the doorways of their little shanties and they are afraid because the dark night has come in from

the sea and brought something old and dreadful and terrible with it. On across the sleeping fields of grass and corn the inexorable night walks and, reaching Charlottesville, it begins to climb and walks on over mountains.[12]

Ghosts are walking abroad in the form of unquiet memories of long-ago frights that may return. Human nature being constant, Hamner expresses here the truth that the undead past will return as surely as night follows day. And how do people respond to this knowledge? Hamner's description of the onset of night is followed closely by a paragraph describing a typical Saturday night in Edensville, a passage strongly reminiscent of Sherwood Anderson's description of a typical autumn night when the county fair comes to Winesburg, Ohio, in the story "Sophistication." Anderson writes:

In the main street of Winesburg crowds filled the stores and the sidewalks. Night came on, horses whinnied, the clerks in the stores ran madly about, children became lost and cried lustily, an American town worked terribly at the task of amusing itself.[13]

Using similar imagery, Hamner writes:

On Saturday night in Edensville the people forget their fear. They walk out of doors, and they go to places where they can gather in groups, to hear a little music, to talk a little talk, to fight a little, to drink a lot, to forget the work they have done all week, to forget the fear, to love and dance and sing. The men get drunk and the women get tired and the children get cross but everybody has a wonderful time and Monday is a long ways off.[14]

Later in the novel, Hamner revisits imagery from Sherwood Anderson's "Sophistication." Before speaking further about Hamner's imagery, it would be helpful to note that "Sophistication" is a story that ends by describing the sense of understanding and spiritual fellowship that blooms between Anderson's protagonist, a teenager and would-be writer named George Willard, and the young woman he adores, Helen White. On the evening of the Winesburg County Fair, as the events of the day are winding down—the horse-races are over, and the town's racetrack has become deserted—George and Helen sit together in the empty grandstands. Each is aware that the other stands on the threshold of adulthood, each is strongly attracted to the other, and each senses that a time of ending and new beginnings has come. After a few minutes pass, they arise from their seats and walk away in the dark. They embrace, but then they become self-conscious and embarrassed:

> They were both embarrassed and to relieve their embar-
> rassment dropped into the animalism of youth. They
> laughed and began to pull and haul at each other. In some
> way chastened and purified by the mood they had been in,
> they became, not man and woman, not boy and girl, but
> excited little animals.
>
> It was so they went down the hill. In the darkness they
> played like two splendid young things in a young world.
> Once, running swiftly forward, Helen tripped George and
> he fell. He squirmed and shouted. Shaking with laughter,
> he rolled down the hill. Helen ran after him. For just a
> moment she stopped in the darkness. There was no way of
> knowing what woman's thoughts went through her mind,
> but, when the bottom of the hill was reached and she
> came up to the boy, she took his arm and walked beside
> him in dignified silence. For some reason they could not
> have explained they had both got from their silent evening
> together the thing needed. Man or boy, woman or girl,
> they had for a moment taken hold of the thing that makes
> the mature life of men and women in the modern world
> possible.[15]

Taking up similar but earthier imagery, Hamner describes Althea running through the night after she leaves the revival tent. She is pursued by Eubank, who catches up with her after she runs into a barbed-wire fence and tears open her dress in the front:

A hand touched her bare shoulder. God had touched her, and in that instant she understood what it was that Moselle had meant. God was real. The hand of God could be felt. She felt the impetus to speak and words came from her in an incoherent babble speaking love and passion and craving.

But the face that confronted hers when she turned was not the face of God. Eubank had followed her from the tent, and now he saw her need and answered it. He had seen cows in heat and had taken them to bulls, and it was more as animals than humans that they came together, brushing aside the confusion of clothes, the falling together on the ground, the wrestling, the search and the delirious discovery of each other. Thus was Althea transported into the land of the unknown tongue.

It was as if two bells had rung together and now, later, they listened together with the diminishing ringing of bells whose tongues had spoken in harmony across the night. . . .

The whole world lay about them. They felt it there, close, somehow at this moment attainable. There were no obstacles between them and any far place.[16]

The sentiments expressed in these parallel passages are remarkably similar, indicating that *Winesburg* exercised a strongly telling effect upon Hamner in terms of imagery, vision, and (in his later novels) style. In each passage, the young lovers are described matter-of-factly, simply, and affectionately. In both instances, the couples are described as adopting the instincts and mannerisms of affectionate animals, temporarily casting aside restraint and propriety to live in the moment. In each case, they temporarily take leave of the drabness and meaninglessness of their daily lives and lay hold of some measure of understanding their place in the world.

Twenty-one years after the appearance of *Fifty Roads to Town*, Hamner assessed this first effort in an interview, saying, "It was my first novel and was very well written for a first novel. It had a great deal of good writing."[17] To this writer he confided that he considered it "probably the best book I've ever written." The novel's outlook, its song to the joy of being alive and in love, is affirmed in another sentiment voiced in poet W. M. Praed's "Chant of the Brazen Head":

> I think that life is not too long,
> And therefore I determine,
> That many people read a song,
> Who will not read a sermon.

The Morning After the First Novel

A man who loves to laugh and tell humorous stories, Hamner has a rich supply of stories from his past. One of his favorite anecdotes about *Fifty Roads to Town* concerns a minor misunderstanding that occurred when two of his beloved aunts read the novel immediately after its publication. These Virginian ladies, Nora Spencer Hamner and Margaret Hamner Meyers, were proper members of the Daughters of the American Revolution and the United Daughters of the Confederacy, and they were affronted by certain plot elements in *Fifty Roads to Town*—such as the scenes of wild abandon at Pentecostal tent services, and poor brain-damaged Hubey Peeler's more peculiar urinary habits—and by a blurb on Random House's first-edition dust-jacket that described the book as "a novel about the strange folkways of Earl Hamner's own people." For his part, Hamner was satisfied with this blurb, as he understood it to mean "a story of the mountain people of Virginia's Blue Ridge." However, his aunts had a different interpretation.

On a visit to Virginia in 1953, Hamner flew to Richmond and was met at the airport by his Aunt Margaret. Upon asking how his family was getting along, Aunt Margaret replied, "They're all fine, Earl. But you'd better go visit Nora. She's taken to her bed after reading your book."

Hamner hurried to his Aunt Nora's house and discovered that, sure enough, all the shades were drawn and his Aunt Nora was lying in bed with the covers pulled up to her chin, a portrait of wounded propriety. He approached her bed timidly and said, "Nora, it's Earl. Do you know me?" She replied, "Yes, I see it's you, Earl. Come up closer, darling, and give me a kiss." He did as she requested. Aunt Nora then looked the young author in the eye and said, "Now, I just want you to know that no matter what you have done to the family, we all still love you." Flabbergasted, Hamner asked, "But what have I done?" With a tinge of frost in her voice his aunt responded, "Earl, we may sometimes have our odd moments, but *nobody* in our family ever worshiped God by leaping upon a piano, and *nobody* in our family ever *voided upon the ground.*"

(Hamner reports that after he explained matters to her, Aunt Nora Hamner recovered her good spirits and left her bed within a few minutes.)

A NOVEL OF EXILE AND HOPE: *YOU CAN'T GET THERE FROM HERE*

"I think that E. B. White summed up what New York offers a writer, or any person really, which is 'the luxury of privacy and loneliness'," Hamner told writer-editor Antoinette W. Roades in 1977. He added, "Being Southern and going to New York, suddenly you don't have the family for solace and comfort. I think that most Southerners are such talkers and such storytellers that simply being there and having nobody to tell the stories to, and to be lonely, you are driven into writing."[18]

Living in New York provided Hamner with the perspective of distance that enabled him to begin creatively synthesizing and organizing the experiences of his upbringing in the South. On some days while he was working at NBC Radio, he and a colleague named Jack Wilson used to periodically banter about small towns and villages they had known in their travels, then pause and lament with mock earnestness, "Well, you can't get there from here!" As Hamner later explained, "What we implied was that the cultural, social, economic, physical differences between New York City and these small towns was so vast that you could not get there from where we were."[19] Out of this light diversion grew the idea for Hamner's third novel, written several years after *Spencer's Mountain* and his migration from New York to California.

Containing echoes of themes found in *The Homecoming, You*

Can't Get There from Here is a hymn to the love of family and community Hamner had known as a boy. Set in New York, it describes a single day in the life of a boy who has just returned to the city from a summer-long trip, taken alone, to visit his father's family in the Blue Ridge region of Virginia, in a village called Schuyler. As described by the boy, Wesley, Schuyler is something like Paradise:

> The way you get there is to fly to Richmond and then take a bus to Charlottesville. In Charlottesville you take another bus out Route 29, the Old Seminole Trail, they call it. At Hickory Creek you get off the bus. Usually somebody meets you, but once or twice I've walked from there. Well, you turn left at Hickory Creek and go on through Faber, and man that's pretty country once you get that far. Little creeks run under rattly old wooden bridges and then just wander off through pastures full of oats and wheat and clover. If you want the feeling of being in Heaven, you fill your lungs with air that sweeps in over a fresh field of clover covered with dew early in the morning.
>
> After you go over the railroad bridge you leave Faber pretty much behind you and you get into the hill country. The air gets still and sweet and if you've been breathing city dust it takes you a while to get used to it. In the spring, which is usually when I go, the road is lined with redbud and dogwood, and as far as you can see, the hills are covered with their white and pink blooms.
>
> After about four miles you come to a fork in the road and you go to the right. You keep going for two more miles on this road and when you get to a place where the road just stops, that's Schuyler.

Having spent an entire summer in bucolic rural Virginia, Wes finds himself thrown without ceremony back into the bustle of life in New York—and a family emergency. Arriving back at his home in Brooklyn, he learns from his kind and loving step-mother, Meredith, that his hard-drinking father, Joe, has just been released from his job as a radio writer and has set out on a series of random visits among old friends in the city, seemingly to square accounts with them. Like Clay-Boy Spencer in *The Homecoming*, Wes sets out to find his father, who might (the boy believes) go on a bender and damage himself as a result of his recent firing. Wes embarks on a day-long odyssey that takes him all over Manhattan and ends with his discovering not only the whereabouts of his father, but also the extent of Joe's love for him and what Thomas Wolfe called "the lost lane-end into heaven." As Hamner himself describes it, the novel "covers a single day during which Wes follows clues left behind by his unpredictable father who seems bent on self-destruction. His search takes him through his father's office in Rockefeller Center, New York City bars, the United Nations, Pennsylvania Station, The Plaza Hotel and finally to a surprising, terrifying and touching climax at the George Washington Bridge when Wes finds out the kind of man his father is."[20]

At every step along the way, the boy finds that he "just missed" his father, a man renowned among his friends as a great storyteller and a generous man who, in a city known for its abruptness and toughness, has left a lingering sense of nostalgic good will with everyone he has met during the day. These people—cleaning women, a former girlfriend, drinking companions, a middle-management businessman, and others—represent a large cross-section of life in New York; and as Wes speaks with them, each seems to remember Joe saying something about a place he knew long ago and wants to find again, a place with the unusual name of Shy Beaver.

Wes has heard his Virginia-born father speak of Shy Beaver many times, and to the boy (and to the reader), it strongly resembles Schuyler. Wes recalls:

> Shy Beaver is this town he heard of or passed through or
> found on a map somewhere and the name really stuck
> with him. He's built up this thing in his mind about Shy
> Beaver, but I'll tell you in confidence that I darn nearly
> believe in the place myself. I guess it's just that I've heard
> Joe talk about it all my life.

It's off the main highway at the end of a winding country road. Along the road are dogwood and redbud trees and according to Joe they're in bloom year 'round. There isn't any sign to tell you where you are, but when you cross a little covered bridge you're in town. Joe put the covered bridge in for Meredith because she fell in love with one she saw in New Hampshire once. . . .

If it sounds like I'm a little hung up on this place myself, you've got to remember that he used to tell me stories about it the way other kids' dads would tell them about Joe DiMaggio.

"Once upon a time in a place called Shy Beaver, there was a little boy named Barney who was celebrating his sixtieth birthday." That was one of the good ones, all about this little kid who liked birthdays so much he celebrated them whenever he liked. Shy Beaver is that kind of place.

But the big thing to Joe about Shy Beaver is that nobody hates anybody else there, little children grow up together no matter what color their skins happen to be, and there aren't any ugly words for people who don't happen to be white Protestants; no hatred, no cruelty, no poverty, no pain. "But then," Joe always finishes each story he tells about Shy Beaver, "you can't get there from here. It's too late. This is the wrong place to start. The road into Shy Beaver has grown over with weeds, and it isn't even on the maps any more."

He always said that if he ever found out how to get there he would paint the directions on the George Washington Bridge.[21]

This place where a person's birthday can be celebrated at any time is a place where time and the timeless intersect. From Wesley's description, it seems a place akin to Heaven. It is evident from Wes's words that in the life of Joe, a man already wounded by being released by his employer and by the dead-end frustrations of working as a radio writer amid the age of television, "the inconsolable wound" of longing for joy, love, and completeness is aching. Joe's day of visiting around is far more than a drinking man's ramblings; it is a search made in hope that the road to Shy Beaver is not entirely lost, and that you *can* get there from here.

And so the boy sets off in search of his father. As it was with Clay-Boy Spencer in *The Homecoming,* Wes finds that there are days when it seems that no good deed goes unpunished. As he makes his way from Brooklyn to Manhattan, crossing New York from east to west and from south to north and back, he finds himself thrown into one adventure-gone-sour after another, amid a landscape that is barren and loveless after a summer spent breathing the "sweet and still air" of Schuyler among loving and accepting relatives. As he travels around New York, he muses upon a painting he has seen on display in the city, Andrew Wyeth's famous work of art titled "Christina's World." This striking, realistic picture, with its strange mixture of forlornness and hope, pain and longing, strikes a chord within the boy, who sees in it a connection between Christina's condition and Joe's yearning for Shy Beaver:

> "Christina's World" is a painting, and I've been looking at it off and on for about the last six years. The first time I saw it, it hurt so much I had to walk away for a while before I could come back and look at it again. Even now it's actually kind of painful to see the picture, but I keep going back to it, the way your tongue will go to the place where a tooth's been pulled no matter how much you try to keep it away from there. . . .
>
> I sometimes think Christina is there in that field at that time of day (around eleven-thirty in the morning you would think from the way the shadows fall) because she is trying to run away. I think she has her own idea of Shy Beaver and that suddenly one day she suddenly felt trapped in that house and cried "Oh God," and ran from that house and there in that golden brown field she fell or tripped or threw herself to the ground. And now in the

painting she has turned back to the house and she knows she cannot run away but still she can't force herself to go back to the house either and she is caught in a terrible moment of anguish where her body is taut and twisted with feeling.

At first I used to believe that in a second she would get up and maybe run on, but these last few summers when I've been back to see the painting I've decided that she knows the field is too big to cross and that in a moment her body will relax, she will resign herself to her world, rise to her feet and go home again where everything will be twice as lonely and as desolate as it was before she tried to run away.

Sometimes I stand and look at the picture and I pretend I can step into the picture. In my dream it is so real I can feel the hot country sun and smell the clover and the wheat and see Christina's hair whipping in the wind. Walking toward her in the dream I think of all the things I will do for her. I will take her a million miles away, buy her pretty dresses, listen to the story of her life, love her, comfort her. But then I say her name and she turns and when I see her face it is not *her* face, but the face of someone I know. Sometimes it is Meredith who looks back at me from the picture, sometimes Joe, and sometimes it is my own face, or a stranger's, and I think maybe it isn't Christina's world, but *the* world, and maybe the figure isn't Christina, but all of us trapped in a barren and loveless landscape unless we find our own Shy Beaver.[22]

Although he is a fairly callow but likeable teenage boy, Wes intuits rightly that the hope, the longing, and the pain of Christina's yearning is universal. Everyone he encounters that day and comes to know to any degree of comprehension beyond a surface knowledge—everyone whether young or old, male or female, rich or poor, white, black, or brown—longs for a place like Shy Beaver. In the meantime, while Shy Beaver remains merely a golden dream, each person must endure the pain of life, with its betrayals, hurts, and losses. Wes recalls a brief dialogue on this matter with his father:

> "'You know what sin is, Wes?'
>
> "'Nope,' I said.
>
> "'There's only one sin,' he said. 'And that's hurting people.'
>
> "That's the closest to a lecture or anything of that type he's ever given me."[23]

Near the novel's end, as night is falling, and after barely missing Joe for roughly the twelfth time in one day, Wes at last learns that his father is prepared to make good on his seemingly offhand promise to paint the directions to Shy Beaver on the George Washington Bridge. Joe has remained hidden from the reader until this point and has lived only through the fond words of his friends, who all speak to Wes of Joe's generosity and good heart. They are grateful to Joe for his storytelling, his friendship, and the fresh sunshine of Virginia he has brought into the heart of New York; they love him for it and express that appreciation to Wes. For his part, Joe has discovered the road to Shy Beaver during his daylong ramble through the city. He learns, as did George Bailey in Frank Capra's 1946 film *It's a Wonderful Life,* that one man's life touches so many others, that when he's not there it leaves an awfully big hole, and that no man is a failure who has true friends. Shy Beaver, then, isn't a geographical place; it's a place in the heart, a community of souls. Having learned this, having learned how to "get there from here," Joe sets out to share that news with others. And so Wes discovers him on the grill-work descending from one of the towers of the George Washington Bridge, paintbrush in hand, while Joe's wife, Meredith, along with numerous police cars and other emergency vehicles converge on the bridge to rescue what appears to be a daredevil—the sort of person who climbs up the side of skyscrapers to get attention—or a potential suicide-jumper. But Joe is no exhibitionist or suicide.

Like Clay Spencer/John Walton in *The Homecoming,* Joe Scott has spent every cent of his final paycheck on gifts for the ones he loves the most: Meredith and Wes. The presents he has purchased, which represent the dearest wishes of his family—a leopard-skin coat for Meredith, who has spent all her married life scrimping, and a typewriter for Wes, who longs to be a writer—are presented to Wes by the police, who found them on the bridge. Having given them everything he has, Joe seeks to deliver one last gift: the knowledge of the way to Shy Beaver.

Waiting until the police on the scene are preoccupied, Wes tries to climb down to his father on the bridge grillwork. The boy falls a short distance, grabs a cable just below Joe's perch, and hangs on for dear life. Joe clambers over to him, gathers the terrified and fainting Wes in one arm, and slowly climbs up the grillwork to where the police and an ambulance are waiting for them. The family threesome is then driven away in the ambulance. Just as Olivia Spencer/Walton half-heartedly scolded her husband for his foolishness and extravagance on a long-ago Christmas Eve, Meredith Scott has a few words to say to Joe:

> Meredith tried to put on her stern expression, but she looked down at the leopard-skin coat she was holding carefully in her lap and smiled in spite of herself.
>
> "Whatever were you thinking about," she asked.
>
> "That," said Joe, and pointed back toward the George Washington Bridge. We were on the West Side Highway by now and framed in the glass of the rear of the ambulance we could see what Joe had written in letters six feet tall.
>
> Joe hadn't gotten to finish painting the directions for getting to Shy Beaver. The letters were kind of squiggly and uneven, but in the lights that were flashing from the boats down below, you could see them for miles and miles. Whatever it was he was going to write, he had put down two words of it:
>
> LOVE IS
>
> We watched until the bridge itself was only a tiny strand of pearls suspended there above the river, and then it was gone from our sight as we turned off the highway and into the city.[24]

Joe did not finish painting the directions as he intended, but he painted enough to provide the answer to the question he had long pursued, and Hamner provides no further clue as to what Joe intended to write: What is the way to Shy Beaver? Love is. Joe's quest to find the way to Shy Beaver represents a response to the human longing for something accepting, loving, and fulfilling that has been lost. As Thomas Wolfe wrote in *Look Homeward, Angel,* "Remembering speechlessly we seek the great forgotten language, the lost lane-end into heaven, a stone, a leaf, an unfound door. Where? When? O lost, and by the wind grieved, ghost, come back again." Shy Beaver, love of God and of others, is "the lost lane-end into heaven."

This novel is written in an earnest, coltish country boy's first-person style, reminiscent not so much of *Huckleberry Finn* but of Sherwood Anderson's horse stories, particularly the story "I'm a Fool." There is that same sense of openness with the reader, the same confessions of failure and bewilderment at the circumstances that come the way of the narrator, the same dead-on mimicry of everyday conversations, such as "Grandpa, why don't you go on to bed instead of sitting yawning?" There is also a sense of something not readily found in Anderson's fiction but pervasive in Hamner's: the half-understood, joyful discovery of what life offers when one is surrounded by humble, honest, and good-hearted people. It is little wonder that in his review of the book, *New York Times* critic Orville Prescott wrote, "It would be as difficult to dislike *You Can't Get There from Here* as to dislike a basket of spaniel puppies."[25] Such was the novel's evocation of a steadily moving, real-life drama and its articulation of the full range of human emotions, that Hamner's agent, Don Congdon, recognized its dramatic potential and took action. He successfully optioned it to renowned Broadway composer Richard Rodgers, who set to work scoring a musical adaptation of *You Can't Get There from Here.* When informed by Congdon that Rodgers wanted to meet the author, Hamner was elated. (He later said, "I felt I had died and gone to Heaven.") He spent an unforgettable afternoon in New York at Rodgers's studio, listening to the man who had written the music for *The Sound of Music, Okla-*

homa! and other memorable Broadway hits run through the melodies he had in mind for his version of *You Can't Get There from Here.* The script for the musical was written by Erich Segal, who would write his best-known novel, *Love Story,* before the end of the decade. But a lyricist was never engaged, other priorities arose, and the stage version of Hamner's third novel was left incomplete at the time of Rodgers's death in 1977.

City of Dreams—and Nightmares: *Murder in Tinseltown*

On occasion, Hamner has quipped that living within a very short drive of the film studios of Hollywood and Studio City is "almost like living in a real place." Standing in stark contrast to the genuineness and down-to-earth realities of Appalachia is the world of Hollywood. On a film set, the "houses" are really facades. What appear to be curtains hanging in the windows of those houses are really artfully arranged scraps of cloth. Characters are really actors who have stepped into a persona and are reciting lines written by someone else. Depictions of the most significant events in life are not real; they are scripted, acted, and breathed into existence by the magic of acting, editing, and computer graphics. If these facts can all be forgotten through "the willing suspension of disbelief" or through ignorance, why, life in Hollywood can indeed be "almost like living in a real place." In his most recent novel, crafted in the form of a murder mystery, co-written with Don Sipes, and published in 2000, Hamner set out to explore this realm, which is so remarkably different from the world of "familism" and love he knew during his formative years.

Murder in Tinseltown started out not as a novel but as a concept for a screenplay that would provide an insider's view of the Hollywood community of writers, producers, directors, and film executives. The world the authors depict is one they knew well, in which the transcendent love depicted in Hamner's earlier novels was stood on its head entirely. Hollywood is a place that creates illusions, films that explore love in all its manifestations. But behind the scenes, in the Hollywood described by Hamner and Sipes, every relationship

Hamner agrees that he looks remarkably like the actor Tony Randall in this portrait taken during the early 1960s.

has its price, and every friendship is a business arrangement and a set-up for opportune betrayal. The novel has an authentic ring, confirmed by first-hand memoirs of life in Hollywood by other insiders. Writing of Hollywood culture, Rob Long, a former producer of the popular series *Cheers* and author of *Conversations with My Agent* (1997), has said, "The definition of 'friend' is so elastic in Hollywood that it includes the definition of 'enemy.' This town is so small that everyone eventually brutalizes everyone else. We're like rats in a coffee can: nowhere to go but at each other."[26] *Murder in Tinseltown* captures this sense vividly.

Hamner and Sipes attempted to shop their concept for a film to be titled *Murder in Tinseltown* in the very community they had portrayed. Not surprisingly, Hollywood had no interest in bringing this screenplay to life. Rebuffed, the authors used their concept to craft a novel instead, which was published by Hawk Publishing in Oklahoma.

A light novel suitable for beach-chair reading, *Murder in Tinseltown* is not merely a murder mystery or even a snapshot of modern Hollywood, though it serves well in both capacities. It is also a depiction of disillusionment and hope, showing a flawed but well-meaning man, a veteran Hollywood director named Emory Goode, drifting perilously close to destroying his marriage to his wife and the life of his daughter through the best of intentions. Emory recognizes his danger in the eleventh hour and then works to redeem the time. While neither Emory nor any of the other primary characters are direct portraits from life, several of the key characters reflect artfully mixed-and-matched aspects of people Hamner and Sipes have known during their many years of living and working in "Tinseltown."

In one short piece of interior monologue, Emory walks through the studio set of a Midwestern town square, all facades and empty appearances:

> "I mustn't stay here long," he said to himself. "This town is a trap."
>
> He knew the city well enough to recognize that the movie set was symbolic of the lives most Hollywood people led. It was all false, all a dream, for some a nightmare. Only a few of them ever woke from the dream long enough to be dismayed. A few others, a very few, woke in time to recognize that it was a nightmare and fled for their lives.[27]

Emory has come to California from New York to work in television. But he has another motive: to save his marriage to his wife, Roberta, and restore his relationship with his daughter, Robin, who has fled to the West Coast ahead of him. Having been preoccupied with his work while residing in New York, he realizes that he has practically driven Roberta and Robin out of his life, and so he has decided to start afresh with them if he possibly can. But for now he is set to direct the pilot for a new series, a nighttime soap opera called *King's Harbor*. He has a strong say in the casting for the series, and he has a particular actress in mind to play one of the leading roles. But when this woman, Lyla Taylor, is found murdered on the set of *King's Harbor* shortly before production begins, Emory and everyone else with a stake in the series becomes a murder suspect: Ariel Smart, Lyla's rival for the starring role; Justin Hargreaves, the prickly writer and creator of the series; Sherwin Fields, the sly assistant to the head of programming; Max Porter, the despicable, boorish producer of *King's Harbor;* and Curtis Hughes, a bona fide stalker of Ariel. Matters become complicated when the only witness to anything unusual on the studio lot on the night of the murder, a guard at the front gate, swears that he saw a car driven by deceased actress Bette Davis exit the front gate at about the time Lyla's death occurred.

The mystery spools out in a well-written, conventional way for nearly two hundred pages, featuring false leads as to the killer's identity, a dollop of steamy sexual activity, diligent investigation of the crime by two streetwise detectives, and the deadly comeuppance of one particularly hateful character. At the novel's end, the murderer is discovered and Emory reconciles with Roberta and Robin.

A watercolor rendering of the Hamner house in Schuyler, painted by Marion Hamner Hawkes in 1972.

What makes *Murder in Tinseltown* a particularly compelling work is not only the opportunity provided to readers to gather clues and unmask the killer, but the inside portrait of Hollywood in all its contradictions: its glamour and its seaminess, its promises and its realities. Further, the authors clothe their characters in the scraps and fragments of speech, dress, and mannerisms faintly reminiscent of people they knew, though there are no portraits in full of anyone. One of the admirable characters, Gloria Blackstone ("the Queen of Talk Television") resembles in some respects a woman Hamner and Sipes have worked with and hold in high regard, Oprah Winfrey. Director Emory Goode, with his white flannel suit and planter's hat, somewhat resembles real-life director Fielder Cook, if only in his sartorial tastes. The persnickety writer, Justin Hargreaves—a complex and irritable man who feels ill-used by everyone—readily resembles no particular real-life personage, though at one point he shares with Gloria Blackstone's audience a view of television that is Hamner's own:

> "I came into television writing with the greatest of hope
> and expectations. I thought it could change the world, and
> I wanted to dedicate my life to it. I felt proud to be part of
> it.
>
> "Television could have been used to inform, to edu-
> cate, and to humanize us all. Instead, it has become a
> cesspool. . . .
>
> "I keep hoping that, in spite of it all, something I write
> might somehow fall on fertile ground and make a small
> difference in somebody's life."[28]

This echoes a point Hamner made in an interview with journalist Lisa Provence in 2003, when he expressed his disgust and anger over what television has become.

> What could have been a medium that might have ele-
> vated, educated, enlightened, and even ennobled all of us
> has become a medium that cheapens the human experi-
> ence, that pictures the procreation of life as a joke or dirty,

that dulls our senses and glorifies violence. More often than not the dramas picture us as ill and in need of a doctor, in trouble and in need of a lawyer, or victims in need of the police. It cheapens our image of ourselves by showing our fellow folks eating worms or plotting to overcome our fellow man/woman through guile, trickery, and deceit or risking life and limb in exchange for a few dollars. Only rarely do we see ordinary human beings whose lives can relate to our own lives.[29]

Murder in Tinseltown is a story of the tearing away of illusions, but it is also a story of victory, for Emory succeeds in taking the first steps toward rebuilding his family. This is accomplished not by wishful thinking or drifting with the tide, but by aggressively acting to reclaim and restore the most important relationships in life—the compact between husband and wife, the fellowship between father and daughter. It is by doggedly rowing against the tide of the prevalent culture in "Tinseltown," by seeking through the love and respect he lavishes upon his wife, children, and friends, and through crafting depictions of "ordinary human beings whose lives can relate to our own lives" that Hamner responds effectively to the human longing for something that sometimes seems nearly lost in the modern world. That is, a sense of fulfilling love and acceptance among good people, the lost lane-end into heaven.

NOTES

1. Hamner to Rusty Coulter, March 28, 1997. I am grateful to Earl Hamner for sharing a copy of this letter, which contains a warm and lively reminiscence about that long-ago summer when he rented the house in Arkansas.
2. "Fifty Roads to Town," http://www.the-waltons.com/booksbyearl.html.
3. "Fifty Roads to Town," http://www.the-waltons.com/booksbyearl.html.
4. *Fifty Roads to Town,* 108.
5. Ibid., 168.

6. Lee, "Mountain Preacher," *The New York Times Book Review,* October 11, 1953, 28.

7. *Fifty Roads to Town,* 298–99.

8. Shinn, "Old-fashioned Revival," *Saturday Review,* October 17, 1953, 44.

9. Bradbury, *Renaissance in the South: A Critical History of the Literature, 1920–1960,* 174.

10. Meeker, "The Youngest Generation of Southern Fiction Writers," in *Southern Writers: Appraisals in Our Time,* edited by R. C. Simonini, 177.

11. Quoted in Margaret Fife Tanguay, "Earl Hamner, Jr.: The Man behind *The Waltons,*" *Authors in the News,* Vol. 2, edited by Barbara Nykoruk, 136. This essay first appeared in the March 1974 issue of *Sky* magazine.

12. *Fifty Roads to Town,* 54–55.

13. Anderson, *Winesburg, Ohio,* 233.

14. *Fifty Roads to Town,* 55–56.

15. *Winesburg, Ohio,* 242–43.

16. *Fifty Roads to Town,* 232.

17. Quoted in Kimberly Dunham, "A Mosaic of the John Boys," *From the Hills* (Charleston, WV) no. 38 (1974): 7.

18. Quoted in Antoinette W. Roades, "Earl Hamner, Jr.," *Commonwealth: The Magazine of Virginia,* April 1977, 26–27.

19. "You Can't Get There from Here," http://www.the-waltons.com/booksbyearl.html.

20. Ibid.

21. *You Can't Get There from Here,* 70–71.

22. Ibid., 97, 99–100.

23. Ibid., 108–109.

24. Ibid., 241–42.

25. Prescott, "Wistful, Whimsical and Pure in Heart," *New York Times,* June 11, 1965, 29.

26. Long, "Our Town," *National Review,* February 23, 2004, 33.

27. *Murder in Tinseltown,* 43–44.

28. Ibid., 151–52.

29. Quoted in Provence, "Earl's World: Almost Like Being in a Real Place," *Charlottesville (VA) Hook,* May 15, 2003, 23.

5

NOTEWORTHY TELEPLAYS:

The Twilight Zone, It's a Man's World, Appalachian Autumn, and The Gift of Love

. . . to transfer from our inward nature a human interest and a semblance of truth sufficient to procure for these shadows of imagination that willing suspension of disbelief for the moment, which constitutes poetic faith.

SAMUEL TAYLOR COLERIDGE, FROM *BIOGRAPHIA LITERARIA*, 1817

Television has an enormous effect in terms of shaping ideas, attitudes, and awarenesses.

DELBERT MANN, 1977, QUOTED IN
TELEVISION: ETHICS FOR HIRE? BY ROBERT S. ALLEY

SPEAK WITH ANYONE ABOUT TELEVISION'S "Golden Age" and soon the conversation will shift to a legendary series created by Rod Serling called *The Twilight Zone*. This program revolutionized the relatively new medium of TV during its initial run (1959–65), offering the viewer well-written dramas on thought-provoking topics, all served up with a healthy dose of the offbeat, the bizarre, and the supernatural. This was a world away from the many musical variety shows, Westerns, and situation comedies that dominated much of television during the Eisenhower-Kennedy years.

In addition to the dramas themselves, who could ever forget Serling's staccato, on-screen narration—and that distinctive, unnerving theme music, all spurring the program's "shadows of imagination" toward a point at which "that willing suspension of disbelief" in the minds of the viewing audience is possible? What many fans of the series might be surprised to learn is that Serling, among his many accomplishments, was responsible for launching Earl Hamner as a television writer.

As was noted earlier, Hamner had begun his career in television during the early 1950s by writing for programs produced live on sound-stages in New York. Seeing that the future of TV lay in taped programming, he relocated to Southern California to be near the center of television filmmaking. After six months of failing to convince anyone in Studio City to give him a chance as a writer of teleplays, he spoke with Ray Bradbury at the MGM commissary in an informal business lunch. The distinguished author recommended that Hamner contact a friend he had met shortly after graduating from college: Rod Serling, who had recently begun producing his new television series. Hamner quickly crafted and submitted two scripts to Serling, whose script committee approved them for production. This provided Hamner with his first paycheck in Hollywood.

Over the next few years, Serling accepted a total of eight scripts by Hamner, and each story was produced. In terms of productivity alone, this placed Hamner fourth in line as one of the show's top contributors—ahead of the great Ray Bradbury and George Clayton

Johnson, but just behind accomplished screenwriters Charles Beaumont, Richard Matheson, and Serling himself.

"The Middle Ground Between Light and Shadow . . ."

Among the scripts Hamner contributed to Serling's program, his favorite and perhaps the most accomplished is one that has become a minor classic among admirers of *The Twilight Zone,* titled "Jess-Belle." This is a well-paced, tightly written story about obsessive love and witchcraft among mountainfolk. It concerns also the awful fruit of jealousy and a theme that pervades so many stories of the supernatural, which can be summed up in a common phrase: Beware of what you wish for.

In the story, Jess-Belle is a comely young woman of the hills who yearns after a marriageable man of her acquaintance, Billy-Ben Turner. But he is already the fiancé of Ellwyn Glover, another beautiful girl. Obsessed with having Billy-Ben for her own, Jess-Belle enlists the services of Granny Hart, an old woman who is known to the locals as a witch. In exchange for an unspecified price, Granny Hart gives Jess-Belle a mysterious potion to drink, which will cause Billy-Ben to become utterly and forever intoxicated with her. The potion works, and Billy-Ben spurns Ellwyn for his new love. But to Jess-Belle's horror, she discovers that the price for the old witch's help was high indeed: She herself has now become a witch as well as a shape-shifter, turning into a panther at midnight and remaining in that form until the morning light, awakening with no memory of what she has done during the nighttime hours. She now possesses the love of her life, but can never sleep under the same roof with him, as she might kill him in the night. Her hold upon Billy-Ben is broken when, in panther form, she is shot by hunters—and vanishes in a cloud of fog. Released from Jess-Belle's hold, Billy-Ben looks with new, loving eyes upon Ellwyn, and the two are married within a short time. However, Jess-Belle's fractured essence takes a new form, assuming the shape of a mouse and then a menacing fog. In a short time Jess-Belle's spirit takes possession of Ellwyn. Taking care to pay Granny Hart in cash (rather than enabling the old crone to trick him by charging an undisclosed price), Billy-Ben learns how to rid the world of Jess-Belle, driving a silver hair-pin into a mannequin dressed in the young witch's clothes. Jess-Belle is destroyed, and Ell-wyn is restored to her husband.

At the core of "Jess-Belle," "distilled from its trappings of folk tale and witchcraft, is a tragic yet classic love story," wrote *Twilight Zone* authority Tony Albarella. He added that the program fittingly aired on Valentine's Day, 1963. However:

> Sadly ironic is the fact that at the time the episode pre-miered, the most popular television series (according to the Nielsen ratings) was *The Beverly Hillbillies.* Earl Hamner worked to present decent, hard-working country people in a real and positive light, showing them to be as gifted and as flawed as members of any other cultural or social class. Shows like *The Beverly Hillbillies, Hee Haw,* and *Green Acres* milked the stereotype of the bumbling, backward yokel for all it was worth. Hamner would later prevail over this mindset by introducing America to *The Waltons;* winning back a huge measure of public respect for "his people" in the process.[1]

Interestingly, Hamner's script for the acclaimed hour-long episode "Jess-Belle" was written in less than a week. (Normally such scripts can take two or three weeks to write.) This came to pass after Hamner received a hurry-up phone-call from one of the program's producers, Herb Hirshman, who was short of material and needed a script within one week. Hirshman specifically requested that, if possible, Hamner write "some of that down-home stuff." During the next few hours Hamner conceived the general idea for "Jess-Belle" and set to work, writing one act per day. (He even wrote the words and tune to a folk-song that recurs periodically throughout the story.) Having promised Hirshman that he could manage writing a script in one week, Hamner delivered it on time, later telling Tony Albarella, "It is risky to make such a promise and I suspect I pulled it off because I was very much at home in the milieu, knew the very special way the people talked and how they might behave in the situations they faced."[2] Strong performances by Anne Francis (best-known for portraying the title character in the detective series *Honey West*) and James Best (who later portrayed Sheriff Roscoe P. Coltrane on *The Dukes of Hazzard*) greatly helped in making "Jess-Belle" one of the strongest episodes of *The Twilight Zone*'s run.

Another well-written script, "The Hunt," concerns a hunter's love for his dog and the eternal consequences of love and loyalty. This story had its origins in Hamner's memories of his father's love for a favorite hunting dog. Earl Sr. accidentally shot the dog one day, and then spent all that night and

PHOTO BY ANTOINETTE W. ROADES

In a photo taken in early 1977, Hamner stands before a tree he transplanted to the backyard of his family home in Schuyler when it was a sapling and he was a boy.

part of the following day searching for the hurt animal, which had run off yelping. When he finally found him, the dog had died. Hamner's father grieved over this accident for the rest of his life, and this heartfelt affection for a faithful dog did not escape the notice of his writer son. In 1953 Hamner wrote an early version of "The Hunt" in the form of a short television play, "The Hound of Heaven," for *The Kate Smith Hour.* This early episode starred John Carradine and featured a then-unknown young actor named James Dean. Rewritten by Hamner for *The Twilight Zone,* the story concerns an old mountain man, Hyder Simpson, who takes leave of his wife, Rachel, to go raccoon-hunting. While out on his adventure, he dies after jumping into a pond while attempting to save his favorite hunting dog, Rip, from being drowned by a raccoon. (The ring-tailed creatures have an ugly, well-deserved reputation for drowning dogs that follow them into water.) Failing to save his dog and himself, Hyder finds himself somewhere outside time and space, walking with his dog on a country road. He is met by a seedy-looking "young man" who escorts the old hunter to an inviting gateway. The guide tells Hyder that he is welcome to enter the gate into the realm beyond, but that the dog must stay outside, as no dogs are allowed. The man chooses not to enter this dogless realm and walks away from the gate. In a while he finds himself before another entryway, where he is told by another young man—an angel, really—that he is welcome, along with his dog. Upon asking why the dog is welcome, the angel tells him that this is Heaven, and that all good people and good beasts are welcome here. Hyder then asks why his dog wasn't welcome at his first stop in the afterlife. That was the entrance to Hell, the angel replies; the guardians of the infernal realm are forever trying to entice the unwary, and they know that a dog will sense the diabolical and try to warn his master to stay away. As the angel tells Hyder, "You see, Mr. Simpson, a man, well he'll walk right into Hell with both eyes open. But even the devil can't fool a dog."

Hamner has a countryman's warm spot in his heart for dogs (and, for that matter, many forms of wildlife). This affection shows through in "The Hunt." As Tony Albarella noted in his commentary on this story, in "The Hunt" Hamner combined his love of dogs "with a dash of the whimsical and a pinch of the fantastic. The result is a charming folk tale that took *The Twilight Zone* into uncharted territory." How so? Albarella explains:

> The series had previously escorted viewers to a wide range
> of disparate settings: the remoteness of the Old West, the
> film noir grunge of the urban city, the facade of normalcy
> in small-town suburbia, the vast reaches of outer space.
> The show had dabbled in suspense, science fiction, comedy, and horror. Hamner put a spin on the old and

EARL HAMNER

brought in a fresh perspective by stepping back to a simpler time and place.[3]

It is noteworthy that Hyder and Rachel Simpson from "The Hunt" are strongly reminiscent of Zeb and Esther of *The Waltons:* two elderly people who are as comfortable with each other as a favorite pair of well-worn slippers. As we know, Zeb and Esther were based upon Hamner's memories of his own grandparents, a blending of both the Hamner and the Giannini sides of the author's heritage. Like Zeb, Hyder refers to his wife of many years as "old woman" and tells her that she's not the boss of him. Rachel stands up to Hyder but gives way in the face of her husband's long-accustomed-to stubbornness in wanting to go out hunting. As Albarella has noted, Hyder and Rachel are based upon characters called "the Old Man and the Old Woman" in a series of short stories Hamner was at work on during the early 1960s. These stories were never published, but the characters themselves came to life in "The Hunt" in January 1962, becoming fully developed a decade later as the lovable grandparents in *The Waltons.*

The third acclaimed episode Hamner wrote for *The Twilight Zone* was titled "Stopover in a Small Town," and it initially aired on April 24, 1964. This is a fairly simple tale that tells of a married couple, Bob and Milly Frazier, who awaken one morning in a room they do not recognize, after a night of heavy drinking at a party. Throughout the rest of the episode, they seek to gain their bearings, wandering through the house and the small town in which they have found themselves, bickering with each other all the while. To their increasing dismay, they discover that they are alone and that all the buildings in the town are facades; it is as if they are lost on the back lot of a movie studio. From time to time they hear the laughter of an unseen little girl, but otherwise it seems the town is deserted. At the very end of the episode, Bob and Milly are scooped up in an enormous hand, as if they were a pair of tiny dolls. The unfortunate couple, along with the viewer, finally discovers the secret behind the mysterious "small town" when the scene changes to reveal a little girl playing dolls with two miniature figures, a man and a woman.

The girl's mother enters the room, and she admonishes, "Be careful with your pets, dear. Daddy brought them all the way from Earth."

This tale of alien abduction, with its surprise ending, predates *The X-Files* by several decades and is a fan favorite. As Tony Albarella has noted, "Stopover in a Quiet Town" succeeds as a drama because it draws the viewer into the story, bringing about the "willing suspension of disbelief" the poet Coleridge famously wrote of. Albarella wrote, "It plays upon some basic fears: loss of control, apprehension of unfamiliar surroundings, a phobia of abandonment or detachment from society, and a fear of captivity."[4] He further states:

> Disbelief cannot be suspended if the characters do not react as would the average viewer under similar circumstances. We relate to Bob and Milly because they respond rationally to each new and surprising development. . . .
>
> They are ordinary people caught in an extraordinary state of affairs.[5]

Of the eight scripts Hamner contributed to *The Twilight Zone,* four were especially good. The fourth and final such teleplay was titled "The Bewitchin' Pool." Originally aired on June 19, 1964, this

At home with his mother, Doris, in early 1977.

PHOTO BY ANTOINETTE W. ROADES

episode concerns two young children, a brother and sister named Jeb and Sport, who live in Southern California. Their parents are in the film industry, well off, and tired of each other. They quarrel loudly and frequently, and are indifferent to their children, insisting that Jeb and Sport be quiet at all times even as they themselves practically bring plaster from the ceiling with their shouting and recriminations. The children long hopefully for a place of peace, joy, and freedom from verbal abusers, and they find it in their backyard swimming pool.

Diving into it and then surfacing, they find themselves climbing from a country swimming hole into a green, pastoral world in which they are welcomed into the house of a kind, grandmotherly woman called Aunt T. She explains to her new arrivals that there are other children about that they have not seen: "They're out there somewhere: the maltreated, the abandoned, the unloved, but eventually they find their way here." Each child, including Jeb and Sport, is expected to perform light chores; but for the most part, this is almost an Edenic world in which gentle humor, fun, acceptance, and peace reign. Upon diving back into the pond, Jeb and Sport soon find themselves back at their own pool in California, listening to the tirades of their parents. Harangued for disappearing from their parents' sight without permission, the children are drawn to the conclusion that they would be much happier with Aunt T, and within a short time, waiting for an opportune moment, Jeb and Sport jump into the pool and disappear from their unhappy home forever, to their parents' sorrow and puzzlement.

Tony Albarella has insightfully noted the similarity between this story and the film version of L. Frank Baum's novel *The Wonderful Wizard of Oz*, with a key difference: "Whereas Dorothy sought the comfort and safety of home while lost in a dangerous dream world, Jeb and Sport seek refuge from the terrors of a shattered family life in a far-off land where they are loved and needed." He adds:

> Aunt T's world is cut from the same cloth as Peter Pan's
> Never Never Land, filled with the "Lost Boys" and girls of
> countless broken homes. In this instance the physical link

between the real and the fantastic, Jeb and Sport's backyard swimming pool, is merely an updated version of
Dorothy's twister or Alice's rabbit hole.[6]

"The Bewitchin' Pool" was far better written than acted, and it is
perhaps for this reason that it is not more widely recognized as one
of Hamner's stronger *Twilight Zone* episodes.

The remaining episodes include "You Drive," which is similar in
theme to Stephen King's novel *Christine*. Inspired by a news story
Hamner had read, it is the story of a man who is tormented by the
strange promptings of his own car after he tries to cover up his role
in a fatal hit-and-run accident. Other scripts include the well-crafted
"Ring-a-ding Girl," a wrinkle-in-time story about a small-town
woman who achieved success in Hollywood and returns to the town
of her upbringing in time to save many lives. This episode is far better written and cleverly conceived than its salute-to-the-Rat-Pack
title suggests. Hamner also wrote "A Piano in the House," which
tells of a magical piano that brings out the most deeply hidden
aspects of its hearers' personalities upon being played. Finally—by
Hamner's own admission—there is a relatively weak effort, "Black
Leather Jackets," which concerns a group of Martian invaders dis-
guised as a biker gang. In an interview with journalist William P.
Simmons, Hamner allowed that if he had to do it over again he
would not have written "Black Leather Jackets," adding "Each of us
is entitled to a lemon!"[7]

In *The Twilight Zone Scripts of Earl Hamner,* the teleplays are
reproduced in full. As such, they provide an immensely helpful look
at the way scripts are written and paced. In each of them, even his
single "lemon," Hamner keeps his dialogue tight and the action moving forward, conforming to the rigid four-act format demanded by
television dramas. Fellow screenwriter Paul Cooper recalls some key
advice he once received: "Earl Hamner . . . told me that after a character speaks sixteen words, the audience stops listening."[8]

Beyond the technical skill that is evident throughout, the text of
the eight *Twilight Zone* scripts demonstrates Hamner's strong imagination and sure understanding of that peculiar realm described by

Serling as "the middle ground between light and shadow, between science and superstition," which "lies between the pit of man's fears and the summit of his knowledge."

IT'S A MAN'S WORLD

When *All in the Family* debuted on CBS in 1971, critics claimed that it was a program ahead of its time in terms of confronting real-life issues in irreverent language, offensive to some viewers. (Some viewers of the show may remember that at the very beginning of its first few episodes, CBS nervously saw fit to include an announcer's voice-over to warn the program's audience that the characters in *All in the Family* sometimes use words of bigotry "just to show how silly they really are.") The program made an immense splash with TV viewers, becoming a hot topic of conversation during the early seventies and laying the groundwork for many of the programs that have been introduced in the years since.

But while *All in the Family* was a pioneering program, it was certainly not the first of its kind. Shows debut periodically that are critically acclaimed but for which the viewing audience is not prepared—one example being NBC's edgy *Buffalo Bill* (1983–84), which starred Dabney Coleman as an obnoxious, self-absorbed TV talk-show host. Almost twenty years before *Buffalo Bill* (and nine years before *All in the Family*), NBC introduced another program that was hailed by critics as groundbreaking, thoughtful, and well-written, but which lasted only half a season. Debuting in the fall season of 1962, this series was called *It's a Man's World*. And Earl Hamner was part of the small writing team that brought this show to life during its short but memorable run.

Created by Peter Tewksbury and James Leighton, *It's a Man's World* concerns the day-to-day life of four teenage boys who live without adult or parental guidance on a houseboat called *The Elephant* which is anchored in the Ohio River off Stott's Landing, near the fictional college town of Cordella. The oldest of the four is Wes McCauley (portrayed by Glenn Corbett), a pre-law graduate who works at a local filling station while awaiting his chance to attend

Hamner proudly displays the commendation he received on Earl Hamner Day in Nelson County, sometime during the 1970s.

law school. Wes is raising his younger brother, Howie (Michael Burns), because they were orphaned after their parents were killed in an automobile accident. Sharing life on the houseboat with the McCauley brothers are one of Wes's former classmates, Tom-Tom DeWitt (Ted Bessell), and Verne Hodges (Randy Boone), a folksinger from the hills of North Carolina, along with a dog named Shadrack. Wes is engaged to a local woman, feisty Irene Hoff (Jan Norris), while Tom-Tom is dating Nora Fitzgerald (Ann Schuyler), an art student. Each episode of the program concerns the boys' struggles to understand and cope with the world they are entering as young adults.

This was not the world of other episodic television dramas; there were no pat endings, morals to be drawn, or appeals to adult wisdom. And, unlike so many other TV dramas, there was no laugh track. Instead there were sardonic discussions of the nation's ills, dark comments about corporate evil and the commercialization of American society—which did not endear *It's a Man's World* to its corporate sponsors—and explorations of sexual freedom and sexual frustration among the young during the Kennedy era. In an article on this extraordinary television series published in *The New York*

Times, writer Kerry Pechter adds, "Fear about the future and anxiety about money are rarely examined in today's teen shows, but *It's a Man's World* frequently addressed both. The boys lived on pork and beans and bought their clothes on sale. When Howie lost $30 in paper route money, the loss was so catastrophic that it pitched him into a flashback of his parents' death. When Wes flunked a law school aptitude test, he walked off his job, got drunk and ended upon crying in Irene's arms."[9]

Hamner wrote one episode for this series, but he is immensely proud of it. The title of it is "A Drive over to Exeter." (Although he wrote this episode, it was apparently revised to some extent by Robert Massing, who is listed in some sources as the sole writer of the teleplay.) The story concerns the unexpected disappearance one evening of Vern and Howie. Tom-Tom and Wes speculate that Vern, who has been brooding and moody for several days, has borrowed the boys' jeep and driven to the nearby town of Exeter in search of sexual adventure—"female companionship," in Tom-Tom's words—and has shamelessly dragged young Howie along with him. From hints dropped throughout the program, the audience is led to know that Exeter is a vile place consisting almost entirely of tattoo parlors, bordellos, adult movie theaters, and beer joints. Wes and Tom-Tom set out for Exeter with Nora and Irene to find the prodigal twosome, with Wes vowing to make things painful for Vern, "that rotten, no good, silly, stupid,

PHOTO BY ANTOINETTE W. ROADES

In January 1977, Hamner is interviewed during a telethon sponsored by station WVIR in Charlottesville for the Martha Jefferson Hospital.

ignorant, corn-fed, guitar-plucking, coon-shouting hillbilly!" At the very moment he is making that rash promise, Vern is treating Howie to a cup of hot chocolate at a roadside diner along the road to Exeter. Within an hour or two the vengeful searchers find Howie outside a tattoo parlor in Exeter and take him back to *The Elephant,* leaving Vern to take his fill of wickedness in the evil town. But when Vern returns later that night, singing and happy, it is revealed that the reason for his disappearance was much more innocent: he was lonely for home and his family in North Carolina, and he had driven over to Exeter because he had heard it was an exciting place that might snap him out of his doldrums. While in town, he had realized the source of his problem and telephoned his parents; and he regales Tom-Tom and Wes with a lengthy catalogue of minor events. One short sample will suffice:

> My Grandma Hodges has been right sick. She was visiting over at Uncle Benny Schuyler's and she was climbing over this stile and she fell down and tore something loose in her side. They had to take her to the hospital in Raleigh, but she didn't want to go. Said she was afraid she'd die down there and she didn't want to go with nothing but a bunch of strangers around her. Mama went down and stayed with her, and now she's on the mend.
>
> My Uncle Luther and his wife, Aunt Honey, were spending the weekend with my folks. My Daddy kind of let on that he'd be glad when they left. Uncle Luther don't talk much. Just sits around and smokes his pipe all the time. Aunt Honey does all the talking for both of 'em. She's a cute old thing, real fat and got the prettiest little face you ever did see and always got these two little spit curls on each one of her ears. . . .[10]

This lengthy explanation—for which Hamner wrote an eight-page monologue, rare in television drama—lifts up the hearts of the other boys at first, but after several minutes of listening to this unending stream of one-way conversation they playfully jump on Vern and bury him beneath a human dog-pile in order to simply shut him up. The final scene fades out on Vern's happy, smiling face.

In this episode the country-boy character, Vern, gives voice to Hamner's own love of home and family. Not surprisingly, "A Drive over to Exeter" was a strong episode of the short-lived *It's a Man's World,* for Hamner endowed it with a strong "human" sense, with a Southern boy, almost a man, making his way in the world but still bound by ties of memory and love to the places and people of his upbringing, haunted by "lost, and by the wind grieved, ghosts." "It seems to me that everything a writer writes is autobiographical," Hamner has said. "Imagination can account for only so much of what we put down on paper." He adds:

> Experience, events, sights, sounds, fears, moments, for-
> gotten things, remembered things, whether we are aware
> of it or not, have to be there in the back of our minds
> when we write. Who and what we are is mysterious and
> random and unknowable except in the most surface way. I
> always loved Thomas Wolfe's observation in *Look Home-
> ward, Angel.* "Each of us is all the sums he has not
> counted: Subtract us into nakedness and night again, and
> you will see begin in Crete four thousand years ago the
> love that ended yesterday in Texas."[11]

As Kerry Pechter has said of *It's a Man's World,* "The show, whose run coincided with the Cuban missile crisis, civil rights clashes and the arrival of Bob Dylan, attracted a minor cult follow-ing on college campuses. But mass audiences weren't ready for its experimental camera work, ironic or bittersweet endings and com-plex writing. NBC cancelled it after only nineteen episodes, citing low Nielsen ratings (and giving rise to an early instance of the sort of viewer protest now common when shows are killed off). Today, *It's a Man's World* is remembered only by the people who made it, their friends, a few classic TV buffs and a smattering of baby boomers who recall watching it as kids."[12] Earl Hamner is especially proud to have had a hand in this program, which he considers to have been very much ahead of its time. He has said, "I was part of a very small number of writers for the series—including Jim Leighton, who wrote many of the episodes. We were allowed a great deal of freedom in what we wrote for *It's a Man's World,* and I'm grateful to have been a part of it."[13]

APPALACHIAN AUTUMN

Where does a person draw the line between the right to live as he pleases and the responsibility to provide for himself and his family when those areas come into conflict? At what point does living on ancestral land and all the elements of long-held traditions need to give way to the demands of necessity and modern life? When does family pride stop being a force for personal orientation and become instead a destructive force? What is the significance of a single human life?

In *Appalachian Autumn,* Hamner explores these questions. Originally written to be aired on *CBS Playhouse* in 1969, it is not comfortable to watch, as it is a piece in which the claims of freedom and necessity, conservative and liberal values, family and community and the world at large, come into sharp conflict—and none is depicted in glowing colors. In this story of the impoverished Harper family of Appalachia, Hamner depicts, to some extent, the grim side of hill-country life—perhaps a side of life viewed quietly and its lessons taken to heart by Clay-Boy Spencer of *Spencer's Mountain.*

The play concerns a large, good-hearted family that in some ways resembles the Spencers and Waltons, but whose circumstances are much more desperate. There is a proud, hard-working father, Rome Harper, who works eighteen-hour days digging in a dangerous, abandoned coal mine in order to gather enough coal to sell to provide for his family. Rome's wife, Virgie, is a faithful, loving wife and mother who desires a better life for her children. Rome's mother, sometimes called "Old Woman," lives under the Harpers' roof and has lived a very long life sustained by her deep faith in God. Like Grandma Walton as portrayed by Ellen Corby, she can be something of a comically humorless, vinegary presence in the household, always quick with a word of reproach or (when affronted by behavior she disapproves of)

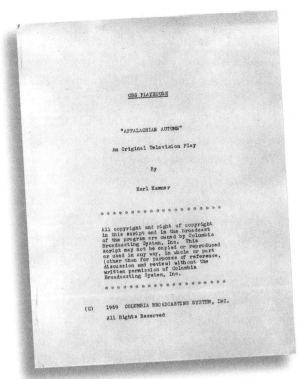

Left, Cover page of Hamner's script for *Appalachian Autumn.* *Below,* First page of the rehearsal schedule for *Appalachian Autumn.*

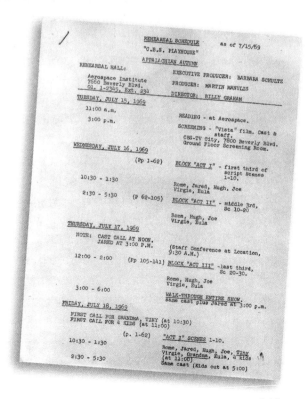

an aptly quoted Biblical passage or scripture-based exclamation, such as, "Sodom and Gomorrah! Fire and brimstone!" There are six Harper children, and one of the older sons, Hugh, is interested in the "impractical" world of art and is the central character in the plot. Hugh is a potter, and he fashions cups, bowls, vases, and other items out of clay, using an old abandoned schoolhouse as his workshop. In memory of his oldest brother, Davey—who was killed in Vietnam alongside many other young men whose circumstances did not allow them to find a refuge from the selective service in college—Hugh has crafted a large clay angel that stands on a hillside overlooking the local cemetery. At one point Hugh explains his passion for pottery, saying, "Sometimes I walk down to the creek where the best clay is, and I bend down and I put my hands on a bed of clay and I can feel a heart beat. It's like the earth has a pulse, and even when I bring the clay back to the schoolhouse, it's like it still has life, just waiten for my hands to shape it into something."

Hugh is beloved by his five brothers and sisters, perhaps especially by one of his younger brothers, Rob, who also has a secret talent as a potter. He is passionately in love with a beautiful young mountain woman, Eula, whose affections are mutual. The happy couple talk privately about marrying someday, traveling to faraway places, and enjoying a full life together.

Into the world of the Harpers comes a shaggy-haired young man named Joe Borden, who is a good-hearted sixties idealist and worker for VISTA (Volunteers In Service To America), one of President John F. Kennedy's "New Frontier" initiatives. With a guitar in his hand and a knapsack on his back, chockfull of good intentions, Joe has showed up in the Harpers' Appalachian community, called Harper's Gap, with hopes of somehow helping to lift the impoverished hill-folk out of poverty. He endears himself to the Harper children but is greeted with varying degrees of suspicion by the community's men, who view Joe as a naïve, do-gooding college-boy who looks down on them and intends to lead them, with the best of intentions, into a world of government handouts and dependence upon charity. Rome, suspicious of the young VISTA man, growls at one point, "Don't talk to me like I'm a dummy, boy."

Joe takes an immediate liking to Hugh and is fascinated by the young mountain man's artistic skill, sensing that *here* might be some sort of key to bringing prosperity to Harper's Gap. Within a short time, he has made arrangements for Hugh to receive business training and further sharpening of his pottery skills at a shop in Bluefield, West Virginia. For his part, Hugh sees little hope in working as a professional artist and mentor of others, but Joe will not take no for an answer: "An artist isn't some jerk who lives in an ivory tower, dabbles at writing or painting or making music. He's a man, Hugh, who digs into the guts of things and comes up with answers. He doesn't say this is where it's at and leave it there. He says: What does this mean? How can I make things better? How can I change what I hate? Hate it good, Hugh, but change it. Change this rotten little poverty pocket into a place where . . . where people can grow, where they can look up at the stars once in a while and not always down at the mud under their feet." Urged on by Joe, Hugh is convinced, and within a short time so is his family, though Rome takes much convincing. In bringing him around, Virgie speaks strongly to her husband for the first time in their married life, shouting, "For once in your life will you forget your pride?" Rome reluctantly agrees to go along with the plan.

Within a few days the community of friends and family come together to sell their various treasures—hand-carved walking sticks, an antique butter churn, and other items—to fund Hugh's trip. A substantial sum is raised, and hope begins rising for Hugh, his family, and the community. Then, on the eve of the young man's departure to Bluefield, Eula confides to Hugh that she is pregnant by him. Hugh arrives at his farewell celebration to announce that he has changed his plans and is not leaving after all; he is instead staying in Harper's Gap and marrying Eula—and nothing can convince him in his Harper pride to do otherwise.

Life returns to normal, the Harper family and their friends return to their day-to-day routines, and Hugh enters into a joyless marriage to Eula, bereft of hope for anything better than a life of scrimping and scraping by. To earn a living for his new wife and unborn child, he sets out against Eula's wishes to work alongside his father in the played-out coal mine, at great risk to his own life. Eula pleads with him to forget his pride and accept public assistance: "What have you got to show for your pride? Will it pay for rent? Put food on the table? Can you trade it at the store?"

On his first day in the mine, Hugh nearly comes to blows with Rome, who wants his son to stay out of the mine and seek some other, safer work. At the moment the two men are about to exchange punches, they collapse in each others' arms, weeping at recognition of their alikeness in stubborn pride and the hardness of their lives. They spend the rest of the day working in the mine together, agreeing that this will be their last day at this type of work: They are ready to take their families from Appalachia to the far-off city of Chicago and make a new living there. They will not accept charity or public assistance, but they will sacrifice their pride to pull up stakes to move where there are better opportunities for all.

At day's end, Rome leaves the mine, sells the family pony to raise money for passage to Chicago, and returns home to learn that Hugh has returned to the mine to remove a particular rock that had caught his eye and might be carved into something pretty for Eula. While the young man is in the mine, there is a cave-in and Hugh is killed. The clay angel he fashioned in memory of Davey will now watch over his own grave. At Hugh's funeral, Joe Borden announces that he is leaving because he can see no hope in his work in Harper's Gap at this point. However, Virgie and Rome convince him to stay on with them, almost as another son, asking that he be patient with them and learn. Virgie pleads, "Honey, learn somethen from us. We've been poor for a long time back here in these mountains. But we've endured. We've learned little tricks to stay alive. We sing hymns, we pray to God, we work hard, we love each other, and we tell ourselves little lies to keep goen from one day to the other. Most of all we keep hopen that a miracle will happen and things will change. If we can keep hope, can't you?" A flicker of hope soon appears, for on the walk home from the graveside ceremony they pass the old schoolhouse, where Hugh's young brother Rob sits working at the potter's wheel.

In this play Hamner emphasizes a truth that he made abundantly clear a few years later in the screenplay he wrote for *Charlotte's Web:* that there is immense, unfathomable value in a single life well lived in virtue, wisdom, and fellowship with one's neighbors, though that life might be lived amid seemingly hopeless circumstances. In *Appalachian Autumn,* this theme is underscored in a moving soliloquy spoken by Virgie as she waits, hoping against hope, while the men of the community sift through the collapsed mine in a vain attempt to rescue Hugh. Wounded by grief at the thought of a second son dying, after losing Davey, she says, "I spent the day watchen one leaf on the crab apple tree. It was the last one left, and it just clung on for dear life, even though the rest of the tree had gone to sleep for the winter. Tonight it fell to earth. I wonder what it is about a single leaf that makes it different from the others. It stayed green long after the others. But when it did turn it was the brightest leaf on the tree." Hugh's life has flamed out, but he has sparked hope in the lives of others, most notably his younger brother, Rob, who may someday grasp the chance once missed by Hugh. Also, Eula will now travel with her in-laws to Chicago, where her unborn child, Hugh's seed, will grow up in a place where his opportunities will be heightened.

The inclusion of Hugh's clay angel as a feature in the play is Hamner's salute to Thomas Wolfe's novel *Look Homeward, Angel.* That work had as a theme the pursuit by Eugene Gant's father, a stonecutter, to carve a perfect stone angel. Old Gant never achieves his goal, though he does carve a beautiful angel that eventually adorns the grave of a prostitute. Hugh Harper's clay angel is crafted not out of pride and ambition, the motivation of Thomas Wolfe's character, but out of love for his dead older brother. In literature, a carved or stone angel represents eternity, remembrance, and loving kindness across generations. Family love is a common theme in the works of Hamner, and in *Appalachian Autumn* he essentially reworked one element of Wolfe's classic, transforming it to reflect his own thematic concerns as a writer. In an article published in *The New York Times* about the play, Hamner asserted that "the play is not about coal or poverty. If I have succeeded, it is a play about love and compassion and sacrifice, a celebration of the triumph of the human spirit."

Appalachian Autumn aired as a presentation of *CBS Playhouse* on the evening of October 7, 1969. The taped play was directed by William Graham, and starred Arthur Kennedy as Rome Harper, Teresa Wright as Virgie, and Estelle Winwood as Grandma. The casting pleased Hamner, who wrote, "The play is not autobiographical, but my own parents' pride and strength and love helped me to create the characters played by Teresa Wright and Arthur Kennedy."[14] And how successful was Hamner's achievement? *New York Times* television critic Jack Gould wrote a mixed review of the program, claiming "*Appalachian Autumn* is not a pillar of dramatic strength; nor is it immune to rudimentary theatrical excesses. Nonetheless it touches realistically and sometimes poignantly on the pride and frustration of a perennially poor family caught in the endless misery of an abandoned coalmining community." Missing entirely the play's latent theme of hope, Gould described the "overriding feeling of futility" that pervades *Appalachian Autumn* and seemed somewhat puzzled that Joe Borden, the VISTA worker, was not presented in a more positive, effectual light. However, he was pleased with the skill the actors brought to the story, and added, "It is not every night that commercial TV comes to grips with an issue such as the reality of poor whites in Appalachia and, more particularly, how the affluent outside world frequently seems incapable of rendering practical aid."[15]

THE GIFT OF LOVE: A CHRISTMAS STORY

Hamner's mother, Doris, was an enthusiastic reader, and her favorite author was Bess Streeter Aldrich (1881–1954). A native of the American prairie states, Aldrich wrote hopeful, upbeat novels that describe humble people who overcome great adversity to achieve some measure of success—mostly in the form of love and the realization that the most valuable things in life are love, friendship, integrity, faith, and the joys of a community of souls. She is best known for her novels *A Lantern in Her Hand* (1928) and *Miss Bishop* (1933), as well as for a handful of short stories, which originally appeared in such magazines as *Ladies Home Journal*, *McCall's*, and *The Saturday Evening Post* during the 1920s and '30s. Aldrich looked back on the stories of her parents and the hardships they overcame on the prairie during the mid-nineteenth century and set out to recount them as stories of people—particularly women—who endured and prevailed. Aldrich records how her own mother brushed aside her well-meant expressions of pity for the merciless difficulties of pioneer life: "Oh, save your pity. We had the best time in the world." Such an underlying theme, of facing adversity and poverty with defiant bravery and a cheerful heart, resonated with Doris Hamner.

Her writer son, Earl, saw possibilities in certain of Aldrich's stories for television movies; and for this reason—and to honor his mother—he set out to bring two of them to life as movies. One of these, *A Lantern in Her Hand,* was his mother's favorite book. But his attempt to render it into a screenplay resulted in the only work that has embarrassed him deeply. He first read the novel, then wrote and submitted a screenplay adaptation for review. Within a short time Hamner was informed by the producer that another writer had been engaged to wrestle the screenplay into final form. The resulting film, inexplicably retitled *A Mother's Gift,* contained little of Hamner's original writing and was embarrassingly poor. Hamner later said that he was glad his mother never saw this wretched film adaptation of her favorite book, which was aired on CBS in April 1995. The script, which was credited to Hamner, Don Sipes, and Joe Wisenfeld, was described as "awkwardly developed" in a harsh review written by Todd Everett in *Variety.*[16] In truth, sad to say, *A Mother's Gift* could not compare with another television movie of the 1990s depicting pioneer life on the American prairie: the superb *Hallmark Hall of Fame* adaptation of Patricia MacLachlan's book *Sarah, Plain and Tall* (1991), starring Glenn Close and Christopher Walken.

But twelve years before *A Mother's Gift,* Hamner had enjoyed much greater success with his adaptation of another of Bess Streeter Aldrich's works. This was the television film *The Gift of Love: A Christmas Story,* which was based upon Aldrich's short story "The Silent Stars Go By" and starred Lee Remick, Angela Lansbury, and

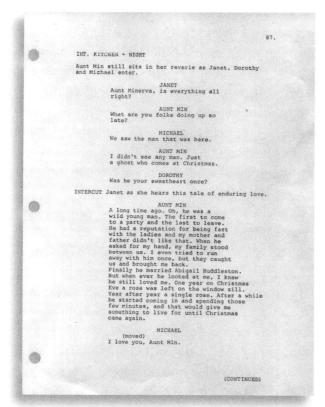

A page from Hamner's script for *The Gift of Love,* originally titled "The Silent Stars Go By."

```
                                            87.

INT. KITCHEN - NIGHT

Aunt Min still sits in her reverie as Janet, Dorothy
and Michael enter.

                      JANET
         Aunt Minerva, is everything all
         right?

                    AUNT MIN
         What are you folks doing up so
         late?

                    MICHAEL
         We saw the man that was here.

                    AUNT MIN
         I didn't see any man. Just
         a ghost who comes at Christmas.

                    DOROTHY
         Was he your sweetheart once?

INTERCUT Janet as she hears this tale of enduring love.

                    AUNT MIN
         A long time ago. Oh, he was a
         wild young man. The first to come
         to a party and the last to leave.
         He had a reputation for being fast
         with the ladies and my mother and
         father didn't like that. When he
         asked for my hand, my family stood
         between us. I even tried to run
         away with him once, but they caught
         us and brought me back.
         Finally he married Abigail Huddleston.
         But when ever he looked at me, I knew
         he still loved me. One year on Christmas
         Eve a rose was left on the window sill.
         Year after year a single rose. After a while
         he started coming in and spending those
         few minutes, and that would give me
         something to live for until Christmas
         came again.

                    MICHAEL
             (moved)
         I love you, Aunt Min.


                            (CONTINUED)
```

Polly Holliday. It was released to popular and critical acclaim during the Christmas season of 1983.

Originally published in 1933, "The Silent Stars Go By" is very short as short stories go—only three pages or so—and Hamner found the need for "an awful lot of invention" to convert the basic germ of the story into a television drama.[17] He set to work on this task in late 1982, and by December he had finished his third draft, which is quite close to what was filmed by Delbert Mann in Vermont during early 1983. Until near the time of its broadcast, the movie retained Aldrich's title, which Hamner considered a memorable one; but as the broadcast date approached, the title was changed at the request of the sponsor (Hamner recalls) to *The Gift of Love.*

Set in the small city of Elyria, Ohio, during the middle of the Christmas season, *The Gift of Love* is the story of Janet Broderick, whose world is quaking on its foundations. Amid all the busyness and bustle of the pre-Christmas shopping season, Janet learns that her husband's department store is going out of business. Her marriage is already shaky, and she must cope with this added stress as well. Further, Janet's mother, Amanda Fenwick—whom Janet adores for her strength and wisdom—suffers a sudden heart attack and dies. Overcome by stress and the effects of pneumonia, Janet collapses and is put to bed. Unconscious to the world, she dreams that she and her two small children are taken back to the small Vermont village of Janet's youth. In the dream, her parents are still living and in vibrant health, as is her maiden aunt, Minerva—"Aunt Min"—and they go about their lives in Janet's childhood home as if prepared to live forever. In time, after some degree of struggle within her dream, Janet revisits the joys of her youth, touches again the love and truths that formed her into a strong, joyful woman, and rediscovers the affirmations of her good family and its love for her; and in that knowledge, she lays hold of an inner strength she never knew she possessed.

The script is one of Hamner's best-crafted efforts, effectively capturing the anguish of a person whose world is collapsing, with all her long-depended-upon supports vanishing. Near the beginning, the screenwriter places Janet at the gravesite of her mother, shortly after the funeral. There she expresses all the fear, sorrow, and lostness that befalls many a person who loses a beloved parent to death, especially a parent whose child has grown to a troubled adulthood:

JANET'S VOICE
I'm afraid, Mother. I don't know how to go on without you. I always felt there was something you knew that would make me strong. I always felt there was some secret you would tell me, and somehow my life would become as rich as yours always seemed to be. Was there something you knew and never told me? I need you, Mother. I need you.[18]

Renowned director Delbert Mann, who had worked with Hamner fifteen years earlier on *Heidi*, brought this new story to life. As Mann recalls, "It is an admittedly sentimental fable about the importance of love and the virtues of the old-fashioned family relationships. The problem, clearly, was how to do it without letting it get saccharine to the point of nausea."[19] Hamner himself admits that this was a challenge, adding that love scenes (in any script) are among the hardest scenes to get right, from the writer's perspective. He is especially proud of a love scene that occurs roughly three-quarters through the story, concerning the normally sharp-tongued Aunt Min and her secret admirer—secret to everyone except Min: an old country storekeeper named Hanibal Prince, who has spent his adult life being put-upon and dominated by his bitter, fault-finding wife, Abigail. Min and Hanibal are childhood sweethearts grown old, and for the short time of their quiet, late-night meeting in the kitchen of Amanda's house, they reminisce about their lives, think about what might have been, and remember romantic scenes from their youth. Each in the presence of the other becomes a better, kinder person. For the occasion of this particular meeting, he has brought her roses. Hanibal's visit is short, and after he leaves Aunt Min sits alone in a memorable tableau. Hamner's script reads:

> He takes her hand for a moment and holds it to his cheek, then turns and exits. For a moment Aunt Min is the loneliest figure we can imagine, but then she picks up the bouquet of roses. She holds them in her arms and sits in a rocking chair.

> Let us HOLD on Aunt Min for a long, long moment as she begins to hum. The song is an old one, and the words to the melody she hums are: "I wandered today to the hill, Maggie, to watch the scene below. The creek and the mill are still, Maggie, where we used to go long ago." She continues to sit reflectively, holding the roses.

At the end of Janet's dream she realizes that the secret she had longed to learn from her mother is the gift of expressing love regardless of adverse feelings and circumstances, and making this gift a "secret place" where she and her husband can rebuild their marriage. At one point in the dialogue around this theme, Hamner's

Three recent Hamner titles: *The Avocado Drive Zoo, The Twilight Zone Scripts of Earl Hamner,* and *Goodnight John-Boy.*

words echo the concluding scenes of *The Homecoming,* where Clay Spencer/John Walton has practically beggared himself to express his love for his wife and children: Janet's husband, Neil, declares, "We've lost everything, Janet. There's no money. There's nothing." To which Janet replies, "There's love." Love as expressed by Love Incarnate is the gift of Christmas, a gift described by the poet T. S. Eliot as "A condition of complete simplicity (Costing not less than everything)."

The television audience loved *The Gift of Love,* tuning in to the drama in large numbers for its initial presentation by CBS on December 20, 1983. Given its impressive rating, CBS brought back the program to be rerun for the next five years during the holiday season.

The critics were less kind, with John J. O'Connor of *The New York Times* writing, "*The Gift of Love* has a tendency to overstate the obvious and underline the banal. The plot encompasses everything from grandma's burnt orange cake to a goose named Brunhilde." Still, he added, this drama "is certainly preferable to the latest fashions in standard action-adventure television," and added that such a presentation as *The Gift of Love*—with its "unabashedly sentimental" elements—could only succeed by being aired during Christmas week.[20] This was echoed by Howard Rosenberg of the *Los Angeles Times,* who claimed, "Now is the time of year when corny, manipulative, teary tales automatically work, and *The Gift of Love* is certainly two hours of that, plus those traditional Christmas symbols snow, sleigh bells, family union and grandma's house." Rosenberg found the drama "far too long and talky, and some of the dialogue a bit thick and gooey even for Christmas."[21] But both critics had high praise for the performances turned in by Lee Remick as Janet, Angela Lansbury as Amanda, and Polly Holliday as the stern but soft-around-the-edges Aunt Min.

Hamner was immensely pleased with the casting of *The Gift of Love.* "At first I had some reservations about our casting Polly Holliday," he later admitted. "I thought everyone would think of her as the wisecracking waitress Flo from the sitcom *Alice.* But I was wrong; in *The Gift of Love* she was *outstanding!*"[22]

As director Mann recalls, "When *The Gift of Love* was aired by CBS, it was taken to task by most critics as being too syrupy. The actors, by and large, escaped condemnation. With the audiences, it was a different story. In the ratings race, the show wound up in fifth place for the week. . . . It played in network prime time for five consecutive years. Maybe its simplistic message wasn't so hard to take after all."[23] Indeed, Hamner himself has stressed on many occasions that he possesses an essentially hopeful outlook on life and that this becomes expressed in his written works—not deliberately or in the form of a "message," but as a latent, underlying presence. As one writer, Cecilia Kirk Nelson, once put it, "While they are primarily to entertain, good stories simultaneously embody an understanding of a glimpse of truth. In conveying wisdom and providing insight, they reveal what it means to be human."[24] For that reason, and with modern critics feeling the need to maintain a certain hardboiled, cynical outlook on television, certain of Hamner's teleplays do not set well with them. But in *The Gift of Love* and certain of his other teleplays, Hamner has crafted works that resonate strongly with the viewing public. Sometimes, to use a cliché, these works are "hated by everyone except the public."

NOTES

1. Albarella, *The Twilight Zone Scripts of Earl Hamner,* 130–31. Any discussion of Hamner's work for *The Twilight Zone* scripts must use as a touchstone the valuable commentary of Tony Albarella, an authority on Serling's classic television series who also co-wrote the above-named book. In addition to reprinting the scripts, Albarella wrote insightful commentaries upon each one. I am indebted to his writings for informing much of my discussion of these scripts.

2. *The Twilight Zone Scripts of Earl Hamner,* 16.

3. Ibid., 43.

4. Ibid., 267.

5. Ibid., 265–66. Albarella's commentary regarding "Stopover in a Quiet Town" is particularly instructive, as he traces close thematic similarities between this *Twilight Zone* episode and one written by Serling himself, titled "Where Is

Everybody?" as well as an episode of *The Outer Limits* called "A Feasibility Study." "Stopover" and "A Feasibility Study" aired less than two weeks apart, in April 1964.

6. Ibid., 301.

7. Hamner, interview with William Simmons, 2004.

8. Cooper, http://www.hollywoodworkingwriter.com/.

9. Pechter, "*It's a Man's World:* Ahead of Its Time, and Ahead of Ours." *New York Times,* January 14, 2001, 38.

10. In recreating these portions of dialogue, I am grateful to Earl Hamner for lending me a holograph of his script for "A Drive over to Exeter."

11. Hamner, interview with William Simmons, 2004.

12. Pechter, "*It's a Man's World:* Ahead of Its Time, and Ahead of Ours." *New York Times,* January 14, 2001, 33.

13. Hamner, telephone conversation with the author, August 6, 2004.

14. Hamner, "We Called It Love," *New York Times,* October 5, 1969, D21.

15. Gould, "*CBS Playhouse* Explores Appalachian Misery," *New York Times,* October 7, 1969, 95. In coming to a better understanding of this made-for-television play, I am grateful to Hamner for lending me a holograph of his script for *Appalachian Autumn.*

16. Everett, "Kraft Premier Movie *A Mother's Gift,*" *Variety,* April 13, 1995.

17. Hamner, telephone conversation with the author, August 17, 2004.

18. In recreating this and other portions of dialogue, I am grateful to Earl Hamner for lending me a holograph of his third revised draft of the script for *The Gift of Love.*

19. Mann, *Looking Back . . . at Live Television and Other Matters,* 321.

20. O'Connor, "*The Gift of Love,* Film on CBS," *New York Times,* December 20, 1983, C19.

21. Rosenberg, "Christmas Story Suits the Season," *Los Angeles Times,* December 20, 1983, VI-10.

22. Hamner, telephone conversation with the author, August 17, 2004.

23. Mann, *Looking Back . . . at Live Television and Other Matters,* 321.

24. Cecilia A. Kirk Nelson, in *The Unbought Grace of Life: Essays in Honor of Russell Kirk,* 59. Cecilia Kirk Nelson is one of the four daughters of American man of letters Russell Kirk and his wife, Annette, who is president of the Russell Kirk Center for Cultural Renewal. Cecilia's essay "'The Box of Delights': A Literary Patrimony" is a charming and informative reflection upon the joys of storytelling and the reading of normative literature.

6

BOOKS AND FILMS FOR THE YOUNG AT HEART:

Charlotte's Web, Where the Lilies Bloom, Lassie: A Christmas Story, and *Heidi*

Each of us is all the sums he has not counted: subtract us into nakedness and night again, and you shall see begin in Crete four thousand years ago the love that ended yesterday in Texas. . . . Each moment is the fruit of forty thousand years. The minute-winning days, like flies, buzz home to death, and every moment is a window on all time.

—Thomas Wolfe, from *Look Homeward, Angel*

ONE AFTERNOON IN 1973, A friend phoned Hamner at his office in Studio City. Quickly the caller discerned that something was wrong. "Earl, you sound all choked up," the man said. "Is something wrong?" To which Hamner replied, "Yes, a spider just died."

At that moment he was putting the finishing touches on a screenplay he had undertaken for Hanna-Barbera's animated version of E. B. White's classic children's tale, *Charlotte's Web.* Hamner began this labor while simultaneously serving as executive producer, writer, narrator, and story consultant for *The Waltons* during that series' first season, making for quite a full plate of responsibilities during 1973. *Charlotte's Web* proved to be Hamner's favorite single work among everything he has yet written for television or motion pictures. It was modestly popular with audiences at the time of its release but gained significant popularity with children and their parents on videotape and DVD during the decades since. The film's superiority lies in that it contains all the ingredients that make for such success: a strong story with intriguing characters; good writing; thoughtful production; the right voicing of the characters; a well-crafted, memorable musical score; and themes that readily capture the imagination of the viewer. As Hamner himself said of *Charlotte's Web,* "It is a marvelous story of miracles, of birth and death, of threat and hope and courage and friendship and regeneration. And on top of all its many other qualities it is funny."[1] In addition to all these qualities, the story also touches on other important themes of life: love and its joys and costs, greed, self-deception, innocence, the changes of life's seasons, the essential loneliness of death, and self-sacrifice on behalf of a friend.

"FIRST, DO NO HARM"

The plot of *Charlotte's Web* is well known. In this simple tale, set on an American farm in the mid-twentieth century, a young pig named Wilbur faces sure death at the edge of Farmer Arable's axe for being a runt, until he is saved by the pleas of the farmer's young daughter, Fern. Later, after Wilbur is sold to another family, the Zuckermans, he grows and puts on weight—which again makes him a target for death, as his new owner sees him as a likely source of bacon, sausage, and ham. But through his unlikely friendship with a spider named Charlotte A. Cavatica, and with the collaboration of other barnyard friends, Wilbur is saved from Farmer Zuckerman's plans. Spinning her webs in the doorway above Wilbur's head, the imaginative Charlotte spells out, in bold letters, such words as *SOME PIG* and *TERRIFIC* and *RADIANT*—which astound the farmer's family as well as neighbors from miles around, who flock to look upon not the amazingly talented spider but, rather, "Zuckerman's Famous Pig." At the novel's end, Wilbur faces a long, happy life on Zuckerman's farm, though he must do so without Charlotte, who dies of old age and exhaustion shortly after traveling with Wilbur to the state fair and spinning the message that secures his future—the word *HUMBLE*—and then finding the strength to lay 514 eggs. But the pig is comforted in the knowledge that although Charlotte has died, he will be a friend to her children and grandchildren, unto many generations. As the narrator remarks at the conclusion of the book, "Wilbur never forgot Charlotte. Although he loved her children and grandchildren dearly, none of the new spiders ever quite took her place in his heart. She was in a class by herself."[2]

When Hamner was offered the chance to write a screenplay adaptation for *Charlotte's Web,* he set to work with a copy of White's book at his elbow and his personal "screenwriter's oath of conduct" in mind, and it is this: *First, do no harm.* By this expression, Hamner means that while the screenwriter will need to cut the story to fit a specific running time as well as alter the story concept agreed upon by the producers, he ought not needlessly change the original author's words or meaning. (This method was especially important while writing the screenplay for *Charlotte's Web,* because in performing the task of screenwriter Hamner was—by an unconfirmed account—the personal choice of the legendary E. B. White himself, who took an active interest in the film's progress.)[3] As a result of his adhering to this rule of conduct, Hamner produced a screenplay that hews remarkably close to White's novel. Whole blocks of dialogue are lifted intact, though some sections of plot and speech were eliminated, and one character—the independent-minded gosling named Jeffrey—was created entirely by Hamner.

Early in the novel, the mother Goose says, "The world is a wonderful place when you're young."[4] These words were retained by Hamner, who revised them to form the film's overarching theme: "It is big and it is frightening at times, but on the whole the world is a wonderful place." Wonderful not in the sense that everything that happens in life is pleasant and enjoyable—for as Charlotte says, "A spider's life can't help being something of a mess, with all this trapping and eating flies"—but wonderful in the sense that in life's greatest losses there can be triumph and that life's greatest gift, love, is bound up not only with pain and great cost, but also with great joy. And in the midst of these paradoxes, there is the truth that in a world in which change seems the only constant, certain things remain. A recurrent theme in Hamner's screenplay is the passing of time through the passing of the seasons: the seasons of the earth's cycle, and the seasons of life. Amid all this change and the losses that come with it, there comes also new life and the eternal certitudes of faith, hope, and love.

"During the writing of the script I came to have the highest regard for Charlotte," wrote Hamner, nearly thirty years after completing this task. "The messages she writes in her web are clever and insightful and effective. She saves Wilbur's life, but she cannot save her own. When she is near death she explains what friendship means, and through her death E. B. White shows us the magic of life regenerating itself."[5]

With his own life no longer in danger, Wilbur asks Charlotte (voiced superbly by Debbie Reynolds) about the meaning of their friendship and their lives on Zuckerman's farm. Hamner took very few liberties with White's text in framing this crucial piece of dialogue:

WILBUR
Why did you do all this for me, Charlotte?

CHARLOTTE
You have been my friend. That in itself is a tremendous
thing. After all, what's a life, anyway? We're born, we live

a little while, we die. A spider's life can't help being something of a mess, with all this trapping and eating flies. By
helping you, perhaps I was trying to lift up my own life a
trifle.

WILBUR

I haven't got your gift for words, Charlotte. But you've
saved me, and I would gladly give my life for you.

Here Wilbur, who throughout much of the story has been concerned entirely about eating, sleeping, and saving his own life, has
reached a point at which he is ready to place the lives of others
above his own. He has fully entered into the "community" of the
farmyard. In the novel, this is a fairly abrupt change. In Hamner's
screenplay, it is a gradual change, with Wilbur taking the time to
become a friend to Jeffrey the gosling, who doesn't care to learn to
swim, and even a friend (of sorts) to the sly, selfish Templeton the
Rat. In both the novel and the film, Wilbur's maturity is due to the
mentoring of him by Charlotte. As in all mentoring relationships,
theirs is a relationship of inherent inequality: Charlotte is the wiser
and the more experienced in the ways of the world; young Wilbur is
a creature in need who has really nothing to offer Charlotte but his
friendship and kind words. Their relationship has been described by
literary scholar Vigen Guroian as one in which, "like a wise teacher
Charlotte gives her pupil as much as he can absorb and not more.
She guides him to the point when he must take possession of himself
and make independent decisions." Guroian continues:

> That process of mentoring comes to a close at the state
> fair when Charlotte's own life is wholly spent and she is
> near death. Until this time there has been little that
> Wilbur could do to reciprocate in kind for what Charlotte
> has done for him. When he realizes, however, that Char-
> lotte will not return to the farm and that there is nothing
> he can do about that, Wilbur takes an initiative that
> bridges the significant gap between mentor and pupil, suf-
> ficient to the requirements of true friendship. Wilbur sees

to it that Charlotte's egg sac is gotten back to the Zucker-mans' farm where it will be safe. Yet even this act of loving reciprocity is conditioned and limited by the enduring qualities of the mentoral relationship itself. It cannot change Wilbur's relationship to Charlotte from "lesser" to "greater." Wilbur cannot teach the teacher; nor is he able to share in Charlotte's experience of being his guide. The mentor stands at both ends of the "mentor-mentee" relationship, the "mentee" only at one end. Wilbur waits through the long winter until the spring to enter into a role toward Charlotte's children that is similar to what she was toward him.[6]

In the hapless life of Wilbur the pig, Charlotte is an unlikely and superb mentor. As was said by a man Hamner deeply admired, children's television personality Fred Rogers, "All of us, at some time or other, need help. Whether we're giving or receiving help, each one of us has something valuable to bring to this world. That's one of the things that connects us as neighbors—in our own way, each one of us is a giver and a receiver."[7] Having received all that Charlotte could possibly give, Wilbur is prepared to take his place in the world as a friend and mentor to Charlotte's progeny.

This, then, is not only an imaginative story in which mentoring is a key element; it is also a story about maturing from childhood and taking one's place in life as a wise and oriented creature—a progression that is made greatly easier with the mentoring of virtuous parents and friends. The prospect of "growing up" is a mysterious and somewhat frightening thing for children to think about. In *Charlotte's Web,* in both the book and screen versions, this transition is portrayed in a lively and imaginative manner, providing readers and viewers of all ages with a sense of hope and encouragement. As Guroian has further written, "If we are able to look back on our lives and say that there was a Charlotte in it, we are most fortunate; but an even greater good fortune is if we become a mentor and friend to someone else, as Charlotte A. Cavatica was for Wilbur the runt pig."[8]

Right, A lifelong fisherman, Hamner stands proudly beside his prize catch: a 44-pound Chinook silver salmon he hooked during a fishing trip in British Columbia. This fish is now mounted on the wall of Hamner's office in Studio City. *Below,* On another fishing trip, this time with a longtime friend, director Harry Harris.

As was mentioned earlier, Hamner introduced one character, Jeffrey the gosling, and deftly altered the personalities of several. Fern Arable's brother, Avery, was transformed by the screenwriter from a fairly insufferable brat into simply a high-spirited, energetic boy, voiced by Danny Bonaduce, best known to audiences of the early 1970s as the quick-witted Danny Partridge on the popular television series *The Partridge Family*. Fern's friend Henry Fussy, who is introduced only near the end of the novel, is more fully developed and integrated earlier into the story by Hamner, who transforms Henry from Fern's unseen "crush" into a fully developed character: a sheltered, bespectacled young boy who matures into a confident, fun-loving older boy. Interestingly, after having read an early draft of the screenplay, White was convinced that by developing Henry's character in this way, Hamner had transformed *Charlotte's Web* from a story of "miracles" into a boy-meets-girl love story. But this is simply not the case. The story of Charlotte's self-sacrificing friendship with Wilbur far outweighs the subplot involving Henry's friendship with Fern.

In White's book, Templeton the Rat is an unwilling ally, somewhat fearsome and utterly untrustworthy; under Hamner's hand, Templeton is softened to become a gluttonous, loveable rogue, whose character is delightfully voiced by Paul Lynde. The waltz-tempo duet, "A Fair Is a Veritable Smorgasbord," sung by Templeton and the stammering Goose (voiced by veteran actress Agnes Moorehead, who is perhaps best known for portraying the meddlesome Endora on the TV series *Bewitched*), is one of the highlights of the film. The choice of Moorehead to provide the voice of the Goose was another master-stroke, as she brings to the role a grand-dame quality that accentuates the humor in the Goose's peculiar speaking style—particularly when she advises Charlotte on the proper spelling of the word *TERRIFIC* by grandly proclaiming, "I think it's double-T double-E double-R double-R double-I double-F double-I double C-C-C." After being corrected by the Sheep (voiced by Dave Madden, another *Partridge Family* cast member), she sniffs, "I still think it's prettier spelled double-T double-E double-R. . . ."

In terms of character depictions, Hamner went so far as to

change even Wilbur the Pig a small bit. In the novel, Wilbur has an occasionally bitter, even sarcastic edge to his personality, though in the film he is, for the most part, a good-hearted innocent—very much like the porcine star of a much later film, *Babe.* In *Charlotte's Web,* Wilbur is voiced by the comic actor Henry Gibson, whose trademark vocal delivery embodies a combination of good-natured earnestness and timidity—qualities quite appropriate to Hamner's interpretation of Wilbur's character.

Hamner was delighted to discover that the veteran songwriting team of Richard M. Sherman and Robert B. Sherman, who wrote the award-winning score to *Mary Poppins* and various other Walt Disney films, agreed to provide the music and lyrics for *Charlotte's Web.* (The decision to contract the Sherman brothers for this responsibility sat uncomfortably with White, who found their music too upbeat for his tastes and untrue to the spirit of New England rural life. In his *Letters,* he states at one point that he would have preferred that the scene of Charlotte's death be accompanied by the music of Mozart.) Aside from the duet mentioned earlier, other memorable songs include the haunting "Charlotte's Web," as well as the sprightly "Chin Up," Wilbur's "I Can Talk," the lilting "Mother Earth and Father Time," Fern's love-song to Wilbur titled "There Must Be Something More," a show-stopping tribute to finding common bonds amid differences called "We've Got Lots in Common," and the resonant barbershop-quartet number, "Zuckerman's Famous Pig."

The story was framed by the voice-overs of a man with one of the best-known narrative voices in American film during the mid-twentieth century (and another Walt Disney alumnus), Rex Allen. The last of American cinema's "singing cowboys," Allen had narrated such films as *Charlie, the Lonesome Cougar; The Incredible Journey;* and numerous Sunday-night episodes of *Walt Disney's Wonderful World of Color.* He brought to these narrations warm, knowledgeable storytelling skills served up with a hint of a cowboy twang, giving the listener a sense that the speaker possesses a great deal of down-home common sense and is a man who can be trusted to tell the honest story. Allen brought this same quality to *Charlotte's Web,* to good effect.

The artists at Hanna-Barbera studios, known for their character-istic simple lines and two-dimensional artwork for Saturday-morning cartoon shows for children (such as *Yogi Bear* and *The Flintstones*), invested much extra effort in their artwork for *Charlotte's Web*. While the characters retain something of a two-dimen-sional look, they show evidence of stronger-than-usual care in their crafting, having been invested with far more detail and realistic fea-tures than Hanna-Barbera normally gave human characters. The backgrounds are exceptionally well rendered in color and detail, bringing to mind the rich, warm backgrounds characteristic of the Warner Brothers cartoons of the 1940s. The artists went so far as to model the Zuckermans' barn after the barn on E. B. White's farm in Maine.

As Hamner summed up, in explaining the appeal of *Charlotte's Web,* it's a film in which all the elements and key details came together to form a compelling work—not the least of these elements being the writing. At the close of the book, E. B. White wrote, "It is not often that someone comes along who is a true friend and a good writer. Charlotte was both." Looking at the motion picture adapted from *Charlotte's Web,* and despite his qualms as the novel's author, he may well have said the same of Earl Hamner.

RETURN TO APPALACHIA: *WHERE THE LILIES BLOOM*

At about the time Hamner began work on the second season of *The Waltons,* he turned his hand to screenwriting once again. He had enjoyed working on *Charlotte's Web* the previous year, and now he took up the task of adapting a novel congenial to his memories and sentiments, *Where the Lilies Bloom* (1969). Written by Vera and Bill Cleaver, this novel is set in the Great Smoky Mountains of North Car-olina and portrays an impoverished but determined family of share-croppers as they struggle to retain their upland farm amid trying circumstances. One of the children, fourteen-year-old Mary Call Luther, is an aspiring writer who assumes a leadership role over her three siblings. As a story, and in light of his then-current work on *The Waltons, Where the Lilies Bloom* seemed tailor-made for Hamner.

The straightforward plot of the book and the film concerns the ordeal of Mary Call as she strives to manage an impoverished household and provide for her ten-year-old brother, Romey, and her sisters Devola, age eighteen, and five-year-old Ima Dean, on a small mountain farm. The story covers one year in the life of the Luther family; and as the story opens, the children's father, the widower Roy Luther, is dying of a wasting illness. During his last days, this good but impractical man places a heavy burden upon the shoulders of the child he considers the most level-headed, Mary Call. He makes her promise that after his death, she is to see that he is buried in secret, without the knowledge of a clergyman or undertaker, as they would expect to be paid for their services by the already dirt-poor family. That, plus the fact that the children would be split up and sent to foster homes if it were known that they were orphaned and alone. (Roy Luther fails to see what Mary Call quickly perceives: that in laying this responsibility upon her, she must contrive to keep her father's death and burial a secret from everyone beyond her siblings.) She also promises her father to do everything in her power to keep the family together, to be proud of her family name, and to prevent Devola from marrying the man who is interested in having her for his wife: the despised, middle-aged man whose land Roy Luther has worked for many years, Kiser Pease. After Roy Luther dies, Mary Call sets out to keep these promises. The rest of the story depicts her desperate attempts to hide the fact of her father's death, to keep Kiser and Devola apart, and to provide for her family. To earn money, she enlists the aid of Romey, Devola, and Ima Dean to go "wildcrafting," which means venturing into the mountain forests whenever possible to find and gather herbs, roots, bark, and flowers that can be dried, bundled, and sold for respectable sums and then processed into natural medicines.

At the story's end, Mary Call realizes that though she has tried extremely hard, the burdens of secrecy and self-sufficiency she has tried to carry are too much for her. She also realizes that she has misjudged Kiser and confesses to him the secret of Roy Luther's death. For his part, Kiser has grown to respect the girl's immense strength of character and ingenuity, and he commends her for faring better than many an adult could have managed under the circumstances. Mary Call finally assents to Devola's marriage to Kiser and faces a life full of better opportunities than the one she prepared for during the long months of deceiving the world about Roy Luther's death while trying desperately to keep utter destitution at bay. Having been encouraged by one of her teachers at the local school to pursue her strong skills at writing, Mary Call can now look beyond her pinched circumstances to the wider world. She, Romey, and Ima Dean will now be cared for by Kiser, who is a better man than anyone in the story suspected.

The film might well have been described in the words used by the distinguished American writer William Saroyan to assess the novel, which he praised for being "immersed in a sense of the deep kinship between human beings, animals and plants, recognized, accepted and rejected or cherished with humor. This is a story of good people, with real natures, living under conditions of hardship, in poverty, in the midst of bereavement, maintaining their independence, wit and dignity."[9] Further, the film was released in 1974, a time when the American reading public's interest in Eliot Wigginton's series of Foxfire books—detailing Southern folk customs, music, recipes, and ways—was at its height. But despite all this, as well as a strong story, the fine bluegrass music of the Earl Scruggs Revue, and the majestic scenery of the Great Smoky Mountains, the film *Where the Lilies Bloom* enjoyed only moderate success upon its release, and it was not widely reviewed among major periodicals.

Hamner's screenplay was not at fault, as it follows the Cleavers' plot and dialogue fairly faithfully, with some customized touches thrown in. Hamner altered the plot itself only slightly, to change the Luthers from sharecroppers living on Kiser's land to tenant farmers living on ancestral land that Kiser had taken from them after Roy Luther defaulted on paying his taxes. As for dialogue, Hamner enlivened it with some homegrown touches. He recalled a down-home quip made by one of his grandfathers and wrote it into the dialogue: At one point, Kiser good-naturedly teases Mary Call, whose face has been pockmarked by bee-stings and mud during an accident in the forest, and declares that the girl "looks like she was shot through an apple orchard and hit every tree."

Aside from this, Hamner also recycled a plot segment from his novel *Spencer's Mountain.* In that book Clay-Boy's teacher encourages him to follow his talents and become a writer rather than staying in the village of New Dominion and becoming a mill-worker. She declares to the boy's father, "If the day comes that I go past the mill and see him stooped over a polishing machine, I think I will give up the teaching profession." In *Where the Lilies Bloom,* Mary Call's teacher urges the girl to follow her own inclinations toward writing, admitting tearfully that she has had her heart broken many times by seeing her few talented and gifted students eventually leave school, turn away from their capabilities and dreams, and return to the hills to settle for less in life than they could have achieved had they pursued their dreams.

Hamner also provided the story with a much more satisfactory ending than the one provided in the book, which ended with first-person narrator Mary Call speaking about how she and her siblings have wildcrafted in the past and will wildcraft in the future. In Hamner's version, Mary Call (portrayed by Julie Gholson, who looks like the actress Sondra Locke must have looked as a teen) stands during the wedding of Devola and Kiser, musing upon what she has learned in attempting to live up to Roy Luther's hard promises. This dissolves into a scene in which she stands alone at Roy Luther's grave, as the haunting melody of the Celtic-sounding folk song "Where the Lilies Bloom" is heard. Against the majestic background of the Smokies, she speaks to her father across eternity, declaring her undying love for him, despite everything that has happened since his death. She also says that while she has endured and prevailed, she will someday leave these mountains to seek her fortune in the world, after she has fulfilled all her responsibilities.

MARY CALL
(voice-over)
It's not an easy thing to say, but Roy Luther was wrong
about Kiser. He's a good man and will be gentle with

Devola. I know now that it is possible to love someone even though they fail you. I still love Roy Luther, and I always will. Perhaps that's the true test of love.

(speaking at Roy Luther's grave)
Kiser's not as bad as we thought he was. I'll keep an eye on him and Devola.

Oh, this is a fair place to spend eternity. The air smells like honeysuckle. The wind in the pine trees makes a joysome sound. Sometimes on the wind, I feel something say my name, telling me to come to some far-off place: "Mary Call! Mary Call!" Once I'm through raising Romey and Ima Dean, I think I'll go.

Beyond this, Hamner changed the emphases of the story in several ways. As written by Vera and Bill Cleaver, *Where the Lilies Bloom* is a testimony to the defiant pride, "guts," and determination of the mountaineer children, who scratch out a hard living in an otherwise beautiful land. Hamner also saw the story of Mary Call Luther and her family as similar in some respects to the story of himself and his family, testifying to the power of love, family, community, and determination to overcome nearly all obstacles. In their quest to keep Roy Luther's death a secret from all people outside the immediate family, Mary Call must painfully remove herself and her siblings from fellowship with everyone else in the community who might have helped them had they known of the children's loss. In the movie this is brought home with poignancy on the children's first day at school in September, when Romey is asked by another boy if he intends to try out for the school basketball team. Romey excitedly agrees, but then hesitates and declines when Mary Call quietly warns him to say no; to try out for the team would commit Romey to an activity that would bring him into close comradery with other boys, which might lead him to reveal their family secret. Likewise, Mary Call engages in some light-hearted gossip with some other girls at the schoolhouse door, but then realizes that this world of close friendship and girlish confidences is closed to her. This breaking of community ties was a world away from the life Hamner had known as a boy growing up in a mountain village where burdens were shared and joys were celebrated across family lines.

To bring this story to the screen, Hamner changed the temperament of the central characters somewhat. While young Ima Dean remains fairly consistent in the transition from page to screen, Mary Call and Romey are rendered more thoughtful and less inclined to outbursts of reproachful temper than in the novel—though they do have their moments of frustration and anger. In the book, Romey is forever threatening to run away and put everyone in his family out of his mind forever or to take his father's shotgun and "blow the head off" Kiser Pease or anyone else who tries to make life difficult for the Luther family. But in the screenplay, he is simply a typical unimaginative boy, who readily accepts Mary Call's leadership in the family. In the novel, eighteen-year-old Devola is depicted as mildly mentally impaired—though she mysteriously "outgrows" this handicap by the story's end. In Hamner's imagination, Devola is simply a quiet dreamer, possessing skills and interests nobody has ever suspected. In both novel and film, Kiser is recurrently described as a worthless, sly, awful man—but we never really see him say or do anything terribly mean to anyone, though crossing swords with feisty Mary Call brings out a streak of prickly annoyance in him. (In the film version, in the eyes of the Luther family, Kiser turned them into tenants working on land they rightfully owned. But in Kiser's own eyes, he saved the Luthers from becoming destitute wanderers, first paying the taxes they could not pay, then allowing them to stay on the land.) In truth, in addition to the themes already mentioned, *Where the Lilies Bloom* is also a story about putting aside false assumptions to see life and people as they really are—and, in embracing that truth, finding hope. In the novel, at a moment of deep desolation, Mary Call summons hope and puts into words the spirit that pervades Hamner's screenplay:

> I thought about man's hold on life, how painful its struggle, and I tried to think of the reason for people like us Luthers ever having been born. There must be one, I

thought. Roy Luther said there was a reason for every-thing. And something within me stirred and my spirits lifted and I thought, By the grace of the Lord we're here and what we make of it is our own affair. It's everybody's affair what they make of being here. The Lord hasn't forgotten us. Those are just Romey's words and he is just a child. This land isn't forgotten and neither are we.[10]

In the film version there were strong performances turned in by several of the actors—notably Rance Howard (as Roy Luther), Harry Dean Stanton (Kiser Pease), and Jan Smithers (Devola Luther). Smithers, an actress who became known to television audiences in 1979 as shy Bailey Quarters on *WKRP in Cincinnati*, reveals a lovely soprano voice in *Where the Lilies Bloom* as she sings a lament over the freshly filled grave of Roy Luther. Hamner himself wrote, "I have known girls (and the women they grew up to become) and I have always admired them. They are strong, scrappy, undaunted, self-reliant, and determined, yet they can be vulnerable and sensitive underneath the surface. I thought Julie Gholson was just smashing in the role [of Mary Call] and I have often wondered what has become of her. She showed such promise."[11] (Miss Gholson was nominated for a Golden Globe award for her performance.)

Despite the film's promising aspects, there are also flaws. From a technical standpoint, the lighting is far too dark in several interior shots, and the sound is muddy in some places, making the characters' dialogue occasionally hard to discern. There is also something "off" in the editing of the film, in terms of timing. Sometimes the dialogue does not flow from the characters naturally; there is often an awkward delay between the time one character finishes speaking and another responds. In some places, the punch line to some snatch of humorous dialogue is almost cut off by a quick fade at scene's end.

Hamner recalls that in order to fit the film into a timeframe that would permit the director to shoot on location in the Smoky Mountains while staying on budget, he had to condense the four seasons of the momentous year in the lives of the Luther children into one season, summer. The resulting backdrop of the Smokies was beautiful in the film, especially so in Mary Call's final scene at her father's gravesite. However, a short time after the film was released, Hamner happened to tune in to a radio interview with Vera and Bill Cleaver, who were asked what they thought of the film. One of them answered, "Well, Earl Hamner, the man who wrote the script, ruined it by condensing all the action into one season." The screenwriter laughs about this today and says, "I thought *Where the Lilies Bloom* was an excellent film."[12]

Jay Cocks, who at the time of the film's release was a movie reviewer for *Time* magazine, wrote that there is "a certain charm and challenge" in the film, but that for the most part *Where the Lilies Bloom* "misses any real sense of the proud and strangled lives it portrays" because the film didn't depict the life of the Luther family as a crushing ordeal of unremitting misery.[13] To some extent Cocks has a point, for the Luther children seem to have a remarkably new-looking wardrobe of clothes for impoverished and orphaned mountain children. But the critic's assessment is too harsh, for he is criticizing the story *he* would have crafted rather than the story Hamner adapted from the original authors, whose tale was grounded in firsthand observation of mountain life and wildcrafting. There is indeed charm and a sense of hope arising in this interesting, well-told story, which makes it enjoyable and well worth viewing despite its few drawbacks.

A BOOK FOR CHILDREN—*LASSIE: A CHRISTMAS STORY*

"If story areas were oil wells Christmas would be a gusher!" claimed Hamner in a letter to this writer early in 2004. "It is a time when we all become children and want to relive the time before magic and beauty turned into cynicism and ugliness. . . . Emotions run high, lurk just below the surface, and can easily be manipulated by writers or songwriters or playwrights. It can reach an adoring public with as gross a work as 'I Saw Mommy Kissing Santa Claus,' or as stupid a song as 'Rudolph the Red-nosed Reindeer.' It can even reach the top of the charts with a song being sung by Alvin the Chipmunk. But underlying all the frivolity, the crowds, the commercialism, is the story of Jesus' birth and it carries with it the beauty and the majesty and the fountain of enduring power that has touched mankind for over two thousand years."

Over the course of his career, Hamner produced several works for page and screen in which Christmas is a central element—notably in *The Homecoming,* but also in several episodes of *The Waltons,* as well as *A Dream for Christmas* (aired in 1973), *The Gift of Love: A Christmas Story* (aired in 1983), and a children's book written with Don Sipes titled *Lassie: A Christmas Story,* published in 1998. In this short book the story of Jesus' birth is written explicitly into the plot of a tale concerning one of the most beloved animals in twentieth-century popular culture.

"Who could ever turn down an offer to write a book about Lassie?" wrote Hamner. "The very name brings images to mind of Roddy McDowell and Elizabeth Taylor as children and Lassie herself, surely the most fabled dog of all time. So when Tommy Nelson Publishing offered Don Sipes and me an opportunity to write *Lassie: A Christmas Story,* we did not hesitate."[14]

While many readers remember the classic Roddy McDowell–Elizabeth Taylor film Hamner alludes to, entitled *Lassie, Come Home* (1943), many also remember the television series *Lassie.* Television viewers hold especially fond memories of that program's early years, aired from 1957 to 1964, when the beautiful collie was owned by a little boy named Timmy Martin and his parents, Ruth and Paul, who lived on a farm. In each week's episode, Lassie proved herself instrumental in saving someone from injury or death, usually by running to the Martin house to bark and whine urgently, until someone would realize, "It looks like Lassie wants us to follow her!" It was this version of Lassie's saga that Hamner and Sipes worked into *Lassie: A Christmas Story.*

A brief summary of this simple story might run as follows: It is Christmas Eve day, and Timmy and his mother, Ruth, decorate the tree, with a little help from Lassie. The family lives in rural Vermont, where Timmy's widowed mother is a veterinarian. Today, heavy snow is falling, so Ruth leaves in the family pickup truck to set out bales of hay for the local deer herd that will starve without it. Timmy stays behind to continue decorating the tree, telling the story of the Christ-child and the first Christmas to Lassie while they work. Outside, on the frozen road, Ruth's truck goes over an embankment after she swerves to avoid a cougar in the road. This creature is Old Scratch, a crafty, vicious predator feared by the locals. Unconscious, Ruth is trapped inside the truck as it is covered with falling snow. When Ruth fails to return home within a reasonable time, a search-party sets out to look for her, but it is Lassie who saves the day: first fighting off Old Scratch at great risk to herself, then finding the half-buried truck and digging through the snow to rescue Ruth. Because of her bravery and instincts, Lassie makes it possible for Ruth and Timmy to enjoy a merry Christmas at home together.

In this book, as was the case in 1933 (when Hamner's father returned home in dramatic fashion), Christmas Eve remains to Hamner a time when strange, unexpected, and wonderful things occur that upset the natural and anticipated flow of everyday life. Accented by colorful and action-filled illustrations by Kevin Burke, *Lassie: A Christmas Story* tells how the same wonder that illuminated the Judean night two millennia ago still retains today the power to surprise, delight, and promise release from entrapment—even while a deadly adversary prowls about seeking whom he might devour. (It is perhaps not entirely an accident that the fierce cougar's name, Old Scratch, is also a Southern nickname for Satan.)

As Hamner recalls, "This book remained at the top of the best sellers in stores featuring Christian books in the country for over a year."[15]

A JOURNEY TO THE SWISS ALPS: *HEIDI*

"Earl Hamner was thrilled when he was hired to adapt Johanna Spyri's children's classic, *Heidi,* into a television movie," wrote journalist Lisa Provence. "Little did he know its airing would become a date that would live forever in pro football infamy."[16]

The year was 1968, one of the most tumultuous years in American history in the years following World War II. It was the year of

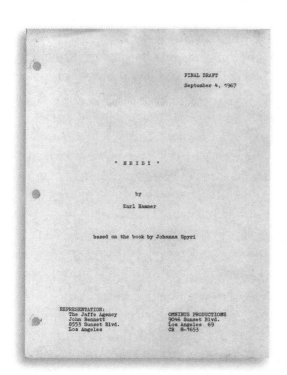

The cover page of Hamner's script for his memorable television film *Heidi.*

FINAL DRAFT
September 4, 1967

" H E I D I "

by

Earl Hamner

based on the book by Johanna Spyri

REPRESENTATION:
The Jaffe Agency
John Bennett
8553 Sunset Blvd.
Los Angeles

OMNIBUS PRODUCTIONS
9046 Sunset Blvd.
Los Angeles 69
CR 8-1653

the height of the Youth Movement, campus unrest, interracial tension, urban riots, and protests against American military involvement in Vietnam. It was the year Robert Kennedy and Martin Luther King Jr. were assassinated—and the year that saw the sudden demise of President Lyndon Johnson as a political force and the rise of another divisive political figure to the presidency, Richard Nixon. It was the year a manned American spacecraft, *Apollo* 8, orbited the moon, and the astronauts' countrymen held their breath in anticipation of the next event in space exploration: a landing on the moon's surface and "one small step for a man, one giant leap for mankind."

Amid all this, Earl Hamner was assigned to revisit a very nonpolitical children's story that many television viewers associated with nostalgia and sweet innocence. As a writer of the screenplay for a new *Heidi,* Hamner knew he faced a steep challenge, for he was quite aware that television audiences would find this movie a marked change in emphasis from the seriousness of America's social and political climate. He knew they would also judge this new version of Spyri's novel against the 1937 Twentieth-Century Fox film that had starred Shirley Temple and Arthur Treacher. These comparisons aside, how would an American audience respond to a sentimental story of a little Swiss orphan girl who wins over her hardhearted grandfather through love and good will alone?

The story of young Heidi Sessemann is familiar to many readers and viewers worldwide. Having lost both parents at an early age, she is taken in hand for a short time by an aunt, Dete Hartzel, who seeks to give the trusting girl a new home with her widowed brother-in-law, Richard Sessemann, in Frankfurt, Germany. Sessemann is the father of Klara, a girl of approximately Heidi's age who has been unable to walk since the day her mother drowned. Unfortunately for Fraulein Hartzel, Sessemann is not at home the day she calls with Heidi in tow, and thus she is unable to arrange for the child to live with her uncle. Turned away by Klara's governess, the severe Fraulein Rottenmeier, Hartzel rebounds from this failure, sending Heidi to live in the Swiss Alps with her reclusive grandfather, Jonas Hartzel. Heidi exudes hopefulness and innocent goodness; and the rest of the story concerns her winning her grandfather's love, gaining a friend in a young goatherd, Peter Distil, and becoming friends with Klara, who visits Heidi in the Alps. There, Klara is inspired by her cousin's spiritually transformed grandfather to literally take her first steps toward walking on her own.

Hamner was pleased to learn that this new version of Spyri's classic would star Maximilian Schell, Michael Redgrave, and Jean Simmons, with Jennifer Edwards—daughter of Blake Edwards and his first wife, Patricia Walker—starring as Heidi. He learned as well that it would be filmed on location in the Swiss Alps, in and near the small town of Sils Maria. With the filmmakers taking pains to make this an authentic-looking production, featuring some of Hollywood's most distinguished names, it behooved Hamner to craft a memorable script. This was his first full-length screenplay since 1963's frothy *Palm Springs Weekend,* and he was anxious to make a good showing in this more serious drama.

"I took a good many liberties with Johanna Spyri's text," said Hamner many years later. "But I believe the liberties I took made the story much more interesting."[17] The result was a script he considered "wonderful." Director Delbert Mann recalls:

In setting forth to do *Heidi* as a show for the whole family, producers Fred Brogger and Jim Franciscus had hired Earl Hamner to write the script. Earl, a gentle and kindly man who hadn't yet created *The Waltons,* did a fine job of reconceiving the story for filming. The book is a classic for children, especially little girls, but holds little interest for adults. The characters are pretty one-dimensional and seem to be rather unmotivated. Earl developed a reason for Grandfather living the life of a recluse, changed the villainous Fraulein Rottenmeier into a sympathetic character, eliminated some secondary story elements, expanded others.[18]

In truth, Hamner did a masterful job in writing this particular script, which bears as its signature theme the importance of striving to retain hope and courage amid even the most discouraging circumstances of life. The emblem of this striving is the eagle, with which Grandfather communes in spirit during long days of meditating quietly at a spot high above his Alpine cottage. At one point he shares with Heidi a key insight he has learned from the eagle: "In all living things there is a reservoir of strength, a courage, a bravery we do not know we possess until the need arises. When we have thought ourselves cowards and find we are indeed brave, that discovery can dazzle the mind, stun the heart, and sometimes cause miracles." By summoning this reserve of courage, Heidi is able to endure her years of feeling unwanted under Dete Hartzel's care, Klara is able to walk again, and Richard Sessemann and Fraulein Rottenmeier are able to thrust aside class distinctions and embrace the love they feel for each other. Encouraged by Heidi, Grandfather is able to overcome the crippling bitterness and resentfulness that have bound him for many years because of Heidi's mother's marriage—of which he did not approve—and to again play the magnificent organ he built at the church in the nearby village of Dörfli.

Hamner's final script for *Heidi* is a model of pacing, character development, and integration of recurring thematic elements. Early on, the viewer wonders why Grandfather is bad-tempered and reclusive; and Hamner supplies a "teaser," with Peter's blind grandmother attempting to explain the reason—and then being interrupted:

GRANDMOTHER

You see, child, your grandfather was once one of the greatest organ builders in all of Switzerland. It took him twenty years to build the organ in Dörfli.

Abruptly Grandfather appears at the door and takes in the scene.

GRANDMOTHER (CONTINUED)

That organ was everything to him, but then one day . . .

GRANDFATHER

(interrupting)
Come!

Heidi is startled for a second, then she obediently picks up her satchel and starts toward the door.

GRANDMOTHER

Jonas? She's only a child!

Grandfather exits without a backward look. Heidi, at the door, turns and smiles a thank you to Peter. Apprehensively she exits.

In this and other sections of the script, Hamner created a sense of suspense and a desire to learn why there is so much unspoken unhappiness in the lives of these characters. A little at a time, in appropriate intervals, the viewer's initial questions are decisively answered.

In addition, an examination of the final script, compared with the finished production, provides the interested film enthusiast a key insight into the filmmaking process, and it is this: The finished script is not necessarily the final word on what will appear in the film. Lines of dialogue are altered and sometimes deleted altogether, depending upon what the director and actors believe will work best. While most of Hamner's final script for *Heidi* is followed to the letter, there are some places in the story where such changes were made. For example, at the point in the film at which Fraulein Rottenmeier and Richard embrace and kiss for the first time, Hamner's script called for Richard to break off their kiss and exclaim that they needed to stop this foolishness and remember their positions. In the film, this same moment of embarrassment and self-consciousness is effectively conveyed not by words at all but by the facial expressions and body language of the pair, played by Jean Simmons and Maximilian Schell.

At another point in the film, near the end, Hamner's script called for Fraulein Rottenmeier, while visiting Grandfather and Heidi with Klara, basically to disappear from the story entirely. Seeking to grow apart from Richard—after all, because of class distinctions, a mere governess and her male employer can have no romantic prospects—it is understood that she is leaving Switzerland for a new position as a governess for a family in England. But in the final version of the film, this is changed. With Richard expected to arrive at the Alpine cottage at any time to collect Klara, Fraulein begins to leave but is stopped by Grandfather and instructed by him to go with Heidi up to his "meditation place" in the High Pasture, where he'll meet them in a few minutes. Grandfather wisely waits until Heidi and Fraulein have gone up the mountain, and then he encourages Klara to at least *try* to walk. He then walks away to join Heidi and Fraulein, deliberately leaving Klara alone in her wheelchair. With nobody around to help her, Klara painstakingly struggles to walk—and succeeds just as her father appears on the scene. Meanwhile, Grandfather delivers the "message of the eagle," regarding the embracing of inner reserves of courage, to Heidi and Fraulein. They gently insist to Grandfather that the eagle's message is intended for him, too. The trio then walks down the mountain together to join Richard and Klara, who has just taken her first steps. From this point through the end of the film, Richard and Fraulein are together, and between them there is no shadow of parting.

In the final scene, at the conclusion of a Sunday Mass, Grandfather himself is deliberately left alone by the others for a few minutes in order to wrestle with his conscience and call upon his own "reservoir of strength," to set aside the bitterness and hurt of many years and to perform music at the keyboard of the church organ for the first time in many years. Grandfather and Fraulein Rottenmeier discover, as did Emery Goode in Hamner and Sipes's *Murder in Tinseltown,* that anything good and worth having in this world must be aggressively pursued and laid hold of. As Grandfather says to the downcast Fraulein at the point where she believes her love for Richard is an impossible dream: "Take my advice: If you want something, you must reach out for it."

In addition to writing the script, Hamner was called upon by director Mann to write two short verses to a song composed by John Williams, writer of the film's musical score. Called simply "Heidi's Song," it was to recur periodically throughout the movie and become the little Swiss girl's theme music. The lilting song, written collaboratively by Earl and Jane Hamner and set in a three-four time signature, runs as follows:

> When I am wishing for dreams to come true,
> All of my wishes are small ones.
> I'll save my big wish for one day
> When I'll find a place of my own.
>
> If I can have only one wish come true,
> If only one dream can find me,
> I'll dream of some place where love is,
> Where I'll find a place of my own.

Mann recalls how actress Jennifer Edwards stayed up late the night before she was to sing the song, memorizing it with the help of her mother. "The next morning on the set Jennie sang it in sweet piping tones, clear and true, and very moving. It was, simply, magic."[19]

"I Hear It Was Great!"

Sponsored by Timex timepieces, Mann's made-for-television version of *Heidi* was scheduled to air on NBC at 7:00 p.m. on Sunday evening, November 17, 1968. But then a problem arose.

In those days before cable and satellite TV, America's three main networks monopolized the broadcasting of professional sports on Sundays. The three networks guarded their "turf" jealously, and NBC was no exception. While ABC aired all manner of sports, talk shows, and movies and CBS aired National Football League games, NBC oversaw the broadcasting of games played by the upstart American Football League. For the most part, then as now, Sunday afternoons in the fall and early winter were devoted to the viewing of professional football on TVs across the United States. In the early evening of November 17, a game between two AFL archrivals, the New York Jets and the Oakland Raiders, was running long on NBC. The network had sold the 7:00–9:00 timeslot to Timex for the broadcast of *Heidi* and was contractually bound to air the movie at the top of the appointed hour. With less than a minute left in the game and the Jets leading 32-29, NBC programming personnel decided to cut away from the game to air *Heidi* exactly on schedule.

Across the nation, children rejoiced, though football fans were outraged. Such was the extent of their anger that, according to a report that ran in the *New York Times* afterward, the circuits of the NBC switchboard were overloaded. *Times* journalist Thomas Rogers noted that in the hours immediately after NBC's decision, irate fans crossed from understandable irritation into the realm of the ridiculous: "Many callers, unable to reach NBC, called the Police Department and tied up the emergency police number for several hours. Operators at The New York Telephone Company and *The New York Times* were also deluged with calls."[20] Writing in the *New York World-Telegram & Sun,* columnist Harriet Van Horne wrote that "for two lovely Sabbath hours, while little Heidi went piping down the valleys wild, the NBC switchboard was besieged by obscene oaths and hoarse cries of outrage. . . ."[21] Syndicated humor columnist Art Buchwald got a huge horselaugh out of the whole affair, writing, "Men who wouldn't get out of their chairs during an earthquake rushed to the phones to scream obscenities at the man responsible for cutting off the game."[22] To add salt to the fans' wounds, during the final forty-two seconds of the game the Raiders scored two quick touchdowns and an extra point, coming from behind in dramatic fashion to win 43-32.

To make matters worse, in the midst of the movie's broadcast, NBC hastily tried to make amends by running a crawler across the bottom of the screen, informing the viewing audience of the game's unexpected outcome. Unfortunately this crawler was run during one of the most emotionally charged segments of the story: the point at which Klara struggles to pull herself to her feet and walk, in a remarkably moving piece of acting by young actress Zuleika Robson. The intrusive message regarding the outcome of a football game was distracting and had a deflating effect upon the story's climactic moment. At this point, there were not only enraged football fans but enraged filmmakers as well: men and women who had labored for months to craft a memorable film drama—and had succeeded in a most unexpected and unwanted manner.

For many years the animus against Delbert Mann's *Heidi* for its unintended affront to professional football far overshadowed the fact of the film's high quality. For roughly a year, the very word *Heidi* was the punchline to a hundred jokes by standup comics on television. But amid all the controversy, reviewers were kind to *Heidi,* with Martin Hogan Jr. of the *Cincinnati Inquirer* hailing the film as "a refreshing and sound essay on the virtues of faith, hope, courage, and love"; while Rex Polier of the *Philadelphia Evening Bulletin* called it "a tonic for the soul, as well as satisfying entertainment for the entire family. . . ."[23]

Ironically, a film of which Hamner was quite proud became perhaps the least-known of his screenplays, though he found the entire kerfuffle both amusing and apropos, saying "In a society where sports figures are glorified, for once a little girl in the Swiss Alps gets some publicity."[24]

The losing quarterback on November 17 became far better known throughout the nation in the years that followed than the quarterback of the winning team. He also had the most memorable commentary on the whole dustup. In a post-game interview, quarterback Joe Namath of the Jets was asked what he thought of this important game being pre-empted by *Heidi.* "Broadway Joe" ruefully replied, "I didn't get a chance to see it, but I hear it was great!"

NOTES

1. Hamner, *The Avocado Drive Zoo: At Home with My Family and the Creatures We've Loved,* 105.

2. White, *Charlotte's Web,* 184.

3. Like many writers who watch their novels and short stories rendered into screenplay form, White was not entirely happy with the result of Hanna-Barbera's *Charlotte's Web.* His letters record that he found the film a bit too full of "jolly" songs for his liking.

4. White, *Charlotte's Web,* 18.

5. Hamner, *The Avocado Drive Zoo: At Home with My Family and the Creatures We've Loved,* 105.

6. Guroian, *Tending the Heart of Virtue: How Classic Stories Awaken a Child's Moral Imagination,* 101–102.

7. Rogers, *The World According to Mister Rogers,* 136.

8. Guroian, *Tending the Heart of Virtue: How Classic Stories Awaken a Child's Moral Imagination,* 102.

9. Saroyan, review of *Where the Lilies Bloom,* in *The New York Times Book Review,* September 28, 1969, 34.

10. Cleaver, *Where the Lilies Bloom,* 144.

11. Hamner, to Person, June 8, 2004.

12. Ibid.

13. Cocks, Review of *Where the Lilies Bloom, Time,* February 11, 1974, 65.

14. Hamner, "Lassie's Christmas," http://www.the-waltons.com/booksbyearl.html.

15. Ibid.

16. Provence, "Earl Hamner's NFL notoriety: How *Heidi* irked Jets-Raiders fans," *Charlottesville (VA) Hook,* May 15, 2003, 24.

17. Hamner, telephone conversation with Person, June 15, 2004.

18. Mann, *Looking Back . . . at Live Television and Other Matters,* 219–20.

19. Ibid., 222.

20. Rogers, "Jets cut for *Heidi;* TV fans complain," *New York Times,* November 18, 1968, 61.

21. Quoted in Mann, *Looking Back . . . at Live Television and Other Matters,* 226.

22. Buchwald, "*Heidi* Fans' Next Game: Swiss Alps vs. Super Bowl," *Los Angeles Times,* November 24, 1968, G7.

23. Quoted in Mann, *Looking Back . . . at Live Television and Other Matters,* 227.

24. Provence, "Earl Hamner's NFL notoriety: How *Heidi* irked Jets-Raiders fans," *Charlottesville (VA) Hook,* May 15, 2003, 24.

7

GUIDING HAND:

Falcon Crest, Brewster Place, Snowy River, and *The Ponder Heart*

Someone asked me recently: What's it like to have all that power? And I said: I don't really know what you mean. And they said: You, as an executive producer of a hit show that's run for five years, have a great deal of power. And I realized that I do. That the networks treat an idea that I submit with a great deal of respect. They don't always buy them. Because . . . that is an aspiration: not to produce a copy of The Waltons, *but something that's meaningful in television.*

EARL HAMNER, IN AN INTERVIEW
WITH ANTOINETTE W. ROADES, 1977

During the opening credits of many television dramas, there is a statement to the effect that this particular program was "created by" a specific person. What does it mean to "create" a series? Hamner once explained, "It was a term that was devised by the Writers Guild of America to describe the person who thought up the concept of the show. 'Created by' means that you came to the network with a concept, characters, time period, a locale, a situation and a challenging kind of overall concept. It also means that you are entitled to certain royalties."[1]

Likewise, many television viewers have no idea what is entailed in the duties of a television producer. Asked this question on one occasion, Hamner replied with a laugh that a producer "does pretty much what he wants to do"—which is to say, the producer wears a number of hats. In a nutshell, the producer does what the job title implies: he or she "makes" the film or program, ensuring that every detail involved in putting a story on film is covered while also ensuring that the production comes in on time and on budget. The many responsibilities associated with a producer's work might involve hiring, advising, and (if need be) firing a program's writers and other key members of the crew, including the directors. For example, on one occasion, while serving as executive producer of *The Waltons*, Hamner strongly differed with a director he had recently hired because the man, without authorization, had taken it upon himself to have the white Walton house painted a bright yellow. The paint job had to be redone, returning the house to its traditional white color.

The producer also takes an active hand in approving the casting of certain roles, making sure the schedules of everyone involved in a production are in accord, comforting actors who feel put-upon by directors or fellow actors (or knocking together some heads, when needed), watching rough-cuts of programs long before they are aired to see how the story is "working," ensuring that the writing is top-notch, approving costumes, approving location, and making sure the program's music is appropriate. And there are other responsibilities: on another occasion, again during his tenure with *The Waltons*,

Hamner had to teach the entire cast the words and music to the Baptist hymn "Bringing in the Sheaves" for a particular scene.

The producer consults with the series creator, who often has the surest and best conception of the characters, how they ought to develop, which plot developments make sense, and how the series might develop over time. If the producer and creator are part of a successful series that will be extended for another season, they can look ahead together and determine, in broad strokes, story ideas for certain seasons and holidays of the year, when to introduce a new character, whether to announce that a program's newlywed characters are going to become parents, and so forth. As creator, producer, and executive story consultant for *The Waltons,* Hamner oversaw some creative changes during the screening of rough-cuts. For example:

> I remember one show that we did. We had a character named Yancy Tucker, and he and his wife were on the verge of divorce. Elizabeth was involved with these people, and she said, "I think you would be happier apart." In fact, she was urging them to get a divorce. When we got it on film and looked at it we said, "That's not the function that Elizabeth should serve. She shouldn't be urging older people to divorce. The Waltons really stand for trying to make a marriage work." So, even after we had gotten this on film, through the most clever editing I've ever seen, the editors made it appear that Elizabeth's attitude changed totally and that she was against this divorce. This was an extreme case.

This particular change was accomplished without reshooting any scenes. As Hamner added, speaking on the film editor's role,

> It was possible through cutting and substituting words, dubbing in new words, that her attitude totally changed. Often, in editing, what you do is trim down to size, take out scenes or parts of scenes that don't work, and sometimes when the whole thing is assembled it has a totally

different emphasis than you wanted when you saw the dailies; so you adjust, and shave, and improve.[2]

Hamner learned his skills as a producer by observing firsthand the work of other producers at their craft, then applying those skills as best he could after being named executive producer of *The Waltons* partway through that series' run. The learning process was not always smooth, but he had much welcome help from friends and colleagues who possessed the requisite know-how. One such person was Rod Peterson, an immensely talented writer and producer who was associated with numerous well-wrought television series, including the popular series *Combat!* during the 1960s, before working with Hamner on *The Waltons.* At Peterson's memorial service in August 2004, Hamner recalled their years together on the series with humorous affection, saying, "I was called the executive producer, but when Rod came aboard he recognized that I had no idea what I was doing. So every morning on my desk he would leave a nicely printed-out priority list. Call so and so, clear this property, attend meeting at 10:00, watch rough-cut at 1:00. I did what I was told, and more than thirty years later the series is still being seen around the world—a testament in part to Rod's devotion and contribution to the series." Their partnership, Hamner added, "continued on *Falcon Crest,* and that series prospered as well."

INTO THE TUSCANY VALLEY

Sometime shortly before *The Waltons* reached the end of its run, Hamner created a new series based upon the California wine industry. He had long been fascinated with this subject matter in general and the story of his vintner Giannini ancestors in particular. At first he crafted the concept for a program called "Fair Exchange," which would examine the lives of winery owners in California and in Italy, alternating the perspective from one country to the next every week. In time Hamner blended the idea for this show with another concept program called "The Barclays" to form a program he intended to call "The Vintage Years." Problem was, key individuals at CBS disliked the title, believing that it implied that the series was about elderly people—not the demographic they were seeking to attract for the program they envisioned. A number of alternative titles were suggested, but none of them was deemed suitable. Then Hamner thought of a house in Studio City called Falcon's Lair. With just a little adjustment to that name he soon settled upon the name of his series, *Falcon Crest,* which debuted in 1981.

In this new series, produced by Lorimar Productions, Falcon Crest is the name of a giant winery located in the fictional Tuscany Valley—modeled upon Napa Valley—north of San Francisco, California. But the story of *Falcon Crest* is about more than agriculture and business: it is about a remarkable family and the persistent pull of that family's heritage upon its members.[3] In terms of background and back-story, the Gioberti family of the series is descended from an Italian gold prospector, Giuseppe ("Joseph") Gioberti, who came to Northern California during the nineteenth century and found not

The first-season cast of *Falcon Crest* poses for a group portrait. Seated at the center is Jane Wyman (Angela Channing), while the rest of the cast, from left to right, includes: William R. Moses (Cole Gioberti), Robert Foxworth (Chase Gioberti), Jamie Rose (Victoria Gioberti), Susan Sullivan (Maggie Gioberti), Chao-Li-Chi (Chao-Li), Margaret Ladd (Emma Channing), Nick Ramus (Gus Nunouz), Abby Dalton (Julia Cumson), Lorenzo Lamas (Lance Cumson).

gold but very rich land. Joseph returned to Italy for a short time with his wife, Tessa, and there they had a son whom they named Jasper. As was the case with Hamner's Giannini ancestors, Joseph came back to America with cuttings from vines in Italy and planted a vineyard on his 50-acre farm in the Tuscany Valley. There he prospered and in time purchased the farms of his neighbors. Soon he was the master of 550 acres, immensely wealthy, and the owner of a large limestone manor house, a winery building, and a Victorian mansion. Because of the many falcons that soar in the air currents over the valley, he called his property Falcon Crest.

Jasper Gioberti was the sole heir of the entire spread. He married a woman who proved unfaithful but who presented her husband with two children, Jason (portrayed in the series by Harry Townes) and Angela (Jane Wyman). Jason grew up to become a wastrel and an alcoholic. Angela grew to be an ambitious, grasping, and conniving woman, petty and vindictive to boot—though she runs the family business expertly, while Jason spends his time idling and drinking. Both entered into unsuccessful marriages. Jason married a French woman, Jacqueline Perrault (Lana Turner), who in time left him and returned to France, taking along their son, Chase. For her part, Angela married a newspaper publisher, Douglas Channing (Stephen Elliot), and they had two daughters, Emma (Margaret Ladd) and Julia (Abby Dalton), before divorcing.

It is at roughly this point in the history of the Giobertis in America that the plot of the series begins. After the death of their father, Jason and Angela shared the Falcon Crest estate evenly. However, upon Jason's mysterious death, a codicil in their father's will takes effect and the estate is reapportioned, with Angela gaining control of 90 percent of Falcon Crest, and the remaining parcel of land coming into the possession of Jason's sole heir, Chase (Robert Foxworth), who is now a grown man and a successful airline pilot. Angela covets that remaining 10 percent of the estate and resents the presence of Chase and his wife, Maggie (Susan Sullivan), who arrive in the Tuscany Valley for Jason's funeral and fall in love with the place. Chase and Maggie Gioberti decide to settle in the Valley and become vintners alongside Angela, who is none too happy about this turn of events. She contrives to cover up all details of her brother's death, fearful that if it should be discovered that Jason died under anything other than natural causes, another clause in her father's last will and testament will take effect, dissolving Angela's control over Falcon Crest.

Over the nine years of its run, then, *Falcon Crest* concerned the intrigues of a large extended family's members for control over the entire estate. A complex web of trickery, deceit, and betrayal is spun by the various Giobertis and Channings as they seek dominance, with Angela—far from angelic, despite her name—sitting at the center of the web. The cast of characters grew large as the series ran its course. The *Falcon Crest* saga pits the few basically virtuous characters in the story—including Chase and his family, Angela's daughter Emma (described by Hamner himself as "the conscience of the show"), as well as Douglas Channing's long-lost son Richard (David Selby)—against a rogues' gallery of connivers. These include Angela's libidinous grandson, with the improbable name of Lance Cumson (Lorenzo Lamas)—a name as suggestive as the name "Manley Pointer" in Flannery O'Connor's short story "Good Country People"; Maggie Gioberti's call-girl sister, Terry Hartford (Laura Johnson); the vengeful heiress of a nearby estate, Melissa Agretti (Delores Cantu and Ana-Alicia); and Angela herself—who is pursued by a Greek businessman named Peter Stavros (Cesar Romero). With the unfolding of each subplot to the ongoing, overall saga, the various players employ an arsenal of lawyers, law-enforcement officers, fellow vintners, and local politicians in their quests for power.

In their novel *Murder in Tinseltown*, Hamner and Don Sipes depict a world in which wealth, power, and influence are the be-all and end-all of life. In this world everything and everyone has a price; each friendship is a prelude to a betrayal, and one's enemies of today might be one's allies tomorrow, and vice versa. To a somewhat lesser extent, this is the story of *Falcon Crest*, too—but with a difference. The difference lies in the depth of character and character development, along with an emphasis upon the bonds of family in the ongoing saga, insisted upon by Hamner from the series' outset. Unlike so many nighttime dramas, Hamner invested his characters with realistic nuances and complexity. The more virtuous characters are not an impossible group of goody-goodies but rather flesh-and-blood people troubled by temptation and failings of every sort. Likewise, Angela and her cohorts are not one-dimensional villains driven by greed and selfishness; they also possess a deep love for their families and a love for the land that goes beyond the fortunes Falcon Crest's rich loam has provided them. In the series' final episode, "villainous" Angela Channing, portrayed by Jane Wyman, steps away from a wedding celebration and walks to a quiet place, where she delivers a moving soliloquy in tribute to the land and her heritage. In words reminiscent of Hamner, though written by another writer (Robert Cochran, who is perhaps best known today as the creator of the Emmy Award–winning series *24*), she speaks as if to the long-dead Joseph Gioberti, saying:

> Grandfather, how long has it been since you came to the valley and planted your first vine from Italy? I remember how you used to hold me on the saddle, riding through the fields, and teaching me about the land and the vineyards, and how precious they are together. Seems like only yesterday. . . .
>
> I'm going to do everything I can to keep the vineyard and the winery the jewel of the valley, just as you always dreamed it would be.
>
> Yes, the past has its place, but I'll keep looking to the future. After all, there's a wedding today; children are playing, more children on the way; and of course, the land—always the land. People come and go, but the land endures.
>
> A toast to you Falcon Crest—and long may you live![4]

These lines, written and spoken long after Hamner had left the series, are reminiscent of Gerald O'Hara's tribute to "the red earth of Tara" in *Gone with the Wind;* but they are more closely reminiscent of a passage referenced earlier in this book: Hamner's concluding narration to the episode of *The Waltons* titled "Founder's Day," when, in the persona of the mature man known long ago to his family as John-Boy, he speaks to his first loves and first guides, saying:

> Grandpa, in memory I touch your face. A distance from
> me now, I feel you near. The coyote will disappear from
> the Earth, and the whooping crane will follow the passen-
> ger pigeon, but you will endure through all of time.
>
> Grandma, I touch your hand and when I do I touch
> the past. I touch all the ships that brought us to this coun-
> try and all the strong brave women who faced the frontier
> and made it home.
>
> [Of his parents, John and Olivia Walton:] Strength
> and love came together here. So not the same they did not
> seem a pair, bound together, they were so much one. All I
> ever want is what they've had so long and lived so well.
>
> [Of his brother Jason:] A brother with an alien name.
> The ancient Jason went searching for the Golden Fleece.
> Our Jason makes voyages every day and never leaves the
> piano.
>
> [Of his sister Mary Ellen:] A first baseman grown to
> wife and mother—soft and stronger as she grew.
>
> [Of his brother Ben:] A temper, always at the ready,
> hides the best of him, but I know my brother as my friend.
>
> [Of his sister Erin:] A pretty girl deepens into beauty.
> Impatient for time to pass and bring her love.
>
> [Of his brother Jim-Bob:] His head most often in the
> clouds causes the rest of him to stumble, but seldom really
> fall.
>
> [Of his sister Elizabeth:] A little sister full of wonder
> and far enough behind to be a joy.
>
> [Of storekeepers Ike and Corabeth Godsey:] And
> close as family were our neighbors linked to us in ties as
> strong as blood.
>
> Gentility and graciousness lived there too. The past
> flowing into the present. The present blending with yes-
> terday.

I have walked the land in the footsteps of all my
fathers, back in time to where the first one trod, and
stopped, saw sky, felt wind, bent to touch Mother Earth,
and called this home. This mountain, this pine and hem-
lock, oak and poplar. Laurel, wild, and rhododendron.
Home and mountain. Father, Mother. Grow, too, the sons
and daughters, to walk the old paths. To look back in
pride in honored heritage. To hear its laughter and its
song. To grow, to stand and be themselves, one day
remembered. I have walked the land in the footsteps of all
my fathers. I saw yesterday and now look to tomorrow.

One Thing After Another

Over the course of its nine-season run, *Falcon Crest* was gifted with
a remarkable cast. In addition to the cast members mentioned earlier, other major actors who played roles on the program included E.
G. Marshall, Cliff Robertson, Ursula Andress, Celeste Holm, Robert
Stack, Kim Novak, Lauren Hutton, Eddie Albert, Morgan Fairchild,
and Gina Lollobrigida, among others. One of Hamner's favorite stories involves his memory of the magnitude of the stars who had a
hand in the success of *Falcon Crest.* The first to agree to appear in a
regular role was Jane Wyman, and Hamner knew that "if you cast
somebody like Jane Wyman, then you're able to attract stars of equal
stature." He adds:

> I think one of the first social occasions we had was at a
> hotel over in Westwood called The Marquee. I was the
> host, and as I looked down the table I thought, My God,
> here I am, a country boy from the backwoods of Virginia,
> a redneck, a hillbilly, who accidentally became educated
> and privileged, and I'm looking down the table where I
> see Cesar Romero, Esther Williams, Fernando Lamas,
> Susan Sullivan, Bob Foxworth—I mean, here I am, the
> host for these brilliant stars! And I am very star-struck;
> even today I look at actors and I keep forgetting that I hire
> actors—and fire them![5]

But with much success came heartaches. During his years as executive producer of *The Waltons,* Hamner had enjoyed a vast amount of freedom in that role, working with little interference from the network as to the feel and direction of the series. At the outset of *Falcon Crest,* as creator and executive producer, Hamner likewise had definite ideas as to how the series ought to develop. For one thing, he intended that *Falcon Crest* would follow in the pattern of *The Waltons* in one key respect: as a weekly series, it would be episodic, with every episode telling a discreet new story altogether unrelated to what happened the previous week. Viewers would not have to "tune in next week" to learn how the central conflict of this week's program was resolved. This put the show in sharp contrast to other nighttime dramas of the era—such as *Dallas, Knots Landing,* and *Dynasty*—which were basically serials, with each week's episode continuing a story from previous weeks, and with episodes often concluding with a cliffhanger ending. The difference between these two concepts might be likened to the difference between reading a collection of short stories, on one hand, and reading through the chapters of a novel, on the other. In the one scenario, the writer starts out fresh with a largely blank slate every week; in the other, the writer must work within a continuum of an ongoing plot.

Also, from the beginning the focus of the new series was to be upon the Gioberti family, centering upon the family matriarch. As originally conceived, "The show was intended to focus on a contemporary family's search for meaning, their flight from a pressured, hectic, high-anxiety urban life to the rural setting of the father's boyhood home. All this was planned, in Hamner's overview, as an 'eight o'clock' show. That is, it would be suitable for children, pitched to families in that time slot when children often control program selection. The focus was changed, in decisions influenced by Lorimar and by CBS. Obviously, the enormous success of *Dallas,* and to a lesser extent, that of *Knots Landing,* had much to do with the choice to make the program a 'ten o'clock' show."[6] As Horace Newcomb and Robert S. Alley noted in their important study *The Producer's Medium:*

The *Falcon Crest* that came to television still focuses on families, on extended networks of them, in fact. At the level of plot we deal with murder and extortion, eager and relatively frequent sexual activity, financial chicanery, and internal family stress. But the differences from the earlier design and certainly from *The Waltons* run deeper than this. Here generation plots against generation in efforts to build or thwart dynasty. The wisdom of age still functions, but now the wisdom is tainted by secret knowledge of past scandals and is directed toward the manipulation of power. The exuberance of youth is marred by ambition and misdirected desire.[7]

This focus upon the doings of a large wealthy family, plagued with all the plottings, betrayals, and machinations characteristic of other nighttime dramas, puzzled many of Hamner's fans who had followed his career during the *Waltons* years. And while Hamner was pleased that the emphasis upon family was retained, he was uncomfortable with the overall change. Still, he insisted that there was a distinct difference between his series and other nighttime dramas, saying, "It's Gothic drama, it's human conflicts. The other series do not have the same dimension that my characters do on *Falcon Crest*."[8] As for his recurrent emphasis upon family, he looked to what had worked well for him in the creation of past concepts, telling Australian writer Alex Paige: "I think a lot of writing is autobiographical. Thomas Wolfe said in *Look Homeward, Angel* that 'each of us is all the sums he has not counted: subtract us into nakedness and night again, and you shall see begin in Crete four thousand years ago the love that ended yesterday in Texas.' To me this implies that our family history goes back longer than we know. Anyway, family has worked for me."[9] These characteristics of *Falcon Crest* have been commented upon by journalist Paige, who wrote: "Depth of characterization and leading characters with a strong moral sense (the Gioberti family) distinguished *Falcon Crest* in its early years from the other nighttime soaps of the period. None of the characters in those other programs had the same emotional depth.

Dallas had characters with a rich back-story, *Knots Landing* had leading characters with strong morals. But *Falcon Crest* was the only program that combined the two to form fully dimensional characters, which gave it a depth none of the others could boast."[10]

But whatever creative freedom Hamner may have envisioned in his role with *Falcon Crest,* things changed very early in the series' run. From the outset there was pressure from Hamner's superiors to make the series a serial, beginning with a recurrent suspense theme—Who killed Jason Gioberti?—being insisted upon for the first season. A subsequent plot element involving Nazi treasure was introduced by the writers and producers, and then eliminated at the insistence of one person at CBS. There was pressure to add more sex and violence, though Hamner was far more interested in developing the characters and telling interesting stories. As Hamner diplomatically said during one interview, "I must say I get more input on *Falcon Crest* than I did on *The Waltons* both from Lorimar executives and from the network. I don't think any of them ever understood what made *The Waltons* work, they sort of left me alone, but I think that they feel more secure in drama like *Falcon Crest.* They have more to say and it's really a script by committee. You negotiate lines of dialogue, you don't write them."[11] For the first three seasons especially, Hamner was able to fend off much of this pressure. However, over time the series began to bend to display many of the trappings and devices of every other nighttime soap opera on TV, and he began to become disenchanted with the show. This downturn in his interest was intensified by a most unwelcome legal action.

In 1982, a writer named Anita Clay Kornfeld brought a lawsuit against Hamner, claiming he had lifted the idea for *Falcon Crest* from her novel *Vintage* (1980). The suit went to trial and saw Hamner vindicated. As he later explained, any writer who sets out to craft a fictional work on the wine industry in Napa Valley will cover ground common to all such works on that topic: large farms, Mexican laborers, an upper-class standard in the way of stores and restaurants, wealthy landowners who display a degree of corruption and the desire to monopolize, and so forth. In this lawsuit, Hamner faced the same heartache of frustration that had beset his old friend

Rod Serling many years earlier, when several science-fiction writers wrongly accused Serling of stealing their material and reproducing it in episodes of *The Twilight Zone.* In the end Hamner was cleared of wrongdoing, but it was a hollow victory; he felt exhausted, distracted, and sickened that his integrity had been brought publicly into question. Laboring under such pressures, he left *Falcon Crest* at the end of the fifth season.

Despite this, Hamner is for the most part proud of his involvement with *Falcon Crest* and especially that it is still being televised in syndication, with a large viewing audience in Germany, especially. As he said in an interview concerning the series, "I left at the end of the fifth season. I never even watched it again, I was not pleased with the direction it was going in . . . and I also was not sympathetic to some of the people that were brought aboard. And I was tired, and being in charge with whatever happens on the show, you take the glory and the credit as well, but I had taken that for so long, about fifteen years with both *The Waltons* and *Falcon Crest,* so I was very tired, and I didn't feel that I was . . . coping as I might. And also I had become extremely well to do and didn't need to work. Although now, I need—not for the money, but to prove to myself and to others in the business that age need not impair one's talent, but on the contrary can contribute the benefit of experience the years have brought and, if we've been lucky, even a small smidgeon of wisdom."[12] As Alex Paige wrote in a recent summary assessment of *Falcon Crest,* it is his impression that "Earl had far less control over *Falcon Crest* than *The Waltons* and that the network and Lorimar executives exerted much greater influence over the former than the latter. Add to this that the concept as originally devised by Earl was intended as a family show and that its move to a later timeslot than initially slated required considerable modification to the pilot script and program direction, and ultimately *Falcon Crest* must be judged as a compromised expression of Earl's vision. It seems each year the compromise became greater until finally Earl decided to leave the program." However, overall the program compares well to other nighttime dramas, such as *Dallas* and *Knots Landing,* says Paige: "In essence it was a far less superficial treatment of the human beings with which it dealt. That this was lost from the program soon after Earl departed gives a fair indication of its point of origin."[13]

BREWSTER PLACE, WITH OPRAH WINFREY

During the 1970s, Hamner attempted to create a new series that would depict an extended black American family. The family would be poor but proud, closely knit, and able to weather the storms of life through faith, humor, determination, and family love. This would be a series designed to spotlight African-American life while appealing to a sense of commonality across racial and ethnic lines, moving beyond the various black sitcoms of the '70s with their non-stop formulaic jokes. Hamner has since referred to his concept as "the black *Waltons*," and it never came to fruition.[14] But he did make several attempts, the first being a series he envisioned and titled "The Douglas Family." The pilot for this series, a television movie titled *A Dream for Christmas,* was aired on December 24, 1973, but it aroused little interest at the time. (Interestingly, after being released on video, *A Dream for Christmas* has attracted the enthusiastic interest of a whole new generation of viewers.) A second attempt to initiate a "black *Waltons*," titled "The Ricky-Ticky Schoolhouse," was filmed but never aired.

But the idea of producing a series that would treat black Americans with respect and dignity never left Hamner's mind. At about the time *Falcon Crest* came to the end of its run, he got his first chance in many years to at least lend his influence toward enabling a more visible African-American presence on commercial television. The program, spearheaded by the immensely popular American talk-show host and film actress Oprah Winfrey, was called *Brewster Place.* It was based upon a 1989 miniseries titled *The Women of Brewster Place,* which was in turn based upon a novel by that name written by Gloria Naylor.

Having been cast in a leading role in *The Women of Brewster Place,* Winfrey served as executive producer of the new television series, assuming a prominent role behind the camera as well. She

Top, The combined post office and train station (now closed) beside the railroad track at Rockfish. This is the only public building in the village. *Above,* In a photo taken in 2004, Audrey Hamner relaxes in the living room of the vastly remodeled private residence that was once the Daniel J. Carroll Memorial Hospital in Schuyler. Audrey, Earl, and two of their siblings were born in the hospital room that once occupied this corner of the building.

sought to bring into being a series that would ride upon the strengths of the miniseries while avoiding its weaknesses. Winfrey shared her responsibilities in *Brewster Place* with two seasoned producers she enlisted as co-executive producers, Don Sipes and Hamner. Expressing hope for the series' success, *New York Times* television critic John J. O'Connor claimed, "Ms. Winfrey has been astute in choosing her own partners for the series. The other executive producers, and the writers of the first show, are Donald Sipes and Earl Hamner. Mr. Hamner created *The Waltons* and clearly knows a thing or two about solid family entertainment built around shared hopes and dramas."[15]

Set in Chicago during the year 1967—a time of immense racial upheaval in the United States—*Brewster Place* is the story of a kind, lion-hearted, middle-aged woman named Mattie Michael who struggles to hold her spirits up and her struggling urban neighborhood together. Winfrey herself starred as Mattie, reprising the role she had played in *The Women of Brewster Place.* In the opening episode of the series, she loses her job as a hairdresser for standing up to her boss, who claims, "I am your superior," to which Mattie defiantly replies, "I have no superior but God." Having lost her job, Mattie is convinced by her friend Etta Mae Johnson (portrayed by Brenda Pressley) to invest her life savings in the down-at-the-heels La Scala Restaurant. Mattie does so reluctantly; and in the few episodes that were filmed during the series' short run—during May and June of 1990—*Brewster Place* depicted her ongoing struggle to hold body and mind together among her friends, with all their foibles, and among those who patronize the restaurant, in a place where hope for tomorrow is in short supply. In the neighborhood known as Brewster Place, faith in one's friends and in God, along with courageous determination, must be actively grasped daily in order to carry on. Among the characters who swim into Mattie's orbit daily are the mean-spirited neighborhood gossip, Miss Sophie (Olivia Cole), the young lovers and social activists Kiswana Browne and Abshu Kamau (Rachel Crawford and Kelly Neal), and La Scala's white cook, Mickey Adriano (John Speredakos).

Television critics were mixed in their assessment of *Brewster*

Place. Writing in the *Wall Street Journal,* Robert Goldberg assailed the program as "full of cheap sentimentality," with each episode seeming "to sag under the weight of a simplistic moral." He added that in Mattie's restaurant, "platitudes are dished out with the grits, and clichés are recited as if they were deep philosophy: 'They say that the Lord works in mysterious ways. . . . The winds of change started blowing through my life.'" However, he praised the program's theme song, performed by the immensely talented a cappella group Take 6, as well as the presence of Winfrey herself, who "fills the screen like an earth mother, a life force."[16]

On the other hand, *New York Times* TV critic John J. O'Connor came to a position entirely different from his counterpart at the *Wall Street Journal,* writing, "The black sensibility that informs this series is not heavyhanded. The details are sketched in lightly, from the street sign urging voter registration to the photograph of the Rev. Dr. Martin Luther King Jr. hanging in Mattie's restaurant. There is also a scene next week in which Mattie tells off Mickey for pouting: 'I feel people are looking at me because I'm white,' he complains. 'I know how you feel,' she assures him. The tables are turned adroitly."[16] But the critics were united in their view that *Brewster Place* offered a vast improvement over the miniseries by portraying African-American men in a positive light, where in *The Women of Brewster Place* all the black men were, in O'Connor's words, "either invisible or downright rotten."

Why did the series not succeed? As Hamner has claimed in the past on occasion, for a television series to succeed, a great many factors need to work, including the casting, the music, the direction, the production, the editing, the chemistry of the actors working with each other, the manner in which the opening credits are presented, and any of many small but important factors, including the time slot in which it is scheduled. (To briefly illustrate this point: One of the most successful ensemble comedies of the 1970s, *Welcome Back, Kotter,* came to an abrupt end when the programming department at ABC changed the day and time of the series once too often, moving it into a Friday night time-slot. In the United States, Friday night is traditionally "date night" for teenagers, who were the program's tar-

EARL HAMNER

get audience. After this scheduling change, the series folded within a very short time.) *Brewster Place* had many advantages in its favor, and it is unclear why it failed. Certainly the success of *The Cosby Show,* which aired during the same era as *Brewster Place,* provided evidence that the American viewing public was ready to accept African Americans in roles involving something other than non-stop wise-cracking and ribald comedy. It may be that critic Robert Goldberg was correct in his concerns about the program's sentimentality and its appeal to a "simplistic" morality—although, strangely, these same qualities worked well for *The Waltons.* For his part, Hamner believes (and, with gentlemanly courtesy, only hesitantly suggests) that it may very well be that *Brewster Place* came to a quick end because its viewer base had certain expectations of the series' star: "I think Oprah's fans expected to see Miss Winfrey in all her very real charm and stylishness and loveliness, and instead she portrayed this sort of dowdy-looking older woman. Now, don't get me wrong! She performed marvelously—but I suspect that what her fans saw was not the Oprah Winfrey they were expecting. And that may have worked against the series." In the end, though, one can only speculate; it may never become clear why *Brewster Place* failed to take wing.

A "WESTERN" FROM DOWN UNDER: *SNOWY RIVER*

Like *Brewster Place, Snowy River: The McGregor Saga* sprang from a successful predecessor—in this case, a movie titled *The Man from Snowy River* (1982), which starred Kirk Douglas. But unlike *Brewster Place, Snowy River* saw some limited success as a series, enjoying a four-season run on the Family Channel from 1993 to 1996. The executive producers of the program were Sipes and Hamner, along with Richard Becker and Russell Becker.

At the very root of both the movie and the TV series was a lengthy poem written by Australian bush-balladist Andrew Barton ("Banjo") Paterson, titled "The Man from Snowy River." This poem is crafted as a ballad celebrating the feats of a legendary young mountain horseman who "hails from Snowy River, up by

Kosciusko's side," and his fearless horse, as they chase down a runaway colt through treacherous terrain; and it is written in a thumping rhythm reminiscent of Rudyard Kipling's "Gunga Din." Loosely based upon Paterson's poem, the television series *Snowy River* centers upon a large cattle-ranching family headed by Matt McGregor (Andrew Clarke), the mature "Man from Snowy River." As in the poem and the movie, horses and cattlemen are central to *Snowy River,* along with such essentials as tests of character and courage amid a harsh but beautiful landscape. To American audiences its general concept was remarkably similar to the Western dramas they had known and enjoyed during the 1960s, such as *The Big Valley, The Virginian,* and *Bonanza.* But *Snowy River* is a saga of cattle-ranching not in the Old West but in Australia, thus tapping into Americans' affection for the land they had become intrigued with through the hugely successful television miniseries *The Thorn Birds.*

But bringing the new series to life was a challenge. A major figure in Australian television-programming production, Lynn Bayonas, was approached by *Snowy River*'s production company, Becker International, to work with Hamner and Sipes to develop the show until the point at which pre-production began. This meant outlining story ideas and working with the series' writers on the first thirteen scripts, assembling a cast, finding the first director and the line producer. In addition, the producers needed to build facades for a complete 1860s-era town, Paterson's Ridge, as well as locate authentic costumes, many horses, and all things associated with period drama. "And just to make it really difficult," Bayonas recalls, "we started the first episode with a steam train!" She adds:

> Together with the writer we chose—Peter Schreck—we
> decided not to try and "redo" the movie (poem) but to
> move the action 25 years down the track and find Matt
> (the man) now widowed with sons. . . . Matt is a powerful
> presence in the town, and each year they hold an event
> that honors his great race to find the "colt that got away."
> The series starts with the arrival of a young man from the
> U.S. Luke has a huge chip on his shoulder and seems hell-

bent on winning the race and in the doing, humiliate Matt. It turns out this is Matt's nephew, and he has a grudge to bear with his famous uncle. The series revolved around Matt, his sons, the nephew, and the widow on the adjacent property.[18]

"The show had a terrific concept," said Don Sipes, adding, "We had a great time, lots of fun" working on *Snowy River*.[19]

The cast of *Snowy River* was admirably talented and well chosen. Matt McGregor's children—Colin (portrayed by Brett Climo), Rob (Guy Pearce), and Danni (Joelene Crnogorac)—brought believability and distinct, colorful personalities to their roles, as did Wendy Hughes, who co-starred as the widow Kathleen O'Neil, who is Matt's love interest. As portrayed by Andrew Clarke, Matt is a quiet, heroic figure, who skillfully oversees life on his family ranch, Langara. He embodies the sort of man who is portrayed in many of Banjo Paterson's poems. A critic described one of Paterson's heroes as "a type of those whose soul's compass points true north in all weathers, in every season. Circumstances do not dominate him, rendering him peevish or melancholy or bitter. He has that simple serenity of heart that can sing in solitude, work unwatched, or laugh because a touch of the infinite exhilarates him with a natural joy."[20] Coincidentally, an individual of this sort bears a marked resemblance to such creations of Earl Hamner as Clay Spencer in *Spencer's Mountain*, John Walton in *The Waltons*, Chase Gioberti in *Falcon Crest*, Joe Scott in *You Can't Get There from Here*, and even Emory Goode in *Murder in Tinseltown*. Interestingly, Lynn Bayonas later claimed, "The Snowy River saga was very much in the tradition of *The Waltons* and *Falcon Crest*." With that said, she considered Hamner the ideal choice to serve as one of the leaders of the creative team for *Snowy River*, adding, "The wonderful thing about Earl was his desire to retain the Australianness of the project. The usual experience when co-producing with Americans is one of struggling not to be just creating an off-shore American product."[21]

Snowy River enjoyed a following large enough to merit its continuation for four seasons. At the end of that time most of the original cast had moved on to other roles in other television programs, with Guy Pearce (in particular) well along in a promising career on the big screen. The series was described by *Multichannel News* as "a horse opera in the TV tradition of *The Big Valley, Bonanza* and *High Chaparral.*" Critic Kim Mitchell described it as a program offering visuals of "beautiful country and beautiful people who can spend a whole week sitting on the back of a horse chasing cattle without breaking into a sweat, much less wrinkling their clothes. Why, even the horses and cattle are spotless and shiny and well behaved. Everyone is very nice and even the bad guy is natty and polite." Still, it was "pleasant family viewing with a gentle sense of humor."[22] Asked what key contribution Hamner brought to the success of *Snowy River,* Lynn Bayonas replied, "Earl's undeniable talent, of course!"

"To Tell, to Connect, to Know": *The Ponder Heart*

After being introduced to the world of modern literature by Paul Nusnick during World War II, Hamner delighted in the fiction of numerous American writers, including Sherwood Anderson, Thomas Wolfe, William Faulkner, Elizabeth Madox Roberts, and Jesse Stuart. Another writer he deeply admired was Mississippi novelist and short story writer Eudora Welty, with whom he maintained a lively correspondence—though the two never met face to face.

Hamner first encountered her work during late 1944, when he was in the U.S. Army and living in Paris. At that time he came upon a copy of Welty's short story "The Petrified Man." As he recalled many years later, "I was raised in the backwoods of Virginia, and I had spent three years in the Army. I recognized vulgarity when I saw it. But never had I seen vulgarity elevated to such high art, and I wrote Eudora a note to that effect. Having no address for her, I addressed it simply to Eudora Welty, Jackson, Mississippi, U.S.A. That could account for the fact that the letter was never acknowledged."[23]

Many years passed, Hamner continued to read and admire Welty's works, and then one day he discovered that one of his cast members from *The Waltons,* Mary Jackson—who portrayed Miss

Above, Nancy Zimpher, President of the University of Cincinnati, presents the Frederic W. Ziv Award to Hamner for outstanding achievement in telecommunication, at a ceremony in May 2004. *Right,* Hamner delivers his prepared remarks.

Emily Baldwin—was a personal friend of Welty. Through Jackson's help, he was able to arrange for Welty to inscribe his personal copy of her novel *Losing Battles.* Not many years later, he read somewhere "that Miss Welty had missed a flight at the Los Angeles airport and had to spend an entire day waiting for the next plane. I wrote to her, sending detailed information as to how she might reach me if such a thing ever happened again. I vowed that I would rush to LAX, bring food or drink, whatever would please her. I waited for years for the phone to ring and for that gracious Southern voice to say, 'I'm at the airport.'"[24] But that call never came.

In time ALT Films, in cooperation with PBS station WGBH in Boston, began plans to film an adaptation of Welty's novella *The Ponder Heart* for an edition of *Masterpiece Theatre.* To Hamner's delight, he was asked by Marian Rees, the executive producer of the venture, to serve on the production team, along with Don Sipes. He accepted eagerly and threw himself into bringing to life *The Ponder Heart,* which was filmed on location in Canton, Mississippi, a small town near Jackson. In addition to his work as a producer of the program, he enjoyed the opportunity of working for a short time near the city where the author of the work lived. Welty was still living at her home in Jackson at the time the filming of her novella took place, but she was too ill to receive visitors. Learning of this, and wishing to respect an author he deeply admired, Hamner drove to her house and simply stood on the sidewalk outside for several minutes, facing her home with his hand over his heart.

In the PBS presentation, *The Ponder Heart* consists of the reminiscences of Edna Earle Ponder, owner of the Beulah Hotel in fictional Clay, Mississippi, as she speaks in a voice-over about her experiences with her uncle, Daniel Ponder. The son of the wealthiest man in Clay County, kind-hearted Uncle Daniel has embarrassed and exasperated his family for many years by simply giving away his money and possessions without a second thought. A small conspiracy of well-meaning family members sets out to tame Uncle Daniel, at the instigation of his exasperated father, Sam ("Grandpa") Ponder. Grandpa is afraid that after he dies, Daniel will give away everything he has ever worked for. He first tries to have Daniel committed to the Whitefield Asylum, a nearby sanitarium. In a humorous mix-up at the front desk, Grandpa Ponder is committed to the asylum, while Daniel, blithely free, is driven home by Narcissa Wingfield, the family maid and chauffer. With the intervention of the Ponder family lawyer, Grandpa is quickly released from Whitefield, and soon he and Edna Earle decide that Uncle Daniel might settle down if he were married. Within a very short time they decide upon the perfect match for him, a respectable widow named Teacake Magee. Daniel is entirely in favor of this arrangement, but on the way to the wedding ceremony he meets a simple, seventeen-year-old country girl named Bonnie Dee Peacock and quickly marries her instead. The marriage takes place so quickly that Daniel arrives at the originally scheduled ceremony and introduces his new bride, Bonnie Dee, to his astonished family, his wedding guests, and the jilted bride herself. This match is the despair of the family, as now Uncle Daniel has not only wed the wrong woman and deeply embarrassed Teacake, but he has also married beneath his station.

Newly married Bonnie Dee becomes the wealthiest woman in Clay County after Grandpa Ponder dies suddenly, shocked by the sight of his new daughter-in-law wearing the wedding gown of his own late wife. "It's the Ponder heart," Edna Earle explains early in the drama. "It's big but it's weak." Marital strains soon develop between the newlyweds, as the Ponder wealth goes to poor Bonnie Dee's head and transforms her into something of a high-living hellcat. But then she dies one night at the Ponder house, frightened to death during a violent thunderstorm when a ball of fire shoots into the house from the chimney. Daniel, who had been the only other person in the room at the time of Bonnie Dee's death, is indicted for murder by the local district attorney, pompous Dorris Grabney, who despises the Ponders. When the case comes to trial, Daniel is defended by the young, not particularly sharp family attorney, who has an unpromising nickname, DeYancey "Tadpole" Clanahan. In the end Uncle Daniel finds himself at the center of a bizarre trial at the Clay County courthouse, where he is vindicated by his reputation and the bigness of the Ponder heart.

The Ponder Heart aired on PBS in the autumn of 2001. The production was one in which everything seemed to blend harmoniously, with a lively musical score—faintly reminiscent of the music from *Driving Miss Daisy* in feel and style—by Van Dyke Parks; a well-crafted, well-paced script by Gail Gilchriest; and a superbly chosen cast. The program starred JoBeth Williams, an accomplished actress who appeared in *The Big Chill* and many other films, as Edna Earle, and Peter MacNicol, perhaps best known for his role as John Cage in *Ally McBeal,* as Uncle Daniel—the principal roles. Other strong performances were turned in by Angela Bettis as Bonnie Dee, Jenifer Lewis as Narcissa, Brent Spiner as the insufferable Dorris Grabney,

Hamner speaks on his experiences to students at the University of Cincinnati College-Conservatory of Music.

Joanne Baron as Teacake Magee, Lenny Von Dohlen as Tadpole Clanahan, B. J. Hopper as Judge Waite, and Victor Slezak as Edna Earle's beau, Ovid Springer. But the relatively unknown actor Boyce Holleman stole the show in his portrayal of Grandpa Ponder. A native Mississippian, he exhibited exactly the right accent and mannerisms of an elderly small-town Southern man with a weak heart and a history of suffering "spells" brought on by exasperation over his son Daniel.

As co-producer of *The Ponder Heart,* Hamner had one key responsibility: Because his specialty is writing, he consulted frequently with scriptwriter Gail Gilchriest on the particulars of the screenplay. "To me it all begins with the script," he said on one occasion. "I know, at least in my case, I am in on the conception of the idea, the discussion of it, and then follow it all the way through in all aspects of the production of the particular script. But in the beginning it is a script, and the producer and the story editor and the

EARL HAMNER

writer have to get it off the ground."[25] In advising Gilchriest he was careful to observe the same rule of thumb he had followed with all other adaptations of which he had been a part: First, do no harm. That is, try to maintain the integrity of the original writer's work. With *The Ponder Heart,* this was a challenge, for as he told interviewer Kirk Nuss, Welty's novella "is a told story, and the narrator is all over the place. The structure that is required for a film is not the same structure that one would use or that Miss Welty used in telling her story. So first I think we had to organize the story in a kind of chronological order and then hang as much as possible of her original work onto that new framework."[26]

In terms of structuring the drama, Hamner first suggested that the role of Edna Earle be similar to that of the Stage Manager in Thornton Wilder's *Our Town:* overseeing the plot and being ever-present throughout the drama. "And she would comment, and she would tell, and she would illuminate what was going on, which would have enabled us to have stuck exactly to the way Eudora told her story within the reason and within the confines of film," added Hamner.[27] But sometime during the pre-production planning for the drama, Hamner was told by his associates that they preferred a more traditional television-drama approach, without a frequently present narrator, and that is how *The Ponder Heart* was filmed initially. But as production progressed, it became apparent to everyone associated with the project that Edna Earle's voice was needed throughout the unfolding drama—as Hamner had originally suggested—and that without it there would be gaps in the story and puzzling leaps in the action that would confuse the audience if not addressed effectively. Thus, in the finished production, the viewer will notice what Hamner termed "occasional comments, narration, and insertions of her voice to keep her presence there as storyteller." Edna Earle's presence is vital throughout, from her opening words, "My Uncle Daniel is just like your uncle, if you've got one. Only he has one weakness: he loves happiness. And sometimes he gets carried away." As Hamner notes, "She is the once-upon-a-time voice."[28]

From a writer's perspective, one of the more difficult points in the film adaptation lay near the very end, at the conclusion of the courtroom scene. The situation is this: During a dinner break, while all the participants in the trial are enjoying lunch at the Beulah Hotel, Daniel goes downtown alone and closes out his account at the local bank. No reason is given for this action. All the audience knows is that Uncle Daniel did not murder his young wife. Later, back at the courtroom, the trial comes to an end and the jury is charged by the county judge. At that moment, Daniel rises, faces the jury and spectators, and announces, "I guess I won't be needing this where I'm going!"—and proceeds to dip into his jacket pockets and fling handfuls of cash into the air among the townspeople present. There is a mad scramble for the money, and Judge Waite gavels for order. When order is finally restored, the jury foreman announces that the jury has already reached its verdict and has found Daniel Ponder not guilty. There is jubilation throughout the courtroom, and Daniel hugs even the radiantly happy Teacake Magee, who had earlier testified bitterly against him at trial because he had jilted her.

Hamner and Gilchriest were determined to see this scene written in such a way that Daniel's reckless throwing away of his cash would not be interpreted as a flamboyant bribe, and they believe they succeeded. Hamner said of this scene, "I don't think that Miss Welty intended it to look like a bribe, so we had Uncle Daniel go to the bank beforehand sort of convinced that he was going to be convicted even though he knew he was innocent, and we gave him a line saying, 'I won't need this where I am going,' and he throws huge piles of money into the air. And it's after that, that he is pronounced innocent. I think it is open to interpretation, and we chose that interpretation."[29]

Actor Peter MacNicol has said that in his portrayal of Daniel Ponder, he envisioned Uncle Daniel as "God's fool." Hamner thought this an entirely appropriate interpretation of the role, as it explains Daniel's hilarious generosity throughout his life, his gentle friendliness, his complete forgiveness of Teacake Magee and Dorris Grabney, and his giving away of every bit of his money at the very end of the story. As to this last-named act, this must have resonated with Hamner as a variation on Clay Spencer's giving away of his entire paycheck on Christmas Eve in *The Homecoming*—an episode that had its origin in a story in his own family history. To be "God's fool" means to place others before oneself, to live joyfully amid self-sacrifice, and to hold loosely to the things of this world while the world calls you crazy. Either Daniel Ponder is on to some sort of essential secret to life or else the tight-lipped, humorless Dorris Grabneys of the world are the natural lords of life. This is something to ponder.

COURTESY OF EARL AND JANE HAMNER

Earl and Jane Hamner.

Hamner was very pleased with the completed project, having found that *The Ponder Heart* adapted very well to film. He told Kirk Nuss, "I think we stayed in fact and in spirit close to the original, to the written version. Somehow when a book gets up off the page and onto the screen there is a whole other defining version of it. Once you see it, you can't imagine it anymore. It exists as you have seen it."[30] The biggest difference between page and screen lay in the cause of Bonnie Dee's death: in the book, Daniel accidentally tickled her to death in a vain attempt to calm her during the thunderstorm; in the film version, Bonnie Dee was literally frightened to death during the storm when the "ball of fire" entered the house through the chimney. Other differences include the change of the district attorney's surname from Gladney to Grabney, and the transformation of Edna Earle from a gossipy chatterbox of a narrator in the book to a fairly level-headed, straightforward storyteller onscreen.

A strong reason why the transferral of *The Ponder Heart* from page to film was so successful may lie in Hamner's great respect for Welty as a literary artist and his close identification with Southern storytelling. He declared, "I feel kinship with everything Eudora Welty has ever written. And I don't know whether it's the similar background of small town or whether it's just that she writes with such a universal voice. I know in [her novel] *Losing Battles* a family gets together, and I think they are celebrating the birthday of an elderly lady—she may be going on a hundred or something. But everybody talks at once. It reminds me so much of my own family which is a big sprawling clan of Southerners, and if you get together at a funeral, or a birth, or a birthday, everybody talks at once, and it's impossible to make any sense of what any single person is saying. It's a chorus of voices, and it's comforting, and it's exalting and wonderful. And you don't have to know what a person is saying. It's just all those voices blending together and telling. The Southern need to tell, to connect, to know. I know you, you know me, you are learning about me through my talk. I know to an outsider it sounds like babble, but to those to whom it belongs, it's communication and loving and exciting."[31] Further, "Just as one writer working with another writer's work enriches the one who is the lesser writer, I am a better writer for having worked with Eudora Welty's work. It is something ineffable. But it enriches one's own work."[32]

NOTES

1. Quoted in Irv Broughton, ed., "Earl Hamner, Jr.," in *Producers on Producing: The Making of Film and Television,* 192.

2. Hamner, quoted in Irv Broughton, ed., *Producers on Producing: The Making of Film and Television,* 201. The episode of *The Waltons* to which Hamner refers is "The Obsession," written by Juliet Packer and originally broadcast on October 19, 1978.

3. For this key insight, and for much of the *Falcon Crest* background that follows, I am indebted to the information posted on the world's premiere Web site devoted to the program, www.falconcrest.org. This site is maintained by the Deutsher *Falcon Crest* Fanclub/German Falcon Crest Fan Club.

4. Quoted (in part) in "Earl Hamner, Creator of *Falcon Crest* and *The Waltons* Interviewed by Alex Paige, July 31, 2004," http://www.arthurswift.com/experiences/earl_hamner_interview_by_alex_paige.html.

5. Ibid.

6. Horace Newcomb and Robert S. Alley, in *The Producer's Medium: Conversations with Creators of American TV,* 160.

7. Ibid.

8. Quoted in Horace Newcomb and Robert S. Alley, *The Producer's Medium: Conversations with Creators of American TV,* 164.

9. Quoted in "Earl Hamner, Creator of *Falcon Crest* and *The Waltons* Interviewed by Alex Paige, July 31, 2004," http://www.arthurswift.com/experiences/earl_hamner_interview_by_alex_paige.html.

10. Paige, letter to the author, October 29, 2004.

11. Quoted in Horace Newcomb and Robert S. Alley, *The Producer's Medium: Conversations with Creators of American TV,* 164.

12. Quoted in "Earl Hamner, Creator of *Falcon Crest* and *The Waltons* Interviewed by Alex Paige, July 31, 2004," http://www.arthurswift.com/experiences/earl_hamner_interview_by_alex_paige.html.

13. Paige, letter to the author, October 29, 2004.

14. Perhaps the closest network television ever came to bringing such a program to life was the comedy *227,* starring Marla Gibbs and a respected veteran of *The Waltons,* Hal Williams. This is not to slight the remarkable *Cosby Show,* which featured a large extended family, the Huxtables, who were nevertheless far more upscale than the Jenkins family of *227.*

15. O'Connor, "Show about Black People, with Winfrey in Charge," *New York Times,* May 1, 1990, C13.

16. Goldberg, "Breaking out of the TV Ghetto,"*Wall Street Journal,* May 7, 1990, A12.

17. O'Connor, "Show about Black People, with Winfrey in Charge," *New York Times,* May 1, 1990, C13.

18. Bayonas, letter to the author, September 21, 2004.

19. Sipes, telephone conversation with the author, September 22, 2004.

20. Archie James Coombes, in *Some Australian Poets,* 84.

21. Bayonas, letter to the author, September 21, 2004.

22. Mitchell, "Family Offers Horse Opera," *Multichannel News,* August 23, 1993, 16.

23. Hamner, "Presenting *The Ponder Heart,*" *Eudora Welty Newsletter* 25, No. 2, Summer, 2001, 8.

24. Ibid., 9.

25. Quoted in Horace Newcomb and Robert S. Alley, *The Producer's Medium: Conversations with Creators of American TV,* 163.

26. Quoted in Kirk Nuss, "An Interview with Earl Hamner, Jr.," *Eudora Welty Newsletter* 25, no. 2, Summer 2001, 10.

27. Ibid., 11.

28. Ibid., 12. In the novella, Edna Earle claims that her gregarious Uncle Daniel is fond not of happiness, but of society.

29. Ibid., 14.

30. Ibid., 14.

31. Ibid., 12.

32. Ibid., 15.

8

THE SIGNIFICANCE OF EARL HAMNER'S WORK

*[I] think that those mountainous walls which his imagi-
nation vaulted gave him the vision of an America with
which his books are fundamentally concerned.*

MAXWELL E. PERKINS, FROM A TRIBUTE DELIVERED
IN MEMORY OF THOMAS WOLFE, 1947

I tell stories that reflect an affirmative view of mankind.

EARL HAMNER, QUOTED IN *TELEVISION: ETHICS FOR HIRE?*
BY ROBERT S. ALLEY, 1977

IN AN INTERVIEW PUBLISHED IN 1981, the American man of letters Robert Penn Warren said, "Everybody knows a thousand stories. But only one cockleburr catches in your fur and that subject is your question. You live with that question. You may not even know what that question is. It hangs around a long time. I've carried a novel as long as twenty years, and some poems longer than that."[1] As was the case with Warren, Earl Hamner is a son of the upper South who has spent most of his life living away from that region but who has carried with him throughout his life the stamp of the land, its people, and their history. Both writers, for many years, carried "cockleburrs" that found expression in the form of recurrent themes in their works.

In the case of Hamner, the formative influences of his upbringing in a Southern village amid a loving family gave him a lifelong appreciation for the importance of close ties of heritage and trusting friendship, a gracious civility, an aversion to mean-spiritedness and needless violence, a disposition toward honest dealings with others, a knowledge that anything worth having must be actively pursued and grasped, and a passion for storytelling. By their example, his parents illustrated a truth articulated by NBC's *Meet the Press* moderator, Tim Russert, in speaking of childrearing: "You can lecture kids, but they really watch your behavior. You have to be a constant presence. There's no such thing as quality time."[2]

View of the Rockfish River, just south of Schuyler.

EARL HAMNER

The story of Hamner's own father's immense love and generosity toward his family, which saw its most memorable moment when he spent his entire paycheck on gifts for his family on Christmas Eve of 1933, was perhaps the biggest cockleburr that stuck with the writer. The question this episode posed for Hamner has remained with him throughout his life: Is love stronger than fear and death?

During the darkest days of the Great Depression, Doris Hamner taught her young children a song that Hamner remembers to this day:

> There's a merry brown thrush sitting up in the tree;
> He's singing to you, he's singing to me.
> And what does he sing, little girl, little boy?
> Oh, the world's overflowing with joy!

To a cynic this must seem a ridiculous song for anyone to sing during the worst economy in the nation's history. But not so to Hamner's Baptist mother, who intuited that human beings are not economic creatures alone. They are spiritual beings, responsible to each other and to their Maker for the choices they make and the way they live their lives in relation to each other. While Hamner is no regular churchgoer, has his own differences with the shortcomings of the Christian church, and is quite private about his current faith experience, the Baptist church of his upbringing—with its melding of faith and practical action, however imperfect—hovers in the background of his fictions, never far away, though never front and center.[3]

To the vast majority of Hamner's admirers this aspect of his thought first came to the fore in *The Homecoming,* both the book and television versions. Here, wrote scholar George C. Longest:

> Revelation and growth through pilgrimage, as in the legend of the Magi, fuse organically with the theme of love and the importance of community and traditional Christian celebration. Traveling through the snowbound night in search of his father, the hero recognizes the sense of community and time and place that bind mankind together:

"As he made his way past the Negro faces it came to him that he did not really know any Negroes. He knew those in the village, but he had never been in one of their homes and did not know what they yearned for or what their dreams were. He felt a sense of loss that an entire community existed within the larger community and he did not know one of them beyond his name and face." The cohesion of setting and narrative and the tie to Christian myth—the coming of light, knowledge, and love through sacrifice—is admirable.[4]

Hamner's upbringing instilled in him the knowledge that life may very well be full of tragedy but that, in the end, every person is more than the sum of his hardships and possessions. This vision of humanity says that human beings possess great transcendent value, and that through honor, courage, and high character, they can triumph over their circumstances and need not be defined by them.

This is the vision that shines through *The Homecoming, Spencer's Mountain,* and many of Hamner's other works. In these novels and screenplays, there is a sense of what the German Romantics called *sehnsucht,* an intense longing for something half-remembered that is now lost or perhaps merely drowned out by the noise of the modern world or hidden by the world's many distractions. This is a yearning for perfect joy and perfect fellowship, and in Hamner's own life, the closest this was ever realized was in the company of the big, sprawling clan of Southerners into which he was born and in which he was reared. There, as he told one interviewer, at family gatherings of any sort, everybody talks at once; and although it's impossible to make any sense of what any single person is saying, it is meaningful. It is "The Southern need to tell, to connect, to know. . . . I know to an outsider it sounds like babble, but to those to whom it belongs, it's communication and loving and exciting."[5]

Hamner's belief in the essential worth and dignity of man arises from an upbringing that reflected those norms in lives firmly rooted in a village in the Virginia foothills. The sound of Virginia wind and water and folk-song and birdsong are present in his voice and in his writings, speaking of a view of life that is essentially affirmative and hopeful. It does not paper over life's difficulties and grim realities, but rather emphasizes the need to meet those challenges with hope, imagination, courage, and dignity. This is what William Faulkner meant when he spoke of the nature of man and the responsibility of the writer "to help man endure by lifting his heart, by reminding him of the courage and honour and hope and pride and compassion and pity and sacrifice which have been the glory of his past. The poet's voice need not merely be the record of man, it can be one of the props, the pillars to help him endure and prevail."

Hamner sees men and women as a community of souls, with past, present, and future generations bound to each other in an intricate dance of inherited customs, conventions, and ways of continuity: the stories, traditions, and manners of families united in community with their own members and with the larger community outside their immediate circle, living on family land or on long-familiar ground. The novelist Mark Helprin illustrated something of this vision when he wrote, in his novel *Memoir from Antproof Case:*

> I was graduated from the finest school, which is that of
> the love between parent and child. Though the world is
> constructed to serve glory, success, and strength, one
> loves one's parents and one's children despite their failings
> and weaknesses—sometimes even more on account of
> them. In this school you learn the measure not of power
> but of love; not of victory, but of grace; not of triumph,
> but of forgiveness. You learn as well . . . that love can
> overcome death, and that what is required of you in this is
> memory and devotion. Memory and devotion. To keep
> your love alive you must be willing to be obstinate, and
> irrational, and true, to fashion your entire life as a con-
> struct, a metaphor, a fiction, a device for the exercise of
> faith. Without this, you will live like a beast and have
> nothing but an aching heart. With it, your heart, though
> broken, will be full and you will stay in the fight unto the
> last.[6]

This view of life affirms that it is good and purposeful and that the mores of a culture that values virtue and wisdom are to be embraced. It is this view, married to lively storytelling, that has proven so popular with Hamner's audience.

Critics have noted these qualities in Hamner's works and in some instances expressed their disdain about them. "This man's wholesomeness is almost predatory," complained John Leonard, in a review of one of Hamner's series. Strangely, though, some of the same critics who took offense at *The Waltons* and other Hamner programs have insisted in other contexts that we need not be offended by anything we see on television, because there is no relationship between art and life. But in the next breath, these same critics insist that a certain new television program will "improve" and "enlighten" its viewers by offending their middle-class values. This strange contradiction was pointed out by the American man of letters Wendell Berry, who once wrote, "The idea that people can be improved by being offended will finally have to meet the idea (espoused some of the time by the same people) that books, popular songs, movies, television shows, sex videos, and so on are 'just fiction' or 'just art' and therefore exist 'for their own sake' and have no influence. To argue that works of art are 'only' fictions or self-expressions and therefore cannot cause bad behavior is to argue also that they cannot cause good behavior. It is, moreover, to make an absolute division between art and life, experience and life, mind and body—a division that is intolerable to anyone who is at all serious about being a human or a member of a community or even a citizen."[7]

Hamner denies that any such division exists and is one in this belief with his friend, science-fiction writer Ray Bradbury, who has also been criticized over the years for the "moralism" of his work. In a letter to the late Russell Kirk written many years ago, Bradbury wrote some words with which Hamner heartily concurs: "The thing that drives me most often is an immense gratitude that I was given this one chance to live, to be alive the one time round in a miraculous experience that never ceases to be glorious and dismaying. I accept the whole damn thing. It is neither all beautiful nor all terrible, but a wash of multitudinous despairs and exhilarations about which we know nothing. Our history is so small, our experience so limited, our science so inadequate, our theologies so crammed in mere matchboxes, that we know we stand on the outer edge of a beginning and our greatest history lies before us, frightening and lovely, much darkness and much light."[8] This is not to deny the reality of evil as an active force in the world, for Bradbury also wrote that each one of us has "a private keep somewhere in the upper part of the head where, from time to time, of midnights, the beast can be heard raving. To control that, to the end of life, to stay contemplative, sane, good-humored, is our entire work, in the midst of cities that tempt us to inhumanity, and passions that threaten to drive through the skin with invisible spikes."[9]

Novelist Henry Miller once described Sherwood Anderson, author of *Winesburg, Ohio,* by saying, "In Anderson, when all is said and done, it is the strong human quality which draws one to him and leads one to prefer him sometimes to those who are undeniably superior to him as artists."[10] So it is with Earl Hamner, whose "strong human quality" is made known through the retelling of incidents from life that many people, across many cultures, can identify with in a manner that connects not only with the head but with the heart as well. One of his frequent correspondents, Rev. Tom Fowler of the Schuyler Baptist Church, indicated one such example in a letter to this writer, pointing to a tree-felling episode in *Spencer's Mountain.* The scene depicts Clay Spencer and his oldest son as they work to bring down a towering oak:

> The tree was supported now only by the delicate threads of wood that had been in the first decades of its life. They had pierced now to its core, had sawed through wood and time until the tons of wood and leaves and branches and twigs that stood above them were held almost by a slender thread.
>
> "She'll come down, now," said Clay to the boy. "You get back."
>
> "All right, Daddy," the boy said.

"You go all the way over yonder in the center of the field," his father said. "I won't drive the wedge in till you get there."

"Yes sir," the boy said, and ran. When he reached the center of the field he raised his hand and waved. He could not see his father any longer because he was lost in the shade of the tree, but in a moment he heard the pounding of a sledge hammer against the iron wedge. He watched with a mixture of melancholy and awe as the tree began to tremble at the top and then, like the folding of a gigantic fan, lean, then drop and explode with a great crashing sound back to the ground where it had started so long ago as a seed.

Clay-Boy ran back to the base of the tree. He found his father sitting on the raw stump. He was smoking a cigarette and looking at the tree thoughtfully.

"I felt it when she hit the ground," said Clay-Boy. "Way over there in the middle of the field I could feel it when she hit."

"A tree is a sorrowful thing to see layen down on the ground that way," observed Clay.

The tree had not yet settled against the earth. Even now a strong limb, caught in some awkward strained position, would snap; a branch would straighten itself out and fling its leaves out of the broken mass like a stricken arm trying to pretend that its trunk was not dead. Gradually a stillness came into the mass of broken limbs, no sound or movement came from it, and it was dead.

Fowler describes this passage as depicting "Classic Earl Hamner. I have seen this sight many times; have sat on the stump, and have regretted the death of the tree—haven't you?"[11]

With this strong ability to connect down-to-earth experiences with his readers and viewers, Hamner is nevertheless forever surprised by well-meaning people who have written to commend him for the "message" in a particular episode of *The Waltons* or *Snowy*

River or any of his other works. He denies there is any message. As Hamner has said on numerous occasions, "I've always considered myself a storyteller, and little more than that. I could never preach at people." (Ironically, he was given the opportunity to be trained as a Christian clergyman during his years at the University of Richmond, where his undergraduate scholarship was awarded for ministerial training. Hamner turned down that chance, claiming that he never could have endured trying to fill that vocation.) He is well aware of film mogul Samuel Goldwyn's famous dictum for screenwriters: "Pictures are for entertainment, messages should be delivered by Western Union."

It has been said by one writer that all life is an allegory that can only be understood through parable. So it is that the truths that appear within Hamner's imaginative works, woven entirely but unconsciously into their very fabric (rather than pinned on like an ornament), resound so effectively with the readers and the viewers of his work.

FROM WALTON'S MOUNTAIN TO TOMORROW

C. S. Lewis once wrote, "Humanity does not pass through phases as a train passes through stations; being alive, it has the privilege of always moving yet never leaving anything behind." And so it is with Hamner. It would be a mistake to assume, as some have, that he "outgrew" the Spencers and Waltons, attaining maturity in *Falcon Crest* and other later works. In truth, Hamner retains—amid all his success and through eighty-plus years—a sense of close identity with the sensibilities and belief systems he grew to embrace as a boy in Schuyler long ago, at a time and amid a milieu nearly forgotten today. Those mountainous walls that his imagination vaulted long ago, but to which he periodically returns, gave him the vision of humankind with which his books and screenplays are fundamentally concerned: "that we are all human, and that no matter how different we may seem from each other—by race or color, nationality or religion—we are all related by common bonds and concerns. We may be ordinary creatures, and fragile, but we

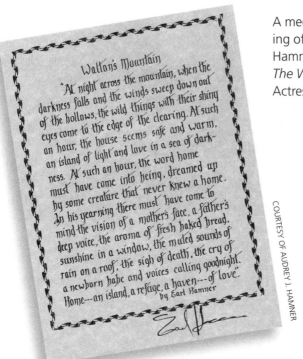

Walton's Mountain

"At night across the mountain, when the darkness falls and the winds sweep down out of the hollows, the wild things with their shiny eyes come to the edge of the clearing. At such an hour, the house seems safe and warm, an island of light and love in a sea of darkness. At such an hour, the word home must have come into being, dreamed up by some creature that never knew a home. In his yearning there must have come to mind the vision of a mother's face, a father's deep voice, the aroma of fresh baked bread, sunshine in a window, the muted sounds of rain on a roof, the sigh of death, the cry of a newborn babe and voices calling goodnight. Home---an island, a refuge, a haven---of love."

by Earl Hamner

A meditation on the meaning of *home,* written by Earl Hamner for an episode of *The Waltons* titled "The Actress," in 1972.

are still capable of strength and sacrifice and wonder and love, and, yes, even nobility."[12]

In speaking of the rightness of love, wonder, and nobility, Hamner steps into his long-accustomed role as "Mister Walton." He is pleased about and proud of his work on *The Waltons*—but yearns for recognition for his many other interests and accomplishments: "I'm fine with being 'Mister Walton,'" he has said, adding with a chuckle that "there's more to my career than that. I also want people to think of me as 'Mister *Twilight Zone*' and 'Mister *Charlotte's Web*' and any number of other names that reflect my work."[13]

Whether this desire will be fulfilled has yet to be seen. What is certain is that over the course of a half-century, Hamner has delighted, comforted, affirmed, and entertained several generations of readers and television viewers through well-told novels and programs that have bespoken a belief that love, generosity, patience, justice, and forgiveness—the qualities of his own upbringing—are key to a fulfilling life, rather than lust, betrayal, cynical indifference, greed, and vengeance—which are arguably the staples of much modern fiction and television. It takes much more patience, diligence, and self-discipline—and, therefore, time—to practice virtue than to simply default to cynicism, betrayal, and evil. In the same way, it takes many years to grow an oak, though toadstools can become fully grown overnight. The question really focuses upon which direction human beings wish to take.

In the years to come, will the norms and values reflected in *The Waltons* and Hamner's other works continue to find receptive audiences? In an essay written in the *Blue Ridge Chronicle,* Hamner himself wrote that "as more and more time goes by the lives we led on Walton's Mountain will seem distant, quaint and primitive to the people living in space colonies or whatever kind of abode people will be living in the year 2509." He adds:

> Certainly we won't see New Year's Eve of 2509, but many of us will live well into this coming century, and we will take with us some of the qualities we admire in the Walton family. Hopefully these values will still work in the strange new world ahead. Hopefully we can adapt these values so that they will still apply, still have real meaning, and still be sustaining to our descendents.[14]

To borrow and adapt one of Hamner's own titles, it *is* possible to get there from here. But to do so will require imagination, faith, memory, allegiance to the "permanent things"—the timeless norms that humanity ignores at its peril—that are illustrated in Hamner's life and work and married to prudent action, and a willingness "to fashion your entire life as a construct, a metaphor, a fiction, a device for the exercise of faith," in Mark Helprin's words. "Without this, you will live like a beast and have nothing but an aching heart. With it, your heart, though broken, will be full and you will stay in the fight unto the last."

To those who read or view Earl Hamner's work, home is a place that is always within memory and within reach of daily life. The decisions and actions taken by any one person or a small group of persons can ripple outward and affect other lives, whether one is working in the home, in the factory, in the office—or in the world of television. During an interview conducted at Lynchburg College at an event associated with a reunion of the Waltons International Fan Club, Hamner encouraged the telecommunications students in the audience to work in their local communities rather than gambling all on achieving success in New York or Hollywood:

> I have one piece of advice . . . that I do pass on to young people, which is: Don't go to New York; don't come to Hollywood, because the competition is so fierce that you're probably going to end up waiting tables—and there's nothing wrong with that—or being a car-hop—and there's nothing wrong with that—but it's not what you came there to do.
>
> Why not take advantage of whatever town you belong to, wherever you live, and create a theater, or do your own film, or write what you see, what you care about, what you know about? But do it where you are and where you have roots instead of going to New York or Hollywood, where you're just going to be put to terrible tests. Some people make it, some people don't, but the odds are so much against you, while they aren't if you stay home and work where you are. "Brighten the corner where you are," as they say in the old Baptist hymn.[15]

Further, as Hamner told the graduating class of telecommunications students at the University of Cincinnati in 2004:

> You will inherit this medium. I encourage you to remind yourselves of the power you have each time you write, act in, produce, direct, or sponsor a program.
>
> Television has the power and the ability to enlighten, to educate, to lift viewers to new levels of experience, but there is also a lot of vulgarity. Too much of what we see seems to be written from the groin. I urge you to consult another organ.

The Hamner siblings pose at an event held at the Walton's Mountain Museum. *From left:* Jim, Paul, Audrey, Nancy, Marion, Earl.

People want more family programming. They want programs they can watch with their children, without being embarrassed. They want programs about people like themselves, who aren't necessarily criminals or in need of lawyers. I know, because they tell me so, in their letters and in person.

I encourage you to keep creating meaning for television. Only from the heart can come universal truths.

Without courage, honor, compassion, pity, love, and sacrifice, as William Faulkner pointed out, we know not of love but of lust. We debase our audience. But we can ennoble and enrich our viewers and ourselves in our journey through this good time, this precious time, this green and wonderful experience we call life.[16]

Although he no longer lives in the Blue Ridge foothills, Hamner can and does take the love and the virtues of his upbringing with him throughout his travels through life, living out his "immense gratitude that I was given this one chance to live, to be alive the one time round in a miraculous experience that never ceases to be glorious and dismaying." Living life in gratitude for its gift, he can be "at home" wherever he happens to be. "'You can't go home again,' Thomas Wolfe said, a generation ago," wrote Russell Kirk on one occasion. "But some fortunate few of us still can go home—and do."[17]

NOTES

1. Quoted in "Robert Penn Warren, Poet and Author, Dies," *New York Times,* September 16, 1989, 1.

2. Quoted in Alan Fisk, "Russert Writes Loving Memoir of His Dad," *Detroit News,* April 12, 2004, E1.

3. Although he has described himself in a letter to me as "more a pantheist than anything else," Hamner acknowledges the importance of the Christian faith tradition in his development as a man, and is even in negotiations with a company in Nashville to record a CD of spoken hymns, focusing upon the words of the hymns that meant the most to his family during his formative years in Schuyler. He longs to record a hymn that was a favorite of his father, the early twentieth-century piece titled "In the Garden":

    I come to the garden alone,
    While the dew is still on the roses,
    And the voice I hear,
    Falling on my ear, the Son of God discloses.

    And He walks with me, and He talks with me,
    And He tells me I am His own;
    And the joy we share as we tarry there,
    None other has ever known.

4. Longest, *Dictionary of Literary Biography, Vol. 6: American Novelists Since World War II, Second Series,* 130.

5. Quoted in Kirk Nuss, "An Interview with Earl Hamner, Jr.," *Eudora Welty Newsletter* 25, no. 2, Summer 2001, 12.

6. Mark Helprin, in *Memoir from Antproof Case,* 514.

7. Berry, in *Sex, Economy, Freedom, & Community: Eight Essays,* 1993, 159. To anyone interested in understanding what makes for spiritual and economic health within a community—or, for that matter, what makes for true

community—I cannot recommend this book highly enough, especially the essay from which this particular quotation is taken, "Sex, Economy, Freedom, and Community."

8. Quoted in Russell Kirk, *Enemies of the Permanent Things,* 120.

9. Ibid., 118.

10. Miller, *Homage to Sherwood Anderson: 1876–1941,* 115.

11. Fowler, in a letter to the author, September 24, 2004. The episode of the tree-felling he quotes is from *Spencer's Mountain.* Interestingly, Hamner—who tends bonsai trees and is an ardent outdoors enthusiast—describes himself with a chuckle as a "tree-hugger."

12. Hamner, "Coming Home to Walton's Mountain," *TV Guide,* November 20, 1993, 14.

13. Hamner, telephone conversation with the author, January 23, 2004.

14. Hamner, "Welcome 2000: *The Waltons* and the Millennium," *The Blue Ridge Chronicle* 8, no. 1, 2000, 1.

15. Quoted in an interview conducted by Dr. Woody Greenberg with Michael Learned, at Lynchburg College, Lynchburg, Virginia, October 19, 2002.

16. Quoted in Deborah Rieselman, "Write Way to Hollywood: Electronic Media's Brightest Star Shines Light on How to Reach the Top Without Losing One's Values," in *The University of Cincinnati Horizons,* September 2004, 13.

17. Russell Kirk, "The Homing Impulse" (syndicated column), September 1, 1965. Despite differences in temperament and certain interests—Kirk, for example, held a very low opinion of television in general—I strongly suspect Kirk and Hamner would have enjoyed each other's company, what with each possessing a fondness for storytelling and good conversation, a strong belief in the central importance of family, and a fervent love of trees, nature, and natural conservation, among other similarities.

Hamner at work in his office in Studio City, March 2004.

EARL HAMNER

9

REFLECTIONS ON HAMNER'S ACCOMPLISHMENTS

We love the things we love for what they are.

FROM "HYLA BROOK," BY ROBERT FROST

EARL HAMNER IS FOND OF telling about the time he spoke before a civic group about one of his recent projects and told one or two stories from his life and career. At the conclusion, he asked if the members of the audience had any questions. As he recalls, one woman stood up and said, "I've got a question, Mr. Hamner."

He replied cheerfully, "Yes, ma'am."

She asked, "How come you talk so funny?"

Hamner paused for a moment and then explained, "All Virginians talk a little bit funny, but I talk funnier than most because I've been educated."

Everyone laughed, and the woman started to sit down, but then straightened. Something was still on her mind, and she declared reproachfully, "And you don't *look* the way I thought you would." Hamner had never heard this one before.

"Well, what did you think I would look like?"

She said, "I've heard your voice on television and I thought you would look like a skinny Colonel Sanders."

The audience tittered and Hamner replied that he had never looked like the famous fried-chicken entrepreneur, and that he hadn't been skinny since he stopped smoking many years earlier. Having said this, he was alarmed to see that the woman was still standing. She paused as if searching for the right words.

"But," she finally said, "you *seem* real sincere."

After that, there didn't seem much more to be said. One of Virginia's favorite storytellers now had another story to add to his repertoire.

The woman in this story simply wanted to know more about Hamner. His family members, admirers, and many friends from the world of television—actors, writers, producers, and directors—have their own assessments of the man and his work, and they have been immensely generous in investing the time and effort to share their own assessments of Hamner with me. What follows are those assessments, which further inform the portrait of the man and his works.

Harper Lee

Miss Lee is an American literary legend and the author of To Kill a Mockingbird. *In 1961 a letter she wrote to the Dial Press in praise of* Spencer's Mountain *was reprinted in full on the back cover of the novel. In late November 2004, she sent the following words to the author of this book.*

Since *Spencer's Mountain* I have followed Earl Hamner's career with much interest and much satisfaction, having picked a winner.

Judy Norton

Best known for her role as Mary Ellen in The Homecoming *and* The Waltons, *Ms. Norton has continued to work as an actor in the years since* The Waltons *ended its run. She has appeared in* Millennium, Stargate-SG1, *and many other programs. In addition, she served as the co-artistic director for two theaters in Canada and collaborated as a writer and director of more than forty shows that have been mounted across Canada's western provinces.*

Earl brings humor, compassion, and an understanding of human character to his writing. On a television series, corporate pressure can often bring about a deterioration of integrity for the original intent of the program. Earl always fought to maintain the heart and soul of the program: to keep the core values and dimensions of the characters. He knew these characters intimately and strove to bring them to life for the audience with their various strengths and flaws. He truly cared about the show and I believe it showed in the final product.

It was an honor and a pleasure to be a part of *The Waltons.* At the time we were filming we had no idea of the impact the show would have on so many peoples' lives. I am continually touched by the personal stories I hear regarding ways in which *The Waltons* helped people through difficult times in their lives. For example, a cancer survivor who told me that watching *The Waltons* comforted her during her chemotherapy. She looked forward to watching the show while recovering. Or the family members for whom *The Waltons* provided a role model of a caring, supportive family life. Our family "goodnights" have become legendary and I constantly hear people say that they share that tradition in their own families now. I am very proud of the quality of the show and feel it is deserving of a place in television history.

Tony Albarella

Co-author of The Twilight Zone Scripts of Earl Hamner, *Albarella is a noted authority on* The Twilight Zone *and Rod Serling.*

People are often shocked to learn that Earl Hamner's first work in Hollywood was the development of eight original scripts for Rod Serling's *The Twilight Zone.* A quick perusal of those scripts, however, reveals traits that the author both perfected and personified. Earl brought a country sensibility and an appreciation of family life to Serling's anthology, and his work complemented the talents of the series' other writers.

As the co-author of *The Twilight Zone Scripts of Earl Hamner,* I know firsthand the degree to which Earl and his roots are intertwined. While a love of the people of Virginia is evident in his work, his connection goes far deeper; Earl's very soul springs from the earth where he was born and raised. This upbringing has instilled a sense of pride in who he is and a measure of compassion so vast that Earl is compelled to share it with all who know him. The privilege of his friendship is a true blessing.

Several years ago, hoping to bring out some interesting information for *Twilight Zone* fans, I sought out Earl in his capacity as a writer. What I found was so much more: a gifted mentor, a cherished friend, a spirit bubbling with humor and bursting with infectious energy. Though separated by the breadth of the country (Earl lives on the West Coast and I on the East), we established a singular rapport and compiled our book via long, glorious sessions on the telephone and computer. At no time did it *ever* feel like work.

This professional and personal relationship was cemented when my wife, Cindy, and I first visited California to meet with Earl and Jane (his magnificent bride of fifty years, and nowhere on Earth can you find two people more loving and deserving of each other). The Hamners treated us not as newly established friends but as extended family members.

The book you now hold explores and celebrates Earl's charm, candor and wit. Readers will be reassured to know that although he's a part of movie and television history, Earl Hamner remains happily insulated from the Hollywood life. In his work and in his life, what you see is what you get. And you get quite a lot. From the feistiness of *Falcon Crest* to the imagination of *The Twilight Zone* to the warmth and tenderness of *The Waltons,* Earl's fiction is an extension of himself. His writing is alive because he lives within it.

Ellen Geer

Daughter of the late Will Geer (Grandpa Walton), Ellen Geer is an actor and Artistic Director of the Will Geer Theatricum Botanicum in Topanga, California. She herself appeared in two episodes of The Waltons: *"The Ceremony," in 1972, and "The Pledge," in 1980. Below, she responds to the question, "What did your father think of Earl Hamner?"*

I only know that Pop loved Earl. They were and are remarkable men. Pop and Earl came from the same source: a great curiosity about life, and along with this fascination, a dedication and skill to share all aspects of the human condition without fear and an abiding belief in justice, equal rights. As I remember, they never had to spend time in "talk" about the character or direction of the script: they both intuited an understanding of these things.

It is a rare gift that Earl has of allowing his heart to speak without covers and it is combined with his unique writing, which tells a story both true and involving. *The Waltons* gave the next generation the history of a family that lives and works together, and cares about one another each happy or difficult step along the way. Its simple truths are needed by Americans in 2005. American culture has a desperate need of the human values that live in Earl Hamner.

William Schmidt

A native of a blue-collar town near Pittsburgh, Pennsylvania, Schmidt came to Hollywood in the early 1980s as a young, inexperienced writer. He was mentored in the writing of teleplays by E. F. ("Ernie") Wallengren, who was himself mentored by Hamner. Schmidt wrote for Falcon Crest; Dr. Quinn, Medicine Woman; *and several other series and TV movies. He is currently writing for and producing* Carnivàle *for HBO. In the following excerpt from a lengthy telephone interview, Schmidt speaks of Hamner's work as a mentor of writers.*

When I was at Northwestern University, I decided to go into TV writing, so I wrote about forty letters to people out here [in Hollywood]—executives, studios, whoever I could think of. Only one person sent a nice letter back, and that was Earl. He told me basically, "It's hard breaking in, but Northwestern is tops, and if you're ever in Hollywood stop by." So I came out, and he had me in for an interview.

He himself didn't have time to formally mentor me. But there was a twenty-five-year-old story editor he had groomed whose mother, Claire Whitaker, worked with Earl. He went to this man, Ernie Wallengren, and said, "Look, as payback for me helping you, I'd like you to help Bill." And, thanks to Ernie, when it came time to get launched in my career, I was able to do it myself. I was at Universal for about a year and a half, and then Ernie asked me to go into *Falcon Crest*. The first few years of that run, Earl, and Ernie, and Rod Peterson and Claire, and I were the staff. (Rod and Claire were like second parents to me.) I credit all of them for my success.

Of course Earl mentored Ernie, who then mentored a number of us. The team of William Rabkin and Lee Goldberg just wrote a book on TV craft, and they dedicated it to Ernie, because he was their mentor. Earl also mentored one of the best writers in this town; her name is Karen Hall. And there are others he mentored I haven't even met. It takes a very special person to mentor, someone with a good heart. After a time Ernie said to me, "Now, *you* have to mentor." So I do as much mentoring as I can. It was just one of those things, like dropping a pebble in the water. Earl was that pebble.

Falcon Crest was a fun, glamorous show (especially with Jane Wyman heading the cast) that appeared during the time of the prime-time soaps. For a young guy—only twenty-six years old—well, they put me through my paces. I'll never forget my first script for *Falcon*. I had seen Earl's notes on it, which I think Ernie wanted to shield me from. I was devastated. But the craft that he taught me is the craft I teach others: We all go from the fount of Earl. And by the time I was done, I had written fifteen episodes of *Falcon Crest*.

As a writer, I've never met anybody who had a more natural sense of what makes drama work. I have other heroes, like Rod Serling and people like that, but nobody understands the form as well as Earl does. And also there's a confidence there. I think because he wrote these terrific novels, there's an assuredness about his writing that made him very secure. And in this town, where insecurity runs the show, that was a very unique *something*. (When I just said the word *very* I could almost hear Earl saying, "The word *very* should be cut out of the English language!") There's so much poetry in his writing. And you know Earl's style: he's never arrogant. He gently let you know what he considered good drama.

Sometimes, as a producer, Earl was, frankly, too nice a guy. He was extremely conciliatory—and there were times, I have to admit, that I wanted him to knock some heads together—we all did—but he had (and has) his own way. It's a way you don't see any more, and I mourn the passing of his way in this business: this way of getting your point across and being a wonderful guy, but being very strong about it. So I guess I would say his style was softer than other styles I've seen. And yet I think we produced a hell of a show. He had this fabulous way of making the cast feel very good. Because Earl is such a gentleman and treated everybody with respect, everybody there treated each other with respect.

During the *Falcon Crest* years, he always said to me as a writer, "Clean lines . . . clean lines." He always said to the art directors and the costumers, "Clean lines." And I think these guys didn't even know they were seeing clean lines, but they knew they liked it. That's kind of it in a nutshell, what he was about as a producer.

A little story: The head of the TV film department at Northwestern was Dr. Martin Maloney. After I wrote my initial letter to Earl, I spoke to Dr. Maloney because Earl had mentioned he went to Northwestern for a short time. And I said to Dr. Maloney, "You were head of the department when Earl was here. What did you think of him?" He said, "Oh, he was a wonderful writer. When he was here I told him, 'Earl, you've got to stop writing this stuff about these poor people in Virginia—otherwise you're not going to get anywhere.'" And Maloney added, "Fortunately he didn't take any of my advice!"

John McGreevey

McGreevey is one of the most respected television writers in America, with writing credits extending back to the 1950s. A longtime close friend of Hamner, he wrote more than twenty episodes of The Waltons, *more than any other writer for that series. According to information posted at Ralph Giffin's* Waltons *Web site, McGreevey is responsible for creating two of the most memorable characters in the series: Verdie Grant and Corabeth Walton Godsey.*

Earl is a master of character detail. In the development of the script he was constantly on the alert for the false note—eliminate it!—tireless in his pursuit of the true. When you're sure you have found it, underscore it. It is the genuineness of the characters that won *The Waltons* its original audience and is delighting millions of people still today.

I sat in dozens of story meetings with Earl over the many seasons of *The Waltons.* When we would have rejected this springboard or that story germ and our creative juices seemed stagnated, after a long pause, Earl would sit up abruptly. "How about this? The Baldwin ladies wake up one morning, look out onto their lawn. They see—(very dramatic pause) a camel!" Earl is grinning impishly and the story editor, producer, and I are groaning, laughing. "No, Earl. No! Not the camel again! Please!" That story meeting would adjourn. The camel story was never written.

Ronnie Claire Edwards

Best known for her role as Corabeth Walton Godsey on The Waltons, *Miss Edwards is a distinguished director and actor who has appeared in many television programs, including* Dynasty; Designing Women; *and* Murder, She Wrote—*in addition to Hamner's own short-lived series* Boone. *She is the author of a remarkable memoir,* The Knife Thrower's Assistant: Memoirs of a Human Target *(2000).*

Earl is a gentleman—a gentleman at work in a world in which he and the rest of us are often surrounded by barbarians. And because he is a gentleman, has high expectations of those he works with, and knows how to handle difficult situations in a gracious manner, you don't want to disappoint him!

Beyond that, I think one of his key strengths is that he understands—more so than most writers and producers—what an actor does, how an actor works, how an actor handles material. And that is so unique among television people, and such a gift to those of us who have worked with him.

Paul Hamner

Earl Hamner's only surviving brother, Paul, lives in New Jersey, where he has worked for many years in the shoe business. He remembers growing up in the same household of love, mutual support, laughter, and loyalty recounted so memorably by his writer brother.

Earl was influenced by my parents, and with God's blessing he saw Mom and Dad thrive and never give up during very trying times. He saw our parents as part of a network of close relatives and friends. With thanks to Mom and Dad and a higher power, I must say I am very happy to call Earl Hamner my brother.

Patricia Neal

Legendary actress Patricia Neal is a native Kentuckian who has roots in Hamner's home state of Virginia. Having co-starred with Gary Cooper in The Fountainhead *(1949), with John Wayne in* Operation Pacific *(1951), with Paul Newman in* Hud *(1963), and in numerous other motion pictures and television programs, she portrayed Olivia Walton in* The Homecoming *in 1971. She spoke with the author by telephone in November 2004.*

Earl Hamner is a very good writer—he really is—and a divine man. And I loved the fact that *The Homecoming* and *The Waltons* were about his family. I like his wife and his two children, and I liked his mother, whom I portrayed. On one occasion I met Doris Hamner at the Beverly Wilshire, and we had a wonderful time speaking together.

I loved all my "children" in the show and I love the woman who replaced me as Olivia, Michael Learned. You know, the only one of my children I really keep in touch with is my second daughter, Mary Beth McDonough. She's a sweetheart. She worked with me and with Michael Learned on a movie not long ago. I loved every minute of my involvement with *The Homecoming.* I'm very happy about that program, and I watch it every year at Christmas.

Michael Learned

Michael Learned portrayed Olivia Walton in The Waltons. *Aside from that program, she has appeared in* Gunsmoke, Nurse, *and many other series and television movies. She has also starred in a number of stage plays, including* Driving Miss Daisy. *She assessed Hamner's significance in the following, which is excerpted from a telephone interview with the author.*

Earl is just a wonderful guy. I don't know what else to say about him, other than that he's a decent guy, a gentleman, and a poet—and we love him! He has never gotten the respect and admiration he deserves for what he accomplished.

When I think of *The Waltons,* I ask myself, "How many shows can you think of in which the cast members love each other, truly

Hamner shares a laugh with Michael Learned and Dr. Woody Greenberg at the 2002 East Coast meeting of the Waltons International Fan Club, which was held in Lynchburg, Virginia.

love each other, and that love carries over in the years that come after the show ends?" I look back on every moment of it with gratitude and joy.

The show has been noted in passing for its niceness by critics in the media, including the media of television—and niceness is not interesting to our society. We're far more interested in watching programs depicting Paris Hilton, or who's sleeping with whom, or what can you get away with, and that offends me deeply. I'm not talking about being a right-wing radical, but just common morality: it's not recognized or respected anymore. I think this started in the late 1960s, and it's carried on through to today. I said to Earl once, "When you look at how popular and long-lasting *The Waltons* was, and how it's never mentioned in television retrospectives as one of the notable programs of the 1970s, doesn't that just kill you?" And he said yes.

As for niceness, I think the show has been judged unfairly to some extent. To be fair, I think that toward the end of the series, it tended to get sort of soppy and soggy, with a lot of hugging and tender moments. I think young critics and TV executives today remember the final years of *The Waltons* but forget the earlier years when we dealt with all sorts of things like book-burning, child abuse, the deaths of close relatives, the whole slew of topics we covered during the years that were concerned about the Depression. I remember we did one episode in which a little African-American boy was sort of adopted by the Walton family, and the little boy became very close to John Walton. And at the end of the episode, the Waltons had to basically give the boy to Verdie Grant, because in those days a white family could not adopt a black child. And there's a scene at the very end where the little boy is standing with his new shoes around his neck watching John Walton walk away, and you can tell by John's back that he's heartsick about giving up this child. That was a powerful bit of acting by Ralph, and it wasn't sentimental or saccharine. Now, if the director had chosen to do a close-up of Ralph's face to show a tear sliding down John Walton's face, that would have been soft and sentimental. It was a wonderful ending, and wonderful acting.

I remember people saying to me that they learned how to be a good mother by watching *The Waltons,* or how to become a good dad, or something good and life-affirming from watching the show, and I think of Earl and wonder: What a great legacy for a man to leave.

Hal Williams

A veteran of nearly forty years of working as an actor in television and film, Williams is perhaps best known for his portrayals of Harley Foster on The Waltons, *Smitty on* Sanford and Son, *and Lester Jenkins on* 227.

I think Earl Hamner is a wonderful person, and I will always be grateful to him for providing the sort of writing that gave dignity and believable character to the actors on *The Waltons,* no matter what their race or background. I've been in this business for almost forty years, and of all the programs I've done *The Waltons* was the first to offer that kind of writing. At the time there was nothing else like it. It was the sort of program that you could watch comfortably with your whole family, regardless of where you came from, what color you were, or whatever economic background you came from. It gave Lynn Hamilton and me opportunities that were unknown in those days, the 1970s. Today you see a mish-mash of I-don't-know-what on TV; I sometimes call modern television a "graveyard of decadence." But today you also see many good parts being written for Denzel Washington and other black stars, for television and the

Actors Lynn Hamilton and Hal Williams pose with Hamner at a Waltons International Fan Club reunion.

EARL HAMNER

movies, and the writing for those parts owes a great deal to the pioneering work Earl performed a generation ago.

Paul Harvey

Known for his distinctive voice and delivery as a speaker, for the strong human-interest nature of his news broadcasts, and for his afternoon radio program The Rest of the Story, *nationally syndicated commentator Paul Harvey is a longtime admirer of Hamner.*

Niceness, too long dormant, is becoming dominant again in theatre, in literature, and in electronic media. "Family values" are respected again. This regeneration of our generation was inspired in the misty shadows of Walton's Mountain.

Author Earl Hamner's influence on our national character has deserved a proper biography. If you find yourself in these pages—good for you.

Don Sipes

Sipes has enjoyed a long and distinguished career in Hollywood. He has been a writer, a producer, president of Universal Television, president and Chief Operating Officer of the MGM Film Company, and president of Lorimar Distribution. He is a friend of Hamner, with whom he has collaborated on numerous films and books, including Lassie: A Christmas Story, The Ponder Heart, *and* Murder in Tinseltown. *In a telephone conversation with the author, he offered the following thoughts.*

I've been in the business a long time, and Earl and I worked together for, oh, seven to ten years. He's a terrific guy. He's probably the easiest and best man to work with in the world. A lot of people in this business will stab you in the back, but Earl's not like that. He's a gentleman, and that's a rarity.

Now, how the two of us co-wrote screenplays and what that division of labor looked like is very difficult to describe. Basically, one of us would sit at the machine, and then we would bat words back and forth. And I'll tell you: as a writer he's terrific—he's "A"-Number One!

Harry Harris

One of the giants among television directors, Harris has worked in the business since the mid-1950s. He has directed episodes of many well-known series, including Gunsmoke, Hawaii Five-O, Kung Fu, *and* Falcon Crest. *He directed more episodes of* The Waltons *than any other director who worked on that program. In a telephone interview with the author, he shared the following insights on his longtime friend, Earl Hamner.*

Earl is a kind of a wonder, truly one of a kind. He's a man who comes from a particular point in time, from the closeness of a family that taught him the value and the cost of love. He was a country boy who grew into a wonderful writer who was able to translate the experiences of his life into a form that touched the lives of many people. He told a story of what families had to go through during the Depression to survive and come through, and the story he told in *The Waltons* is basically accurate and true. I know because I lived through those times, too.

He's a wonderful person, one of a kind. He's always an upper, never a downer. Even in times when things were bothering him, he never treated you badly because of it. That doesn't mean he was a pushover. If he was deeply bothered by something about some aspect of a show, he'd be very firm and up-front about it; he'd go and speak directly to the person responsible for the problem. But I can't say enough good things about Earl. He's a wonderful, ingenuous man. When Earl Hamner considers you his friend, you're proud of it!

I was proud to work with Earl on many of the shows he created, including *The Waltons, Apple's Way, Falcon Crest,* and others. *Falcon Crest* was interesting. It was the story of a wealthy family living in the wine country of Northern California, in a place very much like the Napa Valley. It was certainly a departure from *The Waltons!* The series itself was pretty damn interesting, and the writing was good. Working on the series was fun, but when Earl left, things changed. It wasn't fun any more, and I left a few years after Earl. We just didn't like the people who were coming aboard the series and trying to take over. And the show didn't fare well after Earl left. The bright spot was the star of the program, Jane Wyman. She's a marvelous lady I still visit fairly frequently. She enjoyed *Falcon Crest* and adored Earl. She still does!

Alex Paige

Paige is an Australian journalist who has written insightfully about Hamner and Falcon Crest.

To my mind the most important thing about Earl's work is that he has demonstrated by example that it is possible to be a successful writer in a variety of media while writing from the heart.

The combination of his heartfelt, passionate writing and the skills he took the time to learn and internalize enabled him to produce quality work whether he was writing a novel, a radio play, a screenplay, or a television script. All these are very different media and budding writers are often told they are mutually exclusive and that if you have a talent for one you may well be unable to produce quality work in another.

Many young people like myself who dreamed of becoming writers watched *The Waltons* and identified with the John-Boy character. In fact, it's the only time I can recall that what is today regarded as a decidedly "unsexy" ambition, that of becoming a writer of "serious fiction," was presented as an admirable, attractive one by way of it being the goal of the leading character in a high-rating TV series.

That Earl, as the narrator of the program, was also playing the part of the adult John-Boy, resonated with us too. It showed us that—as opposed to what we were taught by many of our teachers and the custodians of "high culture"—that creating and producing a TV drama series was not incompatible with the goals of the serious novelist. That one could be both a novelist and a TV producer, without compromising one's integrity or one's commitment to either medium, and while still working to the best of one's ability.

Though Earl himself may not have even recognized this, it was a very valuable example he set before us. Many people who have undertaken a basic screenwriting course will be familiar with the series of "test" questions often put forward which supposedly determine whether or not you have a "visual imagination": if you see your story unfolding in your mind like a movie, you are said to have a suitable imagination for scriptwriting; if you don't grow impatient with evocative descriptive passages in books, you are said to have an imagination better suited for prose. Earl's work throws this dichotomy into the trash where it belongs and shows that a strong imagination and writing from the heart enables you to write in whatever medium you want. That to me is his most important contribution.

As to his skills as a writer, these must be assessed based on the medium for which he is writing. As a novelist, Earl's work is distinctive and richly descriptive and compassionate. In the media of television and film, it's much more difficult to assess, as the programs we see on screen are never the work of just one person. But all his work is populated with real people—characters you can believe in, living beings about whom you are led to care.

Richard Thomas

An actor from his earliest years, Richard Thomas has been active in theater, television, and motion pictures for most of his life. At the time of this writing, he is starring on Broadway in the drama Democracy. *Of all his many accomplishments, he is best known to many admirers for his portrayal of John-Boy in* The Homecoming *and* The Waltons. *In a telephone interview with the author, he shared the following thoughts on Hamner's significance.*

Earl is multi-faceted. There are many sides to Earl's vision about what the world is—and they're not all *The Waltons*. His intellect is so keen, and he has a terrific dry wit. He has a wicked sense of humor and a wonderfully dry eye about things when he wants to; and he could just have easily written a parody of *The Waltons* as written *The Waltons* itself. But that's not what he chose. He chose to tell the story the way he did, and to celebrate the family.

Earl was the writer, the executive producer, and the guiding creative spirit of the show, and he set the bar very high—not only with *The Homecoming* but also with the pilot script he wrote that started the series off. In those he created the template and the whole tone and style of the show. And because he was from the source itself, he was sort of a litmus test. Earl could tell you if something was authentic or not, and if it wasn't right, or jarring, or if it didn't fall right on his ear, or if it was inconsistent with the local vision of the piece. And if it was wrong, he wouldn't allow it—and that's important. In a sense he was like the artistic director of a theater company. He was invaluable, the one essential ingredient and irreplaceable element in the show.

Earl was also extremely open to the creative input of the actors on the show in a way that was not only very generous and very gracious but kept the series interesting and alive. His openness to the collaborative spirit was inspirational.

I want to add something about Earl as a creative artist. There's a

Waltons cast members and friends pose for a group picture during "An Evening with Richard Thomas," an event sponsored by the Waltons International Fan Club in June 1998 and held in Hartford, Connecticut. *From left, standing:* event organizer and Fan Club member Ray Castro, fan club president Carolyn Grinnell, David Harper, Eric Scott, Leslie Winston, Joe Conley, and Irene Porter of the Waltons Friendship Society, in the UK. *Seated from left:* Mary Beth McDonough, Judy Norton, Richard Thomas, Lisa Harrison, Brighton Walmsley, and Jon Walmsley.

great strain in the writing of American fiction, in local, regional writing: writing in which the creative spirit is focused on a particular place, a particular part of the country, a particular group of people. And most great American writers have this sense of the specific, in terms of geography and culture. And Earl, for my money, is right up there with fantastic writers like Eudora Welty. Now, I know Earl would blanch at that comparison, but I think the similarity is more there than not. I think Earl's enormous contribution is not simply that he made a heart-warming show which America loved and is beloved all over the world, but I think he also provided a television series with a kind of single-minded, clear, creative point of view, an observation of a time and place in American history, and a group of people, in the form of regional American fiction writing of the highest order. Each of those shows he wrote—and I know he didn't write all the episodes, but I mean especially the ones he wrote—were like well-crafted short stories: like Eudora Welty short stories or Flannery O'Connor short stories or Cheever short stories. His qualities as an artist of a local American region writer needs to be emphasized, because beyond the entertainment business, he really did capture a certain period and a certain way of life in a way whose quality was extremely high. And so I have a lot of admiration for him as an American writer about a certain period and a certain way of life. You could have printed an hour of script for an episode of *The Waltons* in *The Sewanee Review* at any time. It goes beyond just making a good show.

That's not to say that there's anything wrong about having created a warm, family-oriented television show and all the things *The Waltons* is associated with. But just in terms of regional American writing about American life, with a certain kind of language and a certain sense of observation of detail and people and story-telling qualities, it's at a very high level of dramatic literature for television, in my opinion. And that's all to his credit, all of it. Earl owns all those "props" lock, stock, and barrel, for the show.

I owe Earl an enormous debt of gratitude. It can't really be repaid, but it can be acknowledged.

Lisa Harrison, Richard Thomas, and Lynn Hamilton with Jane and Earl Hamner, at a get-together in June 1996.

Lynn Hamilton

A distinguished actor who has appeared on numerous television programs—including Sanford and Son, 227, The Practice, *and* Judging Amy, *among many others—Lynn Hamilton portrayed Verdie Grant in* The Waltons. *In October 2004, she addressed a gathering of the Waltons International Fan Club in Lynchburg, Virginia. She commenced with the following words, which are quoted with Miss Hamilton's permission.*

More than thirty years ago, Earl Hamner decided to share his family with all of us. As one of the [Waltons International] Fan Club members said to me, "I learned so much by watching that show." She said, "It wasn't my family. It was, rather, the family that I wished I had." And indeed it was, because it was a family that exhibited love, courage, discipline, loyalty, and honor: all the things that make a society work. It was an American family. But more than that, it was a universal family. And because it speaks to humanity and its principles and its family values, it was one of the joys of my life to have been part of that world, part of the wonderful work of Earl Hamner.

Jeb Rosebrook

Hamner describes Rosebrook as one of his best and most longstanding friends in the world of writing for television. Rosebrook has written many scripts for the large and the small screen over the years, perhaps the most notable being the screenplay for a motion picture starring Steve McQueen, Junior Bonner *(1972). Hamner mentored Rosebrook to some extent and brought him aboard* The Waltons *as a writer.*

As a writer I was privileged to come aboard during that first important season of *The Waltons*. Over the length of the series I wrote three episodes and one two-hour, which opened the season in 1974 ("The Conflict"). The producers and story editors were great to work with, and while Earl had final say on stories, he gave them the creative freedom they needed to do the job.

Earl is a "natural" writer—by that I mean he's got storytelling in his blood. At the roots of it is his growing up in Schuyler. None of his four novels came from a concept as much as from his own life experiences in Virginia and New York City. Earl brings honest storytelling and character development skills to a television series, and *The Twilight Zone* should not be overlooked in this regard. He has the skills hardest to come by in maintaining a quality television series like *The Waltons*—combining drama and humor with character and event-driven stories—and with all of the cast in *The Waltons* that is quite an accomplishment. And Earl is extremely versatile—although he is spoken of mostly in TV terms, his screenplays for *Charlotte's Web* and *Where the Lilies Bloom* made for wonderful films.

He is also fast, facile, and tireless—and unselfish in sharing with other writers. One time he ran into producer Howard Christie of Universal in the doctor's office—Earl had worked for him on *Wagon Train* and Howard was producing *The Virginian*—and he told Howard about me. And Howard, on Earl's word, gave me my first TV job ever.

When embarking on my first original screenplay we talked it over while walking to our daily afternoon coffee break at the Sizzler in Studio City (he got me an office in his building, where he is still today; I was there from 1968 to 1995). By the time we had our coffee he had helped me work out the story. The screenplay, "Ward Craft," was optioned by the late James Coburn and it was my beginning.

Thoughts that come to mind when assessing Earl's character: strong values, a giver of love and loyalty. For writers mentored by him he inspires us to keep climbing the mountain, to keep improving our skills. And once he is your friend, he is your friend for life. As someone once said of Earl, "He is one of God's good people." Amen.

Kami Cotler

Ms. Cotler portrayed the youngest of the Walton children, Elizabeth, in The Homecoming *and* The Waltons. *Upon completing college, she taught school for several years in Hamner's native Nelson County, Virginia. After this, she and her husband moved to Los Angeles, where she is the co-director of a charter school. The author interviewed her in October 2004 and asked, "What are the key skills and strengths Earl Hamner brings to his work?" She answered as follows.*

First, I would say that he had a very rich experience in his boyhood—and that he was able to recognize the richness of it, and then he was able to communicate it. And I say that because I taught in Nelson County for five years. And I worked with students who were not having the same experience—because it was the 1990s—but still a different experience than a whole lot of the country. And I could never convince them that there was anything singular about it. So, for example, most of my students couldn't really believe that people who didn't live in the area would be amazed by the dogwood. Or that there was something extra special about the mountains. To them, that was just how it was and everybody must know that. So the ability to recognize that there was something special about a situation was one of Earl's strengths.

And then, secondly, he found the language to transmit it. He infused it with real meaning. It was a revelation to me the first time I came to Nelson County, because I had spent my whole childhood saying words about the beauty of the landscape and listening to Will

[Geer] speak lines—Will especially, because whenever he spoke dialogue that was descriptive of nature, he infused it with real meaning, because it was meaningful to him. But it wasn't until I came here that I realized it was true: that it was something special and spectacular that we were talking about on the show.

There's also the fact that he was able to look at all the different characters and personalities he grew up with and find a way to prize them *with their flaws.* People sometimes accused the show of being saccharine, and sometimes it probably was saccharine. But there are moments of human frailty or friction that he also captured, that I think really did resonate with people. And I think that if it was completely saccharine—and we weren't dirty and grubby and barefoot and bickering and noisy and doing all the things real groups of children do—it wouldn't have been as meaningful for people.

And then there's just Earl and his presence. He brings a kind of calm and joy, and a phenomenal speaking voice with a beautiful accent, an accent that is truly ages old. (Nobody says *hoose* any more, for example.) It's special.

Nancy Hamner Jamerson

The youngest of Earl and Doris Hamner's eight children, Nancy Hamner Jamerson served as the model for Elizabeth Walton. She lives in Richmond, Virginia, where she has worked for the Commission of Game and Inland Fisheries. In a telephone interview she shared the following thoughts on her eldest brother.

I'm not sure there's anything I can add to what everyone else has said about Earl! He's a good man and a good brother, and all of us in the family are pleased that he portrayed us so favorably and with such imagination. We're all very proud of him.

Gerald Baliles

A former Governor of Virginia (1986–90), Baliles is currently a partner in the Richmond office of the law firm Hunton & Williams. He is a longtime friend of Earl Hamner, who has said of him, "Jerry Baliles told me that he and I have two things in common: a love of books and a love of fishing!"

Virginia has produced some remarkable individuals of accomplishment, in the realms of the military and politics, and particularly in the world of letters. Earl Hamner is certainly in the front rank among Virginia's writers. He is one of those remarkable individuals who has elevated the reputation of his native state.

I've always thought of Earl as an astute gentleman of engaging gentility. He is a man to whom the word *manners* is not something out of date. I've seen him enter a room full of people in a way that is not so much "announced" as it is sensed.

When Earl and I have spoken in the past, we've sometimes talked of books and fishing—and we discovered there are some interesting parallels between those two worthy enterprises. First, both fishing and books offer opportunities for exploration and imagination. Also, reading and fishing inculcate patience—although it's possible for patience to be broken when you hook a big one!

He is appreciative of natural beauty—and beyond that he senses beauty in ordinary people. He perceives what others cannot see, and through his writings, permits others to see. He knows how to touch the soul and give it the expression of goodness.

To sum up: Earl is a craftsman who possesses a great gift of using language to convey beauty, revealing the wonders and mysteries of life, enriching us all.

Mary Beth McDonough

Ms. McDonough portrayed the middle daughter, Erin, in The Homecoming *and* The Waltons, *and she has continued in the acting profession since leaving the series. She has appeared in numerous programs, including* Ally McBeal, Picket Fences, *and* The West Wing. *In 2000, she wrote and directed a short film,* For the Love of May, *which starred Patricia Neal and Michael Learned. She also is a prominent voice in addressing women's health issues. In a telephone interview with the author, she shared the following.*

Being part of *The Waltons* was a true honor, and I consider myself very lucky to be part of that amazing show. As time goes on, and the older I get, the more I realize that.

I thank Earl all the time for enabling me to be part of it. The writing for the show was incredible. Still, I don't think a program like *The Waltons* can happen again. After *Roseanne,* which depicted another family, a family very different from ours and very real to a sizeable segment of the television audience, there was really no going back to a program like *The Waltons. Dr. Quinn* tried. *Touched by an Angel* was another series that tried to tap into that same audience, and succeeded for several years. And *Promised Land* never made it. Still, our show still holds a special place in people's hearts. People still tape it to watch and remember, and to share with their children and grandchildren.

I adore Earl. He's been such a good friend for all my life. He's been a father figure, a friend, a big brother—he's truly "the real John-Boy" and a wonderful man. He's a gift!

Woody Greenberg

Professor Heywood ("Woody") Greenberg is the Dean of the School of Communication at Lynchburg College in Lynchburg, Virginia. Active in preserving the historical heritage of Nelson County, he is a friend of Earl Hamner and one of the handful of people who founded the Walton's Mountain Museum in Schuyler in 1992.

I think Earl has a real feel for people. When you look at the way *The Waltons* is structured—and I know Earl didn't write every episode— he offered up a framework that the other writers had to work within. And that framework, to my knowledge, was never violated throughout the entire run of the show. And the framework is something that revolves around respect for one another, love for one another, support for one another, protection: all these wonderful human qualities that are the best parts of people.

In the confines of a television program there has to be conflict, so every episode of *The Waltons* revolves around some sort of conflict, where either John-Boy needs to have to figure out how to work through, or one of the kids has to work through, a conflict. And through it all there's always the sense that human values are going to triumph, and that the things that are good about people are going to triumph over the things that are bad about people. That's what I love about it. It's like an innate optimism—and you can see where that would come from in his own life. Earl started out in fairly adverse circumstances (and you couldn't pick a smaller town to come from). But he allowed himself to dream when he was a kid, and he was probably encouraged by his mom, particularly, to dream. And he followed his dreams, and he developed this wonderful, optimistic sense of self and of people in general. And that's what he writes to.

Audrey Hamner

Earl Hamner modeled the character of Erin Walton on his "middle sister," Audrey. Ms. Hamner still lives in western Virginia and is a very active retiree who takes groups of senior citizens on short bus tours all over the eastern United States, sharing with them stories of her family as the original "Waltons."

Earl influenced so many people and so many families. I run into people every day who say how much they enjoyed *The Waltons.* And it's funny: when they find out I'm a "Walton" they want to draw close and talk to me and see if there's some way they can make some of the *Walton* influence rub off on them. I think the appeal is this: Earl brought to the American people the knowledge that while the Depression was a difficult time, there were some families—and they weren't wealthy or powerful—who persevered and enjoyed fulfilling lives in spite of their circumstances. And the knowledge that they need not be defined by their circumstances can be carried over into life today.

Earl is a good brother, a good husband, a good father, he was a good son, and he is a good man. He has worked hard all his life, and my brothers and sisters always looked up to him. He helped all of us with our homework as we were growing up, and he helped us through any personal problems we had. Now that our parents are gone and there are only four of us left from among their eight children, we are closer and more precious to each other than ever. I've always felt close to Earl, and today it's a comfort to me to know that I can call him anytime, tell him or ask him anything, and know that

I'll get an honest and loving response. He's a kind person who feels empathy for people. I've never known him to do anything hateful or unjust toward anyone.

Manfred Wolfram

Professor Wolfram is the division head of Electronic Media at the University of Cincinnati College-Conservatory of Music, from which Hamner graduated in 1948. In 2004, he was instrumental in arranging for Hamner to receive the Frederic W. Ziv Award for outstanding achievement in telecommunication. He shared the following thoughts in a telephone interview with the author.

Television is a very, very difficult profession to get into, and difficult to stay in without compromising one's integrity. After working for fifty years in the business, Earl Hamner has never lost sight of our overall goal: to be an uplifting and positive influence in American life. He belongs to the last honest, good, decent generation of writers who held to that vision. There are very few such people about any more. Earl is an extraordinary role model and a true friend.

Ralph Giffin

Giffin is the webmaster of a key Waltons *Web site and editor of* The Blue Ridge Chronicles, *the newsletter of the Waltons Mountain Museum. He is the co-author (with Earl Hamner) of* Goodnight John-Boy.

Earl was able to put into words the feelings and the things that Americans wanted in their lives. While most of TV and advertising was pushing new, better, and more material possessions, Earl was showing us that being a family together and supporting each other, our neighbors, and our country, was what was important. The Waltons had challenges that they overcame as a family. They worshiped God in church, at the pond, or looking at the sunrise from the top of the Mountain. They respected each other's rights and choices.

Those same values hold true today. As the webmaster for www.the-waltons.com, I have had the opportunity to discuss *The Waltons* with hundreds of young families that love the show. They have related to me how they watched *The Waltons* as children and how anxious they are to give their children the same opportunity today. They want to live in the world that Earl Hamner created: hard work, loving families, respect for God and our country, and the time to cherish and share those values with each other.

Carolyn Grinnell

Founder of the Waltons International Fan Club, which she has served as president since 1992, Carolyn Grinnell is a longtime friend and admirer of Hamner.

What's in a name? When I hear the name Earl Hamner, I think of a young man who dared to dream, who very early in life found beauty and wisdom in books, and who himself grew to become an author, poet, producer, and television and film writer.

In the movie *Spencer's Mountain,* during the graduation ceremony as Clay-Boy receives the scholarship medal, his teacher gives him these words to live by: "The world will step aside to let anyone pass if he knows where he is going." Like Clay-Boy, Earl did indeed know where he was going. This young man loved his family, his home and his community. His love was so genuine that he penned his feelings. He dared to dream and his dreams became a reality.

Earl taught the world through *The Waltons* the importance of home, church, and family togetherness. What touches my heart deeply is when I hear that rich mellow voice with a Virginia accent say,

PHOTO BY PAULINE CRUM

Jim Hamner, Earl's youngest brother. Known for his immense generosity, he lived at the house in Schuyler almost until his death in April 2004.

"When I was a young boy growing up on Walton's Mountain. . . ." With these words, I know I am about to return to an era where "family togetherness" had a special meaning and one's faith in God was strong. There are millions of people around the world who daily glean valuable lessons to live by as they watch the heart-warming, uplifting episodes.

So what's in a name? In the name Earl Hamner there is *inspiration*. An extraordinary man.

Eric Scott

Eric Scott portrayed Ben Walton in The Homecoming *and* The Waltons. *He left show business after appearing in a small number of post-*Waltons *television movies and is now vice president of a business in Hollywood. In a telephone interview, he shared the following thoughts on the series and on Earl Hamner.*

I spent ten years of my life doing *The Waltons,* and I'm more proud of those ten years than any other work I've done in my life. I mean, think of it this way: I was on a show that's meant so much to so many people, and it was lots of fun to do. And that's pretty cool. It was a win-win situation!

Earl Hamner had a vision for the show, and he made it happen! There are not a lot of shows that are on the air today that have their origin in the family life of a man like Earl. He's a dear man and a great talent.

I think his great skill, on the set of *The Waltons,* was that he listened to the actors as people with legitimate concerns and ideas and then made adjustments. (Come to think of it, with so many people in the cast, that may have been the easiest and best way to go!) Earl kept the focus upon the personalities of the characters, allowing them to be themselves and to develop, and that's a tough thing to do.

I think he was aided in this by Ellen Corby, who was an inspiration to me. You may have heard it said that she was concerned that the Waltons were too sweet, that the characters needed to be realistic. She definitely managed to inject just a tinge of vinegar into every scene she appeared in! Well, the thing she emphasized, and Earl did too, was to keep our characters consistent. We would all make suggestions as to how our characters should respond in certain scenes, and then Earl would go back with his writers and make little adjustments, and the result was something great.

And that's another thing: With Earl as a presence, there was a great, creative relationship between the creative and the corporate side of things. You hear so often, about other shows, that the corporate side of the business has a stifling effect upon the creative side. Well, that wasn't the case with *The Waltons*. Earl played a key role in keeping relations between those two areas open and constructive.

Joe Conley

A character actor who has appeared in numerous television programs and movies—including Alfred Hitchcock Presents *and the Tom Hanks film* Cast Away *(2000)—Joe Conley is widely remembered as storekeeper Ike Godsey on* The Waltons.

It's been over thirty-two years since *The Waltons* first blasted onto the TV ratings and began a nine-year position in the "top ten." My memories of the actual production of the show are fuzzy, warm, most pleasant experiences.

The company hired top writers and directors to bring the stories into being and then to film. The casting was absolute perfection. Each actor fitted into the grand scheme as if born to their role. I was filled with enjoyment as I first read each script. As the series aged my role became larger and more important to the show. To an actor, that is a most gratifying memory.

Earl breathed reality into creative stories penned by many different writers. He "watched the store." I'll quote Earl as he described the episodes; he said, "The stories never occurred, but they could have." I believe it was his loyalty to the people, the times, and the location that made the show so loved and appreciated by its audience. He was true to his memories of family and friends and expressed a love for Virginia and its bounty.

Claire Whitaker

A longtime friend and business associate of Hamner, Claire Whitaker has worked in television for many years as a writer, producer, and story consultant. She worked on numerous programs, such as The Waltons, Eight Is Enough, The Fitzpatricks, Falcon Crest, *and many others, collaborating with her writer-husband, the late Rod Peterson.*

There were only a handful of women TV writers when I got into the business in the sixties, and some of those early experiences at male-dominated shows were shatteringly negative. As the women's movement got underway a number of studios decided to take a second look at the feminine point of view, and that's when my husband Rod Peterson and I decided to team up. Our first pitch together was to *The Waltons,* a series we admired greatly. It was a popular show, high in the ratings, and I was intimidated by Earl, whose power as a gifted writer-producer was well known. But as the meeting progressed Earl's willingness to listen, his encouragement, and his flashes of humor convinced me that I could be comfortable writing for him. That first episode was pretty forgettable, but it was a beginning of the most satisfying part of our long careers.

Earl had a talent for putting his finger on the essence of a show. He looked for the "heart-tug," that moment that would draw in the audience emotionally. When Rod and I pitched "The Firestorm," he suggested that at the climax John-Boy reach into the flames of the book-burning and pull out a Bible, from which Mrs. Brimmer would read. For some reason we ignored that suggestion and instead put our own ending on the episode. When we went in for a meeting to discuss the first draft Earl asked, very quietly, "Where is the Bible?" He didn't demand the change or insist on his point of view or criticize us for failing to include his idea, but the way he asked the question told us how much that scene meant to him. We jumped to do the rewrite and if you've seen the episode you know how powerful that moment is. Earl knew his show, he knew what he wanted, and somehow, with kindness and respect—a rarity in the harried world of non-stop television production—he knew how to get the most out of his team.

Earl wasn't doing much of the actual writing by the time I joined the show, but he was fully involved in storylines and loved to tinker with a finished script, adding his touches to dialogue or the direction of a scene. I remember one time when Michael Learned was frustrated by a scene she had at John-Boy's bedside, feeling that it didn't reflect enough color or emotion. I could have tackled the problem, or Rod, but this was a challenge Earl wanted to handle, and so while Michael waited Earl went into his office and banged out a monologue. I remember delivering it to her down on the set. She read through it once. It was beautiful—sensitive and eloquent, Earl at his best—and her reading of it brought tears to our eyes. His instincts as a writer allowed him to cut right to the heart of the scene.

He also has a wicked sense of humor that he often put to use in perking up a flat scene. I loved reading the notes he made in the margins of a script in his bold blue printing because they often made me laugh. In the early days I tended to overwrite. It was Earl who taught me that "less is more," even while adding his own "more" to a script.

I think the key skills that Earl brought to his series involved not only his sensitive writing, but his skills with people. His kindness and generosity were reflected at every level of *The Waltons* so that the morale of that show was higher than any show I had ever worked on. Because of his openness I sometimes thought that people took advantage of him. I complained about that to him once after he graciously conceded a couple of points to an exceptionally nasty network lady. What he said then has stayed with me: "In order to get what you want you have to let others win something. . . ." It was a kind of respect he unfailingly showed for all those he worked with—even when he felt they were wrong.

David Harper

In The Homecoming *and* The Waltons, *Harper portrayed Jim-Bob Walton, who was modeled upon Earl Hamner's youngest brother, James Edmund Hamner. After* The Waltons *ended, Harper continued acting for a short time, appearing as a car thief in* Fletch *and as a doomed young Union sol-*

dier in the TV miniseries The Blue and the Gray. *He left acting in the mid-1980s and now lives and works in Arizona. In a telephone interview with the author, he shared the following about* The Waltons.

The writing of the show portrayed the Depression era accurately. Sure, it could get a little too cute sometimes, but for the most part it was remarkably authentic. People who lived during the 1930s, especially, wrote to us to say so. What Earl presented in *The Waltons* was a reaffirming vision, and reaffirmation is definitely a rare thing that we need very much. Our greatest claim to fame was that other shows made fun of us, but that was really a tribute to us.

It's a real shame that we live in such a mechanized, hurried society today, with our lives complicated by cell-phones, pagers, the 'Net, and other things that don't leave us much time for each other. I mean, how many families actually sit down around the same table and have dinner together these days—much less have three generations together under the same roof, like we did on *The Waltons*? Our show reaffirmed something good that has been largely lost today.

I admire and respect Earl tremendously. Why? Because he's an honest, plain-spoken guy who stands his ground. He knew that in Hollywood you have to go along to get along, to some extent. Well, he stood his ground better than most against the pressure that was put on him by higher-ups who wanted to control his work. He suffered for that, but in the end every one of his programs was not a product but a craftwork. That's an important distinction.

Earl is so personable and has got a lot of wisdom. He accomplished what he did not by being heavy-handed or preachy but by being patient, doing what he could with what he had, and then letting the audience response take care of itself. When I think of him, I envision him as being sort of like Johnny Appleseed: He plants good things for tomorrow, good things that may take time to show results. Like all such people, he accomplishes great things in small, secret ways.

Caroline Hamner

The daughter of Earl and Jane Hamner, Ms. Hamner is a family counselor practicing in California.

I'm supposed to be writing a short piece about my father, but I can't concentrate for all the noise in my neighborhood. There's the motorcycle guy next door who keeps revving his engine. There's the handyman guy down the street using his electric drill. There's the gardener guy mowing his lawn on the adjacent property. And there's the football guy with his TV on full blast watching a game. I suddenly start to wonder: Where are the other hobbyists like the writer guy or the academic guy? Where are they and what are the sounds that accompany those quieter pursuits these days?

One of my strongest memories from childhood is falling asleep to the sound of my father, the writer guy, working into the night on his old manual typewriter. It was a soothing sound, a constant. It was the signal that let me know that all was well with the world: that Dad was home, and we were safe and not alone. I suppose to some people the typewriter would sound like a nuisance, a cause for insomnia, a late-night annoyance, but not so for the daughter of a writer. The rhythm, the determination, the sound of imagination pouring forth onto a fresh sheet of paper was the unique music of my youth.

Sadly, since the invention of computers the typewriter has become a thing of the past. It is an antiquated machine like the washboard or the printing press. And with those outdated inventions go their particular music. Now the sound of writing is a mostly muted event, just a slight tapping on the computer keyboard, a padded clicking of keys. Typewriter music is gone now like a lost language, an ancestry that's come to its end.

Some nights when I can't sleep because I'm overwhelmed by the noise in my head, I try to think of something happy. Christmas usually comes to mind first but with that thought comes shopping anxiety and gift-wrapping worry. Birthdays are supposed to be happy, but these days with the years going so fast and my number growing towards fifty a birthday often sends me into a state of alarm. Travel

Hamner poses with many members of the *Waltons* cast at a Waltons International Fan Club reunion in July 2004. Standing, from left: Tony Becker, Mary Beth McDonough, Michael Learned, Hamner, Hal Williams, Lisa Harrison, Jon Walmsley, Brighton Walmsley, Robert Donner, Joe Conley; Seated, from left: David Harper, Peggy Rea, Martha Nix, Leslie Winston, Eric Scott.

sounds good but then there's the flying part, which terrifies me. So I go back to my childhood bedroom and listen for the sound of Dad typing in the distance. It calms me; it soothes me. I feel safe and young in my heart again.

The Waltons always ended with their ritual goodnights, the goodnight John-Boys and the 'night Mary Ellens. But those are not the sounds of my youth. Instead, I have those magical keys making their music in my memory, the sound of klackety keys, the stories being told. It is a sweeter sound I listen for than the sound of distant voices. It is my father's music I hear in the distance.

Isis Ringrose

A resident of Schuyler, Virginia, Isis Ringrose is a longtime friend of the Hamner family. She and her husband, Tom, live in a beautiful home that was at one time the small community hospital in which Earl Hamner and three of his siblings were born. Asked in an interview to identify the preeminent skills and qualities she perceives in Earl Hamner and his work, she replied as follows.

That's a fabulous question. I may end up telling you things that sound really corny, but they're the truth.

The strongest part, and the part that nobody believes in, is his love. Earl Hamner is capable of transmitting that love of his anywhere, everywhere, to anyone. And that's why the whole world is his family. Psychologists and other people know that good families create a good society. Well, he's the epitome of that. He doesn't know that he's doing that. It's not something put on, or something that he thought out, it's not something that is artificial in any way, shape, or

PHOTO BY DUANE SHELL

Earl Hamner today.

form. He is just that: he loves people. And he thinks of everybody because that's all he knows—sisters and brothers—and so that's how he transmits himself into every issue, every work that he's done.

There is a second thing. The second thing is humility. He has the humility of a saint. (Again, it's corny, but it's real.) He's one of the most humble people that I've ever met. And you look at this person, and the things that he has accomplished; I mean, how savvy do you have to be to get through all the garbage, all the politics, Hollywood, write the books, publish them, and make a show about them? I mean, that takes a lot of savvy. And he just plowed through it because he didn't know any better. He's humble.

Savvy. Wise. I don't know if he's smart, *but he's very wise.* He wrote me a letter about *The Waltons* that said, in essence, "Well, it's a show. You know it's going to end. It's going to be forgotten like so many other shows. It has momentum for the moment, but in time it'll no longer exist in human consciousness, in the present." And I laughed, and I said to him, "As long as there is one family, one human being left on this earth who has the need to belong—which we all do—your show will never die." He didn't know that! I mean, think about that. It's mind-boggling. Everybody wants to belong to the Hamners, to the Waltons, because everybody wants to belong where they're welcome—even with their imperfections—where they can belong and can be loved. Who doesn't want that? And when is it going to stop? It'll never stop. He created something that has its own existence. It's big. It's huge. It's as big as the human spirit.

SELECTED BIBLIOGRAPHY

Primary Sources (Works by Hamner)

Books

Fifty Roads to Town. New York: Random House, 1953.

Spencer's Mountain. New York: Dial Press, 1961.

You Can't Get There from Here. New York: Random House, 1965.

The Homecoming: A Novel about Spencer's Mountain. New York: Random House, 1970.

(With Don Sipes) *Lassie: A Christmas Story.* Nashville: Tommy Nelson, 1997.

The Hollywood Zoo. Ocean Pines, MD: Blue Ridge Publications, 1997; revised and published as *The Avocado Drive Zoo: At Home with My Family and the Creatures We've Loved.* Nashville: Cumberland House Publishing, 1999.

(With Don Sipes) *Murder in Tinseltown.* Tulsa: Hawk Publishing, 2000.

(With Ralph E. Giffin) *Goodnight John-Boy: A Celebration of an American Family and the Values That Have Sustained Us through Good Times and Bad.* Nashville: Cumberland House Publishing, 2002.

(With Tony Albarella) *The Twilight Zone Scripts of Earl Hamner.* Nashville: Cumberland House Publishing, 2003.

"The Driftwood Arrangement" (drama, unpublished).

"Generous Women" (memoir, in progress).

"Odette, the Singing Goose" (children's story, unpublished).

"My Mother Is Alive and Well and Living in the Blue Ridge Mountains of Virginia with Julie Andrews and Maria von Trapp" (drama, in progress).

"Welcome to My Garden; or, There's a Curmudgeon in the Camelias!" (poetry, unpublished).

Teleplays and Other

The Today Show (writer, reporter), 1952–1961.

The Kate Smith Hour (writer, "The Hound of Heaven"), 1953.

The United States Steel Hour (writer, "Highway"), 1954.

The Twilight Zone (writer, "The Hunt," "Jess-Belle," "You Drive," "Black Leather Jackets," "A Piano in the House," "Stopover in a Quiet Town," "Ring-a-Ding Girl," and "The Bewitchin' Pool") 1962–64.

It's a Man's World (initial writer, "A Drive over to Exeter"), 1962.

Mr. Smith Goes to Washington (writer), 1962–63.

Wagon Train (writer), 1962–65.

Gentle Ben (writer, "The Wayward Bear"), 1967.

The Invaders (writer, "The Watchers"), 1967.

CBS Playhouse (writer, "Appalachian Autumn"), 1969.

The Interns (writer), 1970.

Nanny and the Professor (writer, "The Tyrannosaurus Tibia," "A Fowl Episode," "The Haunted House," "The Visitor"), 1970.

The Last Generation (writer), 1971.

Aesop's Fables (writer), 1971.

The Homecoming: A Christmas Story (writer, narrator), 1971

The Waltons (creator, executive producer, executive story consultant, writer, narrator), 1972–81.

A Dream for Christmas (producer, writer), 1973.

(With Jack Miller) *Lassie: A New Beginning* (co-writer), 1973.

Apple's Way (creator, executive producer), 1974.

The Young Pioneers (producer), 1978.

Falcon Crest (creator, executive producer, writer), 1981–86.

A Wedding on Walton's Mountain (executive producer), 1982.

Mother's Day on Walton's Mountain (executive producer), 1982.

A Day of Thanks on Walton's Mountain (executive producer), 1982.

Boone (creator, executive producer, and writer), 1983.

The Gift of Love: A Christmas Story (writer, co-executive producer, based on Bess Streeter Aldrich's short story "The Silent Stars Go By"), 1983.

(With Fred Silverman) *Morningstar/Eveningstar* (co-executive producer), 1986.

(With Don Sipes and Oprah Winfrey) *Brewster Place* (co-executive producer), 1990.

(With Don Sipes, Richard Becker, and Russell Becker) *Snowy River: The McGregor Saga* (co-executive producer), 1993–96.

(With Don Sipes) *The Story of Little Tree* (co-writer and narrator), 1993.

(With Lee Rich and Bruce Sallan) *A Walton Thanksgiving Reunion* (co-executive producer), 1993.

(With Lee Rich and Rich Heller) *A Walton Wedding* (co-executive producer), 1995.

A Mother's Gift (initial writer, based on Bess Streeter Aldrich's novel *A Lantern in Her Hand*), 1995.

(With Lee Rich and Rich Heller) *A Walton Easter* (co-executive producer), 1997.

Night Visions (writer, "The Doghouse"), 2001.

(With Don Sipes) *The Wild Thornberrys* (co-writer, "The Anniversary"), 2001.

(With Don Sipes) *The Ponder Heart* (co-producer, based on the novel by Eudora Welty), 2001.

The Night Before Christmas: A Mouse Tale (writer), 2002.

Screenplays

Palm Springs Weekend. Warner Brothers, 1963.

Heidi. NBC, 1968.

Charlotte's Web. Hanna-Barbera, 1973.

Where the Lilies Bloom. United Artists, 1974.

Other

A Place in History: The Tredegar Iron Works and Its Restoration (narrator), 1989.

Papers

Many of Hamner's archive of scripts and awards are on file in the Hall Campus Center at Lynchburg College in Lynchburg, Virginia. It is expected that this collection will be moved to a new building now under construction on campus and due to open in 2005.

Secondary Sources

Albarella, Tony. "The Forgotten *Twilight Zone* Writer." *The Twilight Zone Scripts of Earl Hamner.* Nashville: Cumberland House, 2003, 9–19. Short introduction to Hamner as an unjustly little-known writer of teleplays for *The Twilight Zone,* followed by a lengthy and insightful interview. Hamner discourses upon his professional relationship with Rod Serling and the other *Twilight Zone* writers, how he conceives ideas for stories, and the seeming conflict between "Mr. Walton" and the writer of off-beat, fantastic stories for Serling's program (and creator of the wealth-and-power-driven Gioberti clan of *Falcon Crest*). Albarella also provides a well-considered summary of each of the eight episodes Hamner contributed to *The Twilight Zone.*

Bell, Joseph N. "The *Real* Waltons." *Good Housekeeping,* November 1973, 68–82. Biographical essay on the Hamners of Schuyler, Virginia, featuring anecdotes of childhood during the Great Depression and short, illuminating statements by Earl Hamner, his siblings, and his mother.

Birmingham, Frederic A. "Meet the Waltons: A Visit on Location with the TV Family Which Has Won the Hearts of the Nation." *The Saturday Evening Post,*

November–December 1973, 69–73, 105–07. Richly illustrated feature story that focuses largely upon the superb casting of the television series. Birmingham credits Hamner with having "given us back something of ourselves, small but important things we may have thought until now we had lost. They constitute, I suspect, the better side of us all. If that is his gift, we owe him, and the Walton family, a vote of thanks."

Broughton, Irv, ed. "Earl Hamner, Jr." In *Producers on Producing: The Making of Film and Television.* Jefferson, N.C.: McFarland & Company, 1986, 191–202. A lengthy, in-depth interview with Hamner covering the creative process in television screenwriting, based upon Hamner's experiences in producing *The Waltons.*

Dunham, Kimberly. "A Mosaic of the John Boys." *From the Hills* (Charleston, WV) no. 38 (1974): 3–11. Special pictorial issue featuring a biographical profile of actor Richard Thomas and a valuable interview with Hamner, who shares his thoughts on his early work, how to become a published writer, the degree to which *The Waltons* is factual, and other matters related to his life and accomplishments as a writer.

Hamner, Earl, and Ralph Giffin. *Goodnight John-Boy: A Celebration of an American Family and the Values That Have Sustained Us through Good Times and Bad.* Nashville: Cumberland House, 2002. Contains in its introductory chapters much autobiographical information provided by Hamner, covering his youth, early career, *Spencer's Mountain,* and the writing, casting, and production of *The Waltons.*

Newcomb, Horace, and Robert S. Alley. "Earl Hamner." In *The Producer's Medium: Conversations with Creators of American TV.* New York: Oxford University Press, 1983, 154–72. Intelligent summary of Hamner's work as the creator and producer of *The Waltons, Apple's Way,* and *Falcon Crest,* as well as a lengthy interview. Speaking of his own accomplishments in television, Hamner at one point laments, "In time it will be tougher and tougher to get acceptance for what I do best. The trend is more and more toward a comic approach to life. . . . It's a leering kind of suggestive television. I hope people get tired of it because I feel like what I do, and not to say that it's wonderful, but I think it's what people really would like, is also necessary."

Prescott, Orville. "Wistful, Whimsical and Pure in Heart." *New York Times,* June 11, 1965, 29. Favorable, insightful review of *You Can't Get There from Here,* in which Prescott focuses approvingly upon "Mr. Hamner's pleas for more loving kindness" and notes, "It would be as difficult to dislike *You Can't Get There from Here* as to dislike a basket of spaniel puppies. In the cold, hard, raucous world of modern fiction there ought to be room for a sensitive plant like this."

Provence, Lisa. "Earl's World: Almost Like Being in a Real Place." *Charlottesville (VA) Hook,* May 15, 2003, 20–25. Retrospective interview with Hamner, containing his impressions of the film version of *Spencer's Mountain* and revealing his personal views on a number of issues related to life and the quality of modern television programs.

Roades, Antoinette W. "Earl Hamner, Jr." *Commonwealth: The Magazine of Virginia,* April 1977, 22–29. An invaluable interview with Hamner, prefaced by an eloquent introduction to his life by Roades. Hamner speaks of his early struggles as a writer, his view of the attraction New York offers the aspiring writer, his hopes for the just-inaugurated American president, Jimmy Carter, and the significance of rootedness in *place* in his own life and works.

Roïphe, Anne. "*The Waltons:* Ma and Pa and John-Boy in Mythic America." *The New York Times Magazine,* November 13, 1973, 40–41, 130–34, 146. Examination of *The Waltons* by a writer at once drawn to the show's appeal and repelled by its "obvious commercial exploitation" who explores the question, "What keeps us watching this obviously corny, totally unreal family?" Roïphe allows that *The Waltons* provides a useful myth, "a good, workable dance to scare away the evil spirits of loneliness, isolation, divorce, alcoholism, troubled children, abandoned elders—the real companions of American family life, the real demons of the living room," and she concludes on a note of tentative hope: "Who knows what the American family can become?"

Tanguay, Margaret Fife. "Earl Hamner, Jr.: The Man behind *The Waltons." Authors in the News,* Vol. 2, edited by Barbara Nykoruk. Detroit: Gale Research Co., 1976, 135–36. A friendly interview with Hamner in which Tanguay describes the plot and style of his lesser-known novels, *Fifty Roads to Town* and *You Can't Get There from Here.* A brief comparison between Hamner's character Wesley Scott (from *You Can't Get There from Here*) with Holden Caulfield (*Catcher in the Rye*) is especially intriguing. This essay is reprinted from the March 1974 issue of *Sky Magazine.*

OTHER REFERENCES

Albarella, Tony. "Earl's the Real Thing." *The Hook* (Charlottesville, Va.) 2, no. 21 (May 29, 2003): 5.

Alley, Robert S. *Television: Ethics for Hire?* Nashville: Abington, 1977.

Anderson, Sherwood. *Winesburg, Ohio.* New York: Penguin Books, 1976.

Anderson, William, ed. *The Horn Book's Laura Ingalls Wilder: Articles about and by Laura Ingalls Wilder, Garth Williams and the Little House Books.* Boston: Horn Book, 1987.

Appel, Paul P. *Homage to Sherwood Anderson: 1876–1941,* Mamaroneck, N.Y.: Paul P. Appel, 1970.

"Earl Hamner Interview." *Archive of American Television.* North Hollywood, Cal.: Academy of Television Arts & Sciences Foundation, Reels 1-6, September 18, 2003.

Atlas, James. "The Case for Thomas Wolfe." *The New York Times Book Review,* December 2, 1979, 52–53.

Aurandt, Paul. *More of Paul Harvey's The Rest of the Story.* Edited by Lynne Harvey. New York: William Morrow, 1980.

Baro, Gene. "Significant Revelation of the Human Spirit." *New York Herald Tribune Book Review*, October 4, 1953, 6.

Berry, Wendell. *Sex, Economy, Freedom, & Community: Eight Essays.* New York: Pantheon Books, 1993.

Bradbury, John M. *Renaissance in the South: A Critical History of the Literature, 1920–1960.* Chapel Hill: University of North Carolina Press, 1963.

Bradbury, Ray. *The Martian Chronicles.* New York: Avon Books, 1997.

Buchwald, Art. "Heidi Fans' Next Game: Swiss Alps vs. Super Bowl." *Los Angeles Times*, November 24, 1968, G7.

Budd, Louis J. "The Grotesques of Anderson and Wolfe." *Modern Fiction Studies* 5, no. 4 (Winter 1959–60): 304–10.

Burns, R. K. Review of *Spencer's Mountain. Library Journal* 87, no. 2 (15 January 1962): 237.

Cavendish, Henry. "Life at the Working Class Level in Virginia." *Chicago Sunday Tribune Magazine of Books*, January 14, 1962, 3.

Cleaver, Vera and Bill. *Where the Lilies Bloom.* Philadelphia: J. B. Lippincott, 1969.

Clemetson, Lynette. "Oprah on Oprah." *Newsweek*, January 8, 2001, 38–48.

Cocks, Jay. Review of *Where the Lilies Bloom. Time*, February 11, 1974, 65.

Coombes, Archie James. *Some Australian Poets.* 1938. Reprint. New York: Books for Libraries Press, 1970.

Cyclops [John Leonard, pseudonym]. "Wholesome Sentiment in the Blue Ridge." *Life*, October 13, 1972, 20.

De Sanctis, Dona. "The Waltons Have Italian Roots." *Italian America,* Fall 2002, 18.

"Waltons Model Home Is Saved at Auction." *Detroit News*, December 8, 2003, 2A.

Donohue, John W. "Arcadia Recalled: *The Waltons.*" *America*, December 23, 1972, 548–50.

Eaton, Phoebe. "The Hollywood Beast Roars." *New York Observer*, February 2, 2004, 1.

Everett, Todd. "Kraft Premier Movie *A Mother's Gift.*" *Variety*, April 13, 1995.

Fisk, Alan. "Russert Writes Loving Memoir of His Dad." *Detroit News*, April 12, 2004, E1.

Freeman, Don. Review of *The Waltons. San Diego Union*, October 5, 1972, n.p.

Goldberg, Robert. "Breaking out of the TV Ghetto." *Wall Street Journal*, May 7, 1990, A12.

Gould, Jack. "C.B.S. Playhouse Explores Appalachian Misery." *New York Times*, October 7, 1969, 95.

Guroian, Vigen. *Tending the Heart of Virtue: How Classic Stories Awaken a Child's Moral Imagination.* New York: Oxford University Press, 1998.

Hamner, Earl. "We Called It Love." *New York Times* , October 5, 1969, D21.

———. "'Waltons' Show the Love Their Author Remembers." *Newark (NJ) Sunday Star-Ledger,* November 5, 1972, IV, 18–19.

———. "Proud Virginian Loves State." *Roanoke Times,* August 5, 1973, n.p.

———. "Coming Home to Walton's Mountain." *TV Guide,* November 20, 1993, 10–14.

———. "Welcome 2000: *The Waltons* and the Millennium." *The Blue Ridge Chronicle* 8, no. 1 (2000): 1.

———. "Presenting *The Ponder Heart*." *Eudora Welty Newsletter* 25, no. 2 (Summer 2001): 8–9.

———. "A Wonderful Journey: The Books of Earl Hamner." http://www.the-waltons.com/booksbyearl.html

———. "A Letter to My Children." http://www.freshyarn.com/1/essays/hamner_letter1.htm

———, and Kami Cotler. "Live Fan Chat: Earl Hamner Jr. and Kami Cotler." http://www.reidland.com/music/green/chat031599.html

———, and Kirk Nuss. "An Interview with Earl Hamner, Jr." *Eudora Welty Newsletter* 25, no. 2 (Summer 2001): 9–15.

———, and Alex Paige. "Earl Hamner, Creator of *Falcon Crest* and *The Waltons* Interviewed by Alex Paige, July 31, 2004." http://www.arthurswift.com/experiences/earl_hamner_interview_by_alex_paige.html

Harrison, W. K., III. Review of *Fifty Roads to Town*. *Library Journal* 78, no. 17 (1 October 1953): 1686.

Helprin, Mark. *Memoir from Antproof Case.* San Diego: Harcourt Brace & Co., 1995.

Hobson, Susan, comp. "New Creative Writers: Earl Hamner." *Library Journal* 78, no. 17 (1 October 1953): 1672.

Holley, Val. *James Dean: The Biography.* New York: St. Martin's Press, 1995.

Houghton, Buck. *What a Producer Does: The Art of Moviemaking (Not the Business).* Los Angeles: Silman-James Press, 1991.

Howells, W. D. *Criticism and Fiction, and Other Essays.* New York: New York University Press, 1959.

Jewell, Tracey, writer and producer. *The Walton Legacy.* Harrisonburg, Va.: WVPT Video Library, 1997.

Jolliffe, Christina. "Author behind *The Waltons* Speaks at Elyria Public Library." *Elyria (OH) Chronicle-Telegram.* http://www.chronicletelegram.com/Archive/Html/2003/September/9-14/Daily%20Pages/Local/HtmL/local2.html

Judge, Frank. "Let's Save a Show." *Detroit News,* September 15, 1972, 14C.

Kelly, Sandra. "'Mrs. Walton, I Presume?': TV Series Brings Visitors to Schuyler." *Roanoke Times,* August 5, 1973, B1–B2.

Kibler, James E., Jr., ed. *Dictionary of Literary Biography,* Vol. 6: *American Novelists Since World War II, Second Series.* Detroit: Gale Research Co./Bruccoli Clark, 1980.

Kirk, Russell. "To the Point: The Homing Impulse." Syndicated column. (1 September 1965).

———. *Enemies of the Permanent Things: Observations of Abnormity in Literature and Politics.* 2nd ed. Peru, Ill.: Sherwood Sugden & Co., 1984.

Klonicki, Elaine. "Reality in a Television Survivor." *Raleigh News & Observer,* January 10, 2001, 9A.

Lardine, Bob. "In a Case of Old Wine in New Bottles, an Angry Author Takes *Falcon Crest* to Court." *People Weekly,* April 12, 1982, 34–35.

Lee, Charles. "Mountain Preacher." *The New York Times Book Review,* October 11, 1953, 28.

Leonard, John. "Gentlewoman's Agreement." *New York,* March 31, 1986, 84–85.

Letofsky, Irv. "TV Times Also Are Tough for *Waltons.*" *Minneapolis Tribune TV Week,* October 8–14, 1972, 3, 6.

Levin, Martin. Review of *You Can't Get There from Here. The New York Times Book Review,* June 20, 1965, 32.

Library Journal 87, no. 4. Review of *Spencer's Mountain* (February 15, 1962): 854.

Long, Rob. "Our Town." *National Review,* February 23, 2004, 32–33.

Lowry, Brian. "Dems Seek *Waltons* Endorsement." *Daily Variety,* August 21, 1992, 3.

Mann, Delbert. *Looking Back . . . at Live Television and Other Matters.* Los Angeles: Directors Guild of America, 1998.

Marc, David. *Demographic Vistas: Television in American Culture.* Rev. ed. Philadelphia: University of Pennsylvania Press, 1986.

Martin, Douglas. "Jerry Goldsmith Is Dead at 75; Prolific Composer for Films." *New York Times,* July 23, 2004, A21.

Matthews, Richard. "Home of *The Waltons.*" *American Profile,* January 18–24, 2004, 8–9.

McClay, Wilfred M. "The Mystic Chords of Memory: Reclaiming American History." *Heritage Lecture,* no. 550. Washington, D.C.: Heritage Foundation, 1995, n.p.

Mitchell, Kim. "Family Offers Horse Opera." *Multichannel News,* August 23, 1993, 16.

Mook, Bea. "Earl Hamner: Walton's Mountain to *Falcon Crest.*" *The Virginian,* November–December 1986, 11–15.

Morris, Barbara. "Prime Time Live." *Washington Post,* October 22, 1997, D9.

Newsweek. "Sleeper of the Year." April 2, 1973, 58.

New York Times. "Robert Penn Warren, Poet and Author, Dies." September 16, 1989, 1, 11.

Nuss, Kirk. "Earl Hamner, Eudora Welty, and Daniel Ponder." *Eudora Welty Newsletter* 25, no. 2 (Summer 2001): 6–7.

O'Connor, John J. "*Apple's Way* and the Search for Human Values." *New York Times*, February 15, 1974, 67.

———. "*The Gift of Love,* Film on CBS." *New York Times*, December 20, 1983, C19.

———. "Show about Black People, with Winfrey in Charge." *New York Times*, May 1, 1990, C13.

———. "A Reunion for the Waltons." *New York Times*, March 28, 1997, D18.

Orange County (CA) Register. "*Waltons* Sweep Emmy Awards." May 21, 1973, A1–A2.

Pechter, Kerry. "*It's a Man's World:* Ahead of Its Time, and Ahead of Ours." *New York Times*, January 14, 2001, 33, 38.

Peden, William. "Southern Hill Folk." *Saturday Review*, March 10, 1962, 26.

Perkins, Maxwell E. "Thomas Wolfe." *Harvard Library Bulletin* 1, no. 3 (Autumn 1947): 269–77.

Person, James E., Jr., ed. *The Unbought Grace of Life: Essays in Honor of Russell Kirk.* Peru, Ill.: Sherwood Sugden & Co., 1994.

———. "All Their Roads before Them: George Willard, Clay-Boy Spencer, and the 'Beckoning World.'" *The Sherwood Anderson Review* 28, No. 1 (Winter 2003): 1–10.

Peterson, Carol Miles. *Bess Streeter Aldrich: The Dreams Are All Real.* Lincoln: University of Nebraska Press, 1995.

Prescott, Orville. Review of *Spencer's Mountain. New York Times*, January 10, 1962, 45.

Provence, Lisa. "Trouble on Walton's Mountain." *Charlottesville (VA) Hook*, June 27, 2002, 12–16.

———. "Earl Hamner's NFL Notoriety: How *Heidi* Irked Jets-Raiders Fans." *Charlottesville (VA) Hook*, May 5, 2003, 24.

———. "Going, Going: Hamner Home Place on the Block." *Charlottesville (VA) Hook*, November 13, 2003, 6–7.

———. "Goodnight: 'Jim-Bob' Hamner Dies at 67." *Charlottesville (VA) Hook*, April 8, 2004, 7–8.

Publishers Weekly. Review of *The Homecoming.* September 14, 1970, 69.

Publishers Weekly. Review of *Lassie: A Christmas Story.* October 6, 1997, 58.

Publishers Weekly. Review of *The Avocado Drive Zoo.* March 22, 1999, 80.

Publishers Weekly. Review of *Murder in Tinseltown.* March 19, 2001, 80.

Rieselman, Deborah. "Write Way to Hollywood: Electronic Media's Brightest Star Shines Light on How to Reach the Top without Losing One's Values." *The University of Cincinnati Horizons*, September 2004, 11–13.

Rogers, Fred. *The World According to Mister Rogers: Important Things to Remember.* New York: Hyperion, 2003.

Rogers, Thomas. "Jets Cut for *Heidi;* TV Fans Complain." *New York Times,* November 18, 1968, 1, 61.

Rosenberg, Howard. "*Christmas Story* Suits the Season." *Los Angeles Times,* December 20, 1983, VI-10.

Rosenberger, Coleman. "'Heaven Right Here,'" *New York Herald Tribune Books,* January 14, 1962, 6.

Sander, Gordon F. *Serling: The Rise and Twilight of Television's Last Angry Man.* New York: Dutton, 1992.

Saroyan, William. Review of *Where the Lilies Bloom. The New York Times Book Review,* September 28, 1969, 34.

Scholastic Scope, eds. *Appalachian Autumn and Other Plays.* New York: Scholastic Books, 1971.

Seibel, Deborah Starr. "The Other Side of the Mountain: A *Waltons* 'Where Are They Now?'" *TV Guide,* November 20, 1993, 18, 20.

———. "John-Boy Says 'I Do'." *TV Guide,* February 11, 1995, 22–25.

Seldon, W. Lynn, Jr. "A Favorite TV Family Lives at the Walton's Mountain Museum." *Grit,* January 2, 1994, 39.

Shinn, H. J. "Old-fashioned Revival." *Saturday Review,* October 17, 1953, 44.

Simonini, R. C., ed. *Southern Writers: Appraisals in Our Time.* Charlottesville: University Press of Virginia, 1964.

Snodgrass, Mary Ellen. *Encyclopedia of Southern Literature.* Santa Barbara, Cal.: ABC-CLIO, 1997.

Spyri, Johanna. *Heidi.* New York: Ariel Books/Alfred A. Knopf, 1984.

Taylor, Ella. *Prime-Time Families: Television Culture in Postwar America.* Berkeley and Los Angeles: University of California Press, 1989.

TVLand. *Moguls of the '70s, Part II,* videocassette (rev. 25 February 2004).

Twelve Southerners. *I'll Take My Stand: The South and the Agrarian Tradition.* Baton Rouge: Louisiana State University Press, 1977.

Variety. Review of *The Homecoming: A Christmas Story.* December 22, 1971, 42.

Variety. Review of *Morningstar/Eveningstar.* April 2, 1986, 66.

Welty, Eudora. "The Ponder Heart." *The New Yorker,* December 5, 1953, 47.

White, E. B. *Charlotte's Web.* 1952. Reprint. New York: HarperCollins Publishers, 1980.

———. *Letters of E. B. White.* Edited by Dorothy Lobrano Guth. New York: Harper & Row, 1976.

Wyllie, John Cook. "A Boy Grows Up in Nelson County, Virginia." *The New York Times Book Review,* January 14, 1962, 40.

Wolfe, Thomas. *Look Homeward, Angel: A Story of the Buried Life.* New York: Charles Scribner's Sons, 1929.

APPENDIX:

AWARDS AND HONORS RECEIVED BY EARL HAMNER

TV-Radio Writers Award, 1967

Outstanding Script Award, Writers Guild of America, for *Heidi*, 1969

Christopher Award, for *Appalachian Autumn*, 1969

Christopher Award, for *Aesop's Fables*, 1971

Christopher Award, for *The Homecoming: A Christmas Story*, 1971

George Foster Peabody Award, 1972

Emmy Award for Outstanding Drama Series, Continuing (for *The Waltons*), 1973

Parks Mason Award: Virginian of the Year, from the Virginia Press Association, 1973

Special TV Award from The American Jewish Committee and the National Ministries of the American Baptist Church, 1973

Plaque presented by the Quill & Scroll International Honorary Society for High School Journalists: The Members of the Earl Hamner Chapter, Nelson County High School, May 11, 1973

Good Citizenship Medal, Southern Baptists Communications Group, 1973

American Exemplar Medal, Freedoms Foundation at Valley Forge, 1973

Broadcast Preceptor Award, Broadcast Industry, Los Angeles, California, 1974

Christopher Award, for *Where the Lilies Bloom*, 1974

National Association of Television Executives Man of the Year Award, 1974

Litt.D. from the University of Richmond, 1974

Virginia Association of Broadcasters Award, 1975

People's Choice Award, Favorite Television Dramatic Series, for *The Waltons*, 1975

L.H.D. from Berea College, 1975

L.H.D. from Loyola University, 1975

D.F.A. from Morris Harvey College, 1975

Christopher Award, for personal achievement as a television screenwriter, 1975

Entry in the Congressional Record, July 8, 1975

Commendation from the Virginia Communications Hall of Fame, 1976

L.H.D. from DePaul University, 1976

Appreciation Award, Goodwill Industries, 1977

Commendation from The National Society of the Daughters of the American Revolution, 1977

Award for Outstanding Service from the University of Richmond, 1977

Plaque from *Who's Who in America*, 1994

Alumni Excellence Award from the Virginia Foundation for Independent Colleges, 2002

Frederic W. Ziv Award for outstanding achievement in telecommunication, from the University of Cincinnati—College Conservatory of Music's Electronic Media Division, 2004

INDEX

EARL HAMNER

Hamner, James Edmund ("Jim"), 6, 35, 235, 265
Hamner Meyers, Margaret, 116
Hamner, Nora Spencer, 116
Hamner, Paul Louis, 6, 35, 74, 107, 235, 247
Hamner, Scott Martin, 17, 25, 84–85
Hamner, Susan Henry Spencer, 11
Hamner, Willard Harold ("Bill"), 6, 35, 74, 107
Harper, David W., 21, 73–74, 80, 255, 269–70, 272
Harris, Harry, 80, 82, 84, 169, 252–53
Harrison, Lisa, 87, 255, 257, 272
Harrison, W. K. III, 32
Harvey, Paul, 251
Hawaii Five-O, 252
Hee Haw, 136
Heidi, xvi, 157, 181–90
Heller, Joseph, 18
Helprin, Mark, xxi, 227, 233, 236
High Chaparral, 212
Hirshman, Herb, 136
Hite, Kathleen, 84
Hogan, Martin Jr., 189
Holleman, Boyce, 216
Holliday, Polly, 156, 160
Holm, Celeste, 200
Homecoming, The, xi, xix, 4–5, 10, 21–22, 31, 59–68, 71–74, 97, 117, 119, 121, 123, 160, 180, 218, 225–26, 241, 247–48, 254, 259, 261, 266, 269
Honey West, 137
Hopper, B. J., 216
"Hound of Heaven, The," 137
House, Silas, ix–xiii
Howard, Rance, 79, 87, 178
Howard, Ron, 79, 87
Howells, William Dean, 27
Hud, 247
Hughes, Wendy, 211
"Hunt, The," 137–39
Hutchinson, Josephine, 74
Hutton, Lauren, 200

"I'm a Fool" (Anderson), 125
Incredible Journey, The, 171
"Invaders, The," 19
It's a Man's World, 19, 143–48, 162
It's a Wonderful Life, 123

Jackson, Mary, 74, 212
Jagger, Dean, 87
Jefferson, Thomas, 23
"Jess-Belle," 135–37
Johnson, George Clayton, 134–35
Johnson, Laura, 197
Johnson, Lyndon Baines, 182
Jones, Claylene, 80
Judge, Frank, 75
Judging Amy, 257
Junior Bonner, 258

Kate Smith Hour, The, 137
Keeshan, Bob, 76
Kennedy, Arthur, 154
Kennedy, John F., 20, 150
Kennedy, Robert F., 182
King, Martin Luther Jr., 182, 208
King, Stephen, 142
Kipling, Rudyard, 210
Kirk, Russell, xvii, 30, 162, 228, 236–37
Kleeb, Helen, 74
Klonicki, Elaine, 85, 93
Knife Thrower's Assistant, The, 246
Knots Landing, 23, 201, 203–4
Kornfeld, Anita Clay, 203
Kung Fu, 252

Ladd, Margaret, 195–96
Lamas, Fernando, 200
Lamas, Lorenzo, 23, 195, 197
Lansbury, Angela, 155, 160
Lantern in Her Hand, A (Aldrich), 154–55
Larson, Doug, 59
Lassie, 180
Lassie: A Christmas Story, 179–81, 190, 251
Lassie, Come Home, 180

ABOUT THE AUTHOR

James E. Person Jr. is a writer and editorial manager who has worked for more than twenty-five years in reference publishing. He has edited and written for many literary, historical, and biographical reference works, including *Twentieth-Century Literary Criticism, Short Story Criticism,* and many other titles. He is also a freelance writer who has published essays and book reviews in the *Virginia Quarterly Review,* the *Detroit News, National Review,* the *Washington Times,* the *Virginian-Pilot,* and elsewhere. In addition, Mr. Person has written and spoken extensively on the American man of letters Russell Kirk and produced the first two books published on this important thinker: *The Unbought Grace of Life: Essays in Honor of Russell Kirk* (1994) and *Russell Kirk: A Criticial Biography of a Conservative Mind* (1999). Born in Virginia, he is a graduate of the University of Michigan and lives in Northville, Michigan, with his wife and two teenagers.